Mystery Kn
and Mystery

The 'winged Victory' from the sanctuary of the Great Gods on Samothrace: symbol of the triumph in the inner struggle of initiation.

MYSTERY KNOWLEDGE AND MYSTERY CENTRES

RUDOLF STEINER

*Fourteen lectures given in Dornach between
23 November and 23 December 1923*

*Edited with an introduction by
Dr Andrew Welburn*

RUDOLF STEINER PRESS
LONDON

Translation revised by Pauline Wehrle

Rudolf Steiner Press
51 Queen Caroline Street
London W6 9QL

First edition, Rudolf Steiner Publishing Co., London, 1943
Second edition, Rudolf Steiner Press, London, 1973
Third edition, 1997

Originally published in German under the title *Mysteriengestaltungen* (volume 232 in the *Rudolf Steiner Gesamtausgabe* or Collected Works) by Rudolf Steiner Verlag, Dornach. This authorized translation published by kind permission of the Rudolf Steiner Nachlassverwaltung, Dornach

Translation © Rudolf Steiner Press 1997

The moral right of the translator has been asserted under the Copyright, Designs and Patents Act, 1988

All rights reserved. No part of this publication may be reproduced, stored in a retrieval system, or transmitted, in any form or by any means, electronic, mechanical, photocopying, recording or otherwise, without the prior permission of the publishers

A catalogue record for this book is available from the British Library

ISBN 1 85584 061 8

Cover: art by Anne Stockton; design by Andrew Morgan
Typeset by DP Photosetting, Aylesbury, Bucks.
Printed and bound in Great Britain by Cromwell Press Limited, Broughton Gifford, Wiltshire

Contents

Introduction: Rudolf Steiner and the Renewal of the Mysteries
by Andrew Welburn   1

Lecture 1
The Life of the Human Soul
23 November 1923   25

Lecture 2
The Working of the Soul on the Human Body
24 November 1923   39

Lecture 3
The Path into the Inner Core of Nature through Thinking and the Will
25 November 1923   55

Lecture 4
The Relation of Human Beings to the Earth
30 November 1923   71

Lecture 5
The Mineral, Vegetable and Animal Creations
1 December 1923   85

Lecture 6
The Mysteries of Ephesian Artemis
2 December 1923   102

Lecture 7
The Mystery Centres of Hibernia
7 December 1923   117

Lecture 8
The Nature of the Hibernian Mysteries
8 December 1923   129

Lecture 9
The Great Mysteries of Hibernia
9 December 1923   141

Lecture 10
The Eleusinian Mysteries
14 December 1923   161

Lecture 11
The Secret of Plants, Metals and Human Beings
15 December 1923   181

Lecture 12
The Mysteries of the Samothracian Kabeiroi
21 December 1923   196

Lecture 13
The Transition from the Spirit of the Ancient Mysteries to the Medieval Mysteries
22 December 1923   211

Lecture 14
The Striving of the Human Soul during the Middle Ages
23 December 1923   225

Appendix 1
Original German Texts of Verses   239

Appendix 2
The Mystery of Transformation in Ovid's *Metamorphoses*   242

Notes   249

Publisher's Note   265

INTRODUCTION

Rudolf Steiner and the Renewal of the Mysteries

by Andrew Welburn

The cycle of lectures included in this book was in some ways the pinnacle of Rudolf Steiner's work as a spiritual teacher. Yet it is as well to realise as we read them that the lectures were held at the site of his recently destroyed masterpiece of sculptural architecture, the Goetheanum, which had been built as the spiritual home of the Anthroposophical Society in Dornach, near Basel in Switzerland. On that same site would rise Steiner's new or Second Goetheanum building in 'eloquent concrete', with its powerful sculptural forms conceived afresh in the more modern medium yet retaining something of the spirit of the old. Already he had been considering the stylistic and spiritual requirements of the future construction, and early the next year, in 1924, produced the first plasticine models from which the design began. In the meantime, at the Christmas Foundation meeting of 1923, he had founded the Anthroposophical Society anew, preparing the members for its different inner reality and its different formal organization in the parallel series of meetings and lectures to which he occasionally refers directly in these.[1]

In inner content the course of lectures, the future building and the refounded Society are all alike the expression of a profound single vision—a renewed presence of the Mysteries in the modern world.

All alike were Rudolf Steiner's response to a period of

endings and beginnings, destruction and spiritual re-creation, the rebirth of the old in new forms, the triumph of the spirit over material change. These lectures on the Mysteries weave together new ideas from themes long familiar to his audiences and from esoteric truths hardly touched on as yet even in Rudolf Steiner's remarkable opening of esoteric knowledge to the spiritually seeking souls of the twentieth century. They help to show that by placing himself at the head of the Society (in which he had previously held no official title) he intended anything but a return to the old form of a secret society. He was rather pouring out what he knew, embodying it in living forms of community, expressing it poetically, scientifically and historically to make it real and available to all those who needed it.

The Mysteries have been since ancient times an expression of the inner triumphing over external forces. In Antiquity they played the role especially of preserving a link with the 'time of the gods', of the primordial revelation. Not in a static way, but by bringing the chosen leaders, prophets or priests to confront the powers of life and death, to discover the deeper needs and potential of the human spirit, the Mysteries had kept humanity in touch with the living foundations of experience. For those who went through their processes, the attainment of wisdom was the culmination of an existential struggle, and the temples of the Mysteries were distinguished from those of the more familiar 'public' divinities in the ancient Graeco-Roman world by the single feature of the 'winged Victory' which adorned the pinnacle of the edifice. The celebrated Victory (*Nike*) from the temple of the Great Gods on the island of Samothrace is a supreme work of art, and also a quintessential embodiment of the spirit of the Mysteries in which Rudolf Steiner continued to work.[2] The theme of the Mysteries had occupied him since writing *Christianity as Mystical Fact* (1902), one of his earliest anthroposophical books. There he had shown Christianity's emphasis on the individual, on the intensity of a personal relationship to Christ and on individual salvation to be a further stage or evolution from the Mysteries' fundamental principle. In losing touch with its Mystery-origins later Christianity seemed to him to be losing its only chance to give meaning to the modern struggle of the individual, which is in fact deeply rooted in Mystery spirituality—little as the secularized world is inclined to acknowledge this.

Ironically, the Churches had abandoned the very element in their spiritual inheritance which should have given them a key role in modern culture. Rudolf Steiner showed the way in which the content of Christianity could be rediscovered out of the Mystery-struggle in contemporary form—in the striving and inner victory, the death and resurrection processes of the attainment to spiritual knowledge. That did not mean that it should not then be shared by a Church, a community, shaped by common needs and a common history. The ideal of universal communion was one of the new developments where Christianity had evolved beyond the older Mysteries, and the inner discovery of Christian truth by the individual would not be a denial of its meaning for the community. Indeed, Steiner's later thought frequently suggests a subtle and dynamic new model of the mutually fructifying relationships between individual knowledge, the 'spiritual interaction' of the Mysteries and the shared values of community. His own threefold vision of society might be expected therefore to help us understand the way he envisaged that in these several spheres a future humanity would again be able to draw upon the resources of spirituality epitomized in the Mysteries. It was grounded in the threefold understanding of human nature, which was central to his mature thinking and is expressed in the 'Foundation Stone' Meditation given at the climax of the refounding of the Society.

Human individuality, the ego, has become crucially important; Rudolf Steiner grasped the momentum of twentieth-century history, which is ever and again revealed to be the striving of humanity to base forms of life on the development and fulfilment of free individuality. His early philosophical work is devoted to the deeper implications of this truth. But the individual does not and cannot exist in isolation. The way through the minefield of the twentieth century must therefore lie in understanding the way in which individuals can engage with the other dimensions of society—the spheres of brotherly-and-sisterly working together and of collective values, the sphere where everyone must be considered equal.[3] Only by understanding these complementary spheres can we steer our way past the attempts to subordinate the individual to collective goals or the exaltation of competitive individualism at the expense of society, which have alike led to so many human tragedies.

Even though Steiner failed (narrowly) to get a hearing for these principles in the restructuring of Europe after the Great War, they remain a key to the finding of a balance in ourselves which is essential to the cultivation of the spiritual life. Each of these spheres is also within us, in our own deeper human constitution, and each sphere has its spirituality as was understood in ancient times when the teaching of the threefold man and his relationship to the universe was still grasped and applied. When Steiner looks back to the world of antiquity and the early role of the Mysteries, it is accordingly not to turn us back from the Christian evolution of ego-consciousness— but it is to remind us that the spiritual life has always adapted itself to changing circumstances, and that the Mysteries need to assume a form that preserves their harmonizing role.[4] The spirituality of each sphere has to change to suit the new, more individualistic emphasis, whose emergence is in turn put into a broader perspective in the evolution of consciousness. The self is not an end itself, but grows through awareness of the deeper history behind modern esotericism, and in particular to understand that special creativity, that self-overcoming of the developed individuality which is called love.

The Three Spheres 1: Oracles, Individuals, Knowledge and Freedom

In an evolutionary sense, therefore, Steiner can look back to former times in order to understand the spiritual potential of the present. If we take ancient Greece, for example, we find that the Mysteries existed there alongside the public cults and also the oracles—three separate institutions, each with a certain parallel to broadly equivalent manifestations today, if we are willing to recognize them. The oldest type of spirituality among them was the oracular. In Atlantean times the oracles had been humanity's primary way of experiencing the will of the gods.[5] The myths, for instance concerning the oracle at Delphi, point to a continuity with those archaic times by relating that after the Flood, Deucalion's ship was left stranded high and dry there, and that following the oracle's instructions he populated the earth anew. It is characteristic of an oracle that its knowledge is specific to a time and a place: a person goes to a holy site, and at a sacred time or season consults the god. Such oracles remained widespread in the Mediterranean civilizations, being scattered through Italy, Greece, Asia Minor (Turkey) and the north African coast. The querent receives in answer a priestly response (i.e. a message from the god), a natural sign (such as the rustling of the leaves of Zeus' sacred oak at Dodona) or a dream-vision that reveals the presence of the god. Usually the response was a prediction. Those who went to consult the Greek oracles asked generally about their health, their own prospects or those of the town or the nation. Thus the oracle answered an individual's need to know; and once armed with the god's predictive knowledge, the person went away again to recover, to solve his personal problem or pursue his career, leaving his thank-offering to the god or the sanctuary behind. But consulting an oracle demanded no spiritual preparation (beyond perhaps a basic purification rite), and no further commitment afterwards; it did not put gratified questioners in touch with each other, but rather gave them freely what they needed to get on with their lives.

Much of the approach and to some extent even the vocabulary of the oracles survives in modern times in a surprising domain, perhaps: namely, predictive science. The technical term *theōria*, including in it the root-word *theos* (god), referred originally to the divine oracle. As the scientific term 'theory' it now designates a method whereby an hypothesis is tested by making certain predictions, enabling it to be the basis of experiment. This essential scientific idea is still oracular, not just in its language of 'theory' but because it likewise demands that we go out to where the god speaks. Science strongly differentiates itself from the kind of deduction and speculative use of ideas that scientists often claim (rightly or not) to be widespread in other domains, and can only be science if it yields a concept that can be tested in the actual world. Just so the ancient oracles had to be consulted *in situ*. Moreover, they rarely or never gave general, philosophical ideas in response to a question, but practical (if somewhat riddling) advice related to specific circumstances, a particular illness, the outcome of a particular contest, the best specific time for an undertaking. And in the ideal, modern science is oracular in that it belongs to no closed community; its truth is accessible to all who are prepared to go and ask for it. (In practice, the ideal may be tempered by other factors.) Scientists often erroneously believe that this makes science 'value free', a truth outside mere human prejudices and opinions. But even if that is hardly the case, it shows how the notion of scientific truth as the voice of a god to mere human beings is capable of tempting even modern-day adherents into excessive, sometimes even fanatical statements.

There are, of course, obvious changes in the whole structure of society and knowledge when we move to the present-day world. The individual who searches for answers, which no-one may reformulate or pre-empt by asking for faith, is in some sense an oracle to himself. If the Atlanteans were entirely governed by oracles, that meant that in the sphere of individuality and individual initiative they were totally undeveloped. Yet the continuing parallels with modern knowledge show that oracular knowledge has not been left behind in subsequent history, but has rather been internalized and even made the basis of the seeking, enquiring self.

The Three Spheres 2: Religion, Shared Values and Community

At the opposite pole to the oracles, the ancient world celebrated the public cults of the gods, especially, in Greece, the Olympian sky-gods whose quality of light and openness makes them the embodiment of the collective, social aspect of spirituality. They dramatize the shared values of the community, whose life they project on a grand plane, exhibiting its essence in their larger-than-life quarrels and reconciliations, rivalries and amours. And the people took part in their worship through festivals, processions and holidays—collective gestures that helped society feel at one, both with itself and the order of the world. There was, however, scarcely what we would now call a religion. To share in the festivals did not signify any special knowledge or set of beliefs, and no special commitment to the god concerned. Collective feeling was thus loose but widespread, and the many local variations of practice did not make anyone feel excluded. It was in fact the adherence with passionate intensity to one God or Saviour which marked out the early Christians in the Roman Empire, and their refusal to take part in the rites that expressed human solidarity with the social gods of hearth, home, sex and vitality made them seem to some to be 'atheists' striking at the roots of society! Only gradually did it become clear that the Christians were organizing a much more powerful social order, a Church that was not a set of overlapping, uncentralized cultic communities with little in the way of strong beliefs to bind them together but a world-wide community united by the demanding conditions of their new faith.

The underlying assumption behind the ancient Greek cults was that everyone everywhere must fundamentally be worshipping the same gods and so share the same values. They evinced little awareness, in other words, of distinctive community. Religious practice was local and unambitious in the sense of wishing to share any particular religious approach more widely. And if there was little awareness of alien values that might challenge theirs, social and religious values at home were therefore basically unquestioned also. Even when, after Alexander's conquests, the Greeks came into contact with a wide range of beliefs and cultures, they continued to hold on to their fundamental attitudes. The ideal of 'syncretism', or identifying one god with another, enabled them to avoid recognition of essential differences and stress the similarities; universally shared values were sought abroad, those who questioned values at home might again meet the fate of Socrates.

The world of the Olympians represented an experience of

universal order, reflected on earth. But the myths spoke repeatedly of the gulf dividing gods and men, and of the *hubris* involved in trying to bridge it; those who attempted to were punished with mind-bending tasks in the underworld, or mocked and tempted to their destruction by 'the envy of the gods'. I.e. no one could enter the world of gods and stand on their level, determining values, shaping society and belief—at least, not through the framework of the public cults or of the oracles. It was possible, however, for the few, through the medium of the Mysteries—the third great division of Greek spiritual life.

The Three Spheres 3: The Mysteries, Transformation and Collaboration

It was in the Mysteries that human beings did not merely throng around the temples in celebration, but entered into the domain of the sacred, took part in the life of the gods. The initiate became a god (divinization, apotheosis, taking the name of a god such as Osiris, Bacchus, Attis, etc.) or even a creator of gods. The process involved ordeals and intensive preparation. 'A special mode of life was one of the requirements for a subsequent initiation,' explains Steiner. 'The senses were to be brought under the control of the spirit; fasting, isolation, ordeals and certain meditative techniques were employed to that end. The stable realities of ordinary life were to lose all their value, and the whole orientation of perception and feeling to be completely altered.'[6] Here then we find that questioning of values, the discovery of the existential value of experience itself, which was lacking or forbidden in the social religions or the oracular sources. Mystery-knowledge was personal and direct, and gave the power where necessary to change things. It was also associated with a certain scepticism and breaking through the inherited boundaries of ideas—not, however, in the nihilistic modern way but as part of the way knowledge originates and is conveyed to society. All the discoveries that enabled human civilization to emerge, such as fire, agriculture, writing etc., were attributed to the founders of the Mysteries who shared the knowledge of the gods. The calendar, which brought society into harmony with the cycle of renewal, was likewise a Mystery-secret that led to the regulation of almost every aspect of life. Above all, the Mysteries brought people to face the enigma of death and to seek meaning in the face of its threatened negation of life. Unlike the timeless Olympians, the Mystery-gods often died and returned to life. Their mythology is violent and unstable, mapping out the upheavals of the soul which their adherents will have to live through if they are to share in their 'higher knowledge'.

Initiates in the Mysteries were bound together by fraternal bonds. Under vows of secrecy, the knowledge of the Mystery-techniques of divinization was handed down as the foundation of human life. It was only the product, the outer result, that was known to society as a whole. The process of the advancement of knowledge, just like the questioning that was one element in it, was made known only to a very few. In this way the Mysteries had already conveyed divine knowledge to those who could make the inner effort to work with it for thousands of years when Greek civilization arose. In contrast to the surprisingly undeveloped state of individual-searching (i.e. oracular knowledge) and of collective identity (awareness of special values uniting groups of people) even in classical Greece, the Mystery collaboration of brotherly-and-sisterly human effort with divine knowledge was highly advanced. The Mysteries were a potent force reaching into every domain as they had already been in the great theocratic cultures of Egypt, Babylon and the East. If anything they were beginning to wane in their influence—although, as Rudolf Steiner demonstrated, philosophy remained dependent upon the Mysteries right through the classical period. And the content of religion, furnishing the values which the ordinary people could not question, continued to originate from the Mysteries down to the time of Christianity when the initiates understood the reality behind the events that, to outsiders, remained enigmatic and obscure—the death and resurrection of a god, but happening now as a fact of history. For those who could see, the Mysteries were then finally revealed to the world. The light shone in the darkness, but the darkness scarcely comprehended it.

It would be a mistake to suppose, on the other hand, that Christianity was simply the Mysteries transferred to outer event. Within the Mysteries, in the secrecy of the temple, had occurred a transformation that showed the actual creative presence of the gods. To revisit the foundations of life, however, to enter directly into the moral and spiritual basis of things and to overcome death was something that happened in the Mysteries in separateness, apart from the conditions of ordinary life. In isolation, the initiate could then give himself up to the gods, dissolve his identity and be remade. He would return to the mundane world with a deeper, direct assurance of the reality behind it. This was not merely knowledge, but *gnosis*, a transforming, liberating recognition of the spirit. Aristotle points out that the initiates in the Mysteries were not so much taught as 'moulded'. Their experience could not be put in the form of ideas, but only recognized by the other initiates who had themselves been through the process. This in itself cannot directly become the power than can appear in external reality and redeem it. The central Mystery-divinity is not so much the Christ as a goddess of wisdom who gives birth to a Christ—but a Christ as little child, not yet grown up in the cosmos, not yet ready to step out into the world.[7] In Egypt it was Isis who revived Osiris and gave birth to his mystical successor, Horus the sun-child; in Greece it is Persephone who dies and returns to life at Eleusis, and bears the divine child Iacchos. The Mysteries are dominated by the great goddesses, who are all versions of divine wisdom, Sophia. In mystical tradition and in the Gospel of John, this divine Sophia is the true Mother of Christ. Mystery-conceptions such as that of the divine *Logos* ('Word of God') link Christianity with the cult of Ephesian Artemis. The Word can sound for the initiate who makes the human soul an image of the goddess Wisdom in one of her several forms; in human life as in the cosmos she will then give birth to the Christ-child deep within us.

But the Mystery-wisdom needs to join together with something quite different in nature if the Christ is to become the uniter of souls throughout the world, to live in the world and to save it. For the Christ to become incarnate and live in humanity, humanity had itself to evolve to the stage of carrying the mystically apprehended divinity within into collective life. The evolution of greater individuality and ego-consciousness is one side of this development. The ancient world had resisted such individualization, except in the controlled sphere of the Mysteries, because it implied on the one hand the increasing fragmentation of society which is in truth all too familiar to us today. On the other hand, it could be taken further in the life of humanity at large if at the same time the uniting power of the Mystery-experience could also go beyond the bounds of the small brotherhoods of *mystai* and bring together the people of the world—as individuals, in freedom, yet united on a deeper level. The life and death of Christ, in Rudolf Steiner's profound interpretation, was the means whereby the divine Mystery which joined the initiates in the Mysteries flowed over into the sphere of universality and was given to mankind. The Christ who in the Mystery-sphere remains a divine child, and where spiritual death and resurrection was a transcendent experience for the few, in their highest initiation, entered into history. 'In the Mystery places the spirit had been poured out upon the *mystai* of old. Through the "Mystery of Golgotha" it was poured out upon the whole Christian community.'[8]

In Paul's letters and other passages of the New Testament the Christian communities are referred to as 'the saints', but the word thus rendered really means simply 'holy (people)'. In sharp contrast to later usage, it carries no connotation of 'an outstandingly holy man', raised above the ordinary believers. That was a rather retrograde notion, brought in later when the court of Byzantium adopted Christianity. In the elaborate hierarchy of the courtiers, one needed to oil many wheels, to have friends who would talk to friends, or finally personal intercessors with God's 'vicar' (substitute) the Emperor. An alternative route was to go via the influential Emperor's mother. Similar routes to obtaining a hearing with God were assumed to exist through ranks of the saints or the Mother of God. But originally the Christians were a holy people as such. Their worship was a 'calling out' of the people (*ekklesia*): the term normally rendered 'Church' basically means the actual assembly or congregation. Gatherings were in some sense like the old festivals, or communal gestures—but with a tremendous difference. For the Christian communities were aware of the need to preach their Gospel, to establish their spiritual values in the face of an alien world. And they felt united in their 'holiness', which was yet a holiness that could be conferred upon anyone who joined them, anyone who wished to share in the destiny of the people of Christ. There had been nothing like this in the ancient festivals and local cults, nor in the Mysteries, whose centres could rarely hold more than a dozen adherents. The widespread communities' amazing sense of solidarity the world over through the Christ who still lived in them did incontrovertibly change the world, making them a force in society that was not based on inheritance, origin or special gifts but on a collaboration of many different people sharing deeply held values and believing in their destiny.

There had been something resembling this in Antiquity only among the Jewish people. Shaken out of the static assumptions of the great sedentary civilizations of the Near East by the repeated disasters of their history, the Jews evolved the first stages of that individual identity, defined by the complexities of changing life-experience, which we have inherited today. It was still a group-identity, comprising all those who had lived through the problems and uncertainties, the vicissitudes of the history of the 'chosen people'. Christian universality, however, would be unthinkable had it not had as a prototype this previous model. Yet the step from a sense of belonging because one has been born into a community and shares its problems and joys to that of sharing in one which comes together by the decision of separate individuals across the world, which is joined essentially only by love of Christ and all those in whom He lives, was still an enormous one. It required that extraordinary new outpouring of the Mystery-spirit upon the world, the death and resurrection of a god upon earth. The Father of Christ was certainly the Jewish God of history who had spoken through the prophets. But Christianity can only be understood in its full meaning when we grasp its esoteric role as at the same time the fulfilment of the Mysteries.

The New Mysteries and the Three Spheres

When he restored this understanding to the modern world, then, it could clearly not have been Rudolf Steiner's intention to reverse history. It is the role of the Mysteries to provide the substance that passes over into the received religions of the peoples. They furnished the myths of the ancient world, in which the ordinary people believed; when humanity's evolution required it, they took the form of an earthly Event so that Christ's presence could unite mankind. The boundary between the brotherhood-Mystery sphere and the equality-universal sphere is not a matter of closure but of transformation. And likewise, in the modern age, the individual must live in both these spheres. But we must learn how to accommodate ourselves to the nature of the sphere in which we work. In the past, it is true, this did in practice limit the interaction of the domains so that they were separate, and people were more restricted in their ability to move between them. But nowadays we are more able to move between the different domains, combining their resources in freedom. The renewal of the Mysteries which Steiner projects in this book is a continuation of the role the Mysteries always had, deepened and extended by the Christian evolution. The universal working of Christ in humanity did not mean the end of the Mysteries, but a new beginning: 'There was still a place for initiation. For whereas faith allows a person to participate unconsciously in the content of the Mystery of Golgotha, initiation leads to a fully conscious connection with the power that streams invisibly from the events depicted in the New Testament, and which ever since then has pervaded spiritually the life of humanity.'[9] He recognized in the widest possible way the working of the Christ, wherever community comes into being from the hearts of free individuals, whether or not they cry 'Lord, Lord'.[10] The esoteric Christianity of the new Mysteries neither wishes to replace the existing Christian Churches and movements, nor to infiltrate them, but to address them in freedom from a sister sphere—one where the truths of religion are tested by individuals, and where the substance of individuals is transformed through working together out of the spirit.

It could be no part of the role of the new Mysteries to found a Church. But when a group of Church-orientated theological students asked for spiritual content to bring about a 'religious renewal' in that sphere, Rudolf Steiner naturally saw in this a creative step in the relation between different yet mutually interacting spheres. The Christian Community movement which resulted represents a Church open to the renewed content of the Mysteries, and with its sacraments shaped by the spirituality of the modern Christ-experience it continues to work for the desperately needed enriching of Church life. But what was wrong with the mainstream of the Church, it is worth stressing, was not that it was a Church but that it had over many centuries come to forget (or suppress) that original impulse from the Mysteries to which it owed its existence. As a result its spiritual essence had lost its inner connection with life, being presented as an authoritative revelation from the 'beyond', requiring submission and blind acceptance. In many ways, traditional churchly Christianity is now paying the penalty for its dogmatic removal of spiritual truth from human knowledge and life—a rift which Rudolf Steiner certainly wanted to heal, not to widen further.[11]

The reassertion of the place of the Mysteries in spiritual life was central to his purpose in restoring the balance of human existence. Torn between alienated, uncertain consciousness or submission to religious 'authority', modern humanity cannot unfold freedom—and, perhaps still more importantly, cannot use that freedom to work together out of spiritual insight. That was essential to Steiner's conception of an anthroposophy that would flow out into education, medicine, agriculture, painting and the arts, into humanizing the way we work in businesses or in banks—all that makes his spiritual approach a power to bring about creative change in the world about us.[12] In earlier stages he had tried to connect with the vestiges of the older Mystery-forms, which in the fraternal sphere of society had continued a shadowy sort of existence right through the Middle Ages in the trade guilds and professional associations. Indeed, the professions were still known, right up to the seventeenth century, as 'Mysteries'. (It is something of a joke in Shakespeare when even the common hangman proudly refers to his 'Mystery'.) If we remember this use of the term today it is usually in relation to the 'mystery plays' of mediaeval England or Germany, so called because each was mounted by one of the 'Mysteries', i.e. professional guilds. But these organizations had also remained the repositories of oral tradition, handing down the practical skills of architecture, for example, with the mathematical knowledge needed to build the cathedrals and to bring together the different elements from carpentry to stained-glass making required for their completion. The 'Mysteries' handed down their knowledge under oaths of secrecy, and it was far from being just mechanical knowledge. Work has become mechanical, dehumanized, in fact, precisely as the Mysteries died away. Their content was on the one hand the knowledge which brought people practically together to achieve a joint work, and on the other it was the spiritual conviction, the deeper meaning behind work which inspired it and gave it inner depths.

The guild Mysteries were still recognizably the working-on of the Mysteries of old. They gave people the spiritual knowledge they needed for their day-to-day lives (unlike the crisis, special knowledge from the oracles), and that meant to a large extent their very identities. In the ancient Mysteries, says Steiner, the candidate 'no longer considered himself a human being at all, but said: "I must first become a human being."'[13]

It has always been through the Mysteries that people acquired the role which gives them human value, the spiritual basis of their contribution to existence. Nowadays, people experience alienation from their work, feeling imprisoned or degraded by the labour they have to perform, or are unable to identify inwardly with the demands made upon them by society, precisely because we have lost that deeper dimension to the pattern of life which the Mysteries provided. Modern initiation, for Steiner, has as its purpose the restoration of this human and spiritual value to life. The Mysteries are the key to working together out of the spirit, in no way a turning-in and away from society.

By the eighteenth century, however, the old Mystery knowledge was clearly disappearing. The changes which have fashioned modern secular society also helped to sweep it away. One exception was the craft-knowledge of Masonry, which had adapted to the needs of the time by cutting its ties with building to become 'speculative' or 'free' Masonry. The greater complexity of social life meant that the knowledge people required was more philosophical, less bound up with specific activity. And from its esoteric core Masonry reached out to continue the ideal of fraternity and the temple, the Mystery-domain. Historians have sometimes been perplexed that Freemasonry was not a revolutionary-democratic movement. It was rather a working in the sphere of fraternity, where people met 'on the level' as partners in the spiritual interaction that should shape society. Its esoteric core is clearly linked, as Rudolf Steiner shows, to the Rosicrucian Mysteries, which had also descended from the Middle Ages but had played an active part in the redirection of spiritual life that had become necessary with the rise of the other great force that would alter human values and life-experience—modern science. The Rosicrucian Mystery-teaching was in this respect a direct precursor of the spiritual-scientific form that Rudolf Steiner was able to give to his anthroposophy, and in the final lectures below, in this book, he follows the trajectory that leads through the Rosicrucianism of the Middle Ages to modern forms of spiritual cognition. But he found that the organizations which remained from past stages of spiritual evolution had largely atrophied, or fallen into the hands of men no longer able or worthy to lead them. He turned instead to the refounding of the Anthroposophical Society, and poured into it the wisdom of his life's experience as an esoteric gift. Freemasonry and related organizations survive today, of course, though their relevance to modern life is not always clear and their emphasis on secrecy and segregation is a dubious persistence from bygone days.[14]

Rudolf Steiner reached back, in the lectures leading up to the Christmas Foundation, to the archetypal forms of the Mysteries and Mystery-wisdom in the ancient world. At the same time, he made his starting-point the kind of individual knowledge, the successor to the ancient oracles, which springs from freedom and openness. He had found the way to do so through his growing awareness of a further development in that sphere connected with quite recent times—since the year 1879. I mentioned previously that science sometimes presents itself, mistakenly, as if it could speak like a god in this sphere. That is not the case. But the spiritual worlds do reach out to the individual who seeks them, offering a true path suitable to our times rather than a distorted continuation of the old. This path is Michael's: his slaying of the dragon is a spiritualized Imagination equivalent to Apollo's defeat of the Python to win oracular knowledge. The dragon to be slain is precisely the hardening of knowledge into forms that were once appropriate but are no longer right. The freedom of individuals depends upon constantly avoiding this ahrimanic trap. Formerly it was done for us by the ever new responses of a god but nowadays we are called upon to share in the work with Michael, the Regent of the Cosmic Intelligence who since 1879 stands in a special relationship with human development; through it we are able to give scientific knowledge a place in our spiritual life. Rudolf Steiner had spoken explicitly in many lectures of the Michael Age and of the School of Michael in its preparation for the spirituality of the free individual.[15] But in a deeper sense his own work in this sphere goes back to his earlier philosophical writings. Already in *The Philosophy of Freedom* he had explored the relationship between knowledge and freedom, and sought to show a path of knowledge that would lead people to awareness of their 'spiritual activity'— and it is to this philosophical and introspective knowledge, characteristic of modernity, that he appeals in the opening lectures here on 'The Life of the Human Soul'. It is the path which he was eventually to extend in the *Anthroposophical Leading Thoughts*, which culminate in the 'Michael Letters' that lead us most profoundly into the meaning of our individual task of knowledge today.

The image of Michael and the Dragon brings us to apocalypse. Apocalypses have mostly come from Jewish and Christian tradition, and unlike the myths or teachings of the Mysteries they express the individual vision of a seer who looks into the future and already takes part in its struggles. The canonical instance is the Apocalypse of John in the New Testament. But contrary to the popular notion that the future is fixed, like an impending doom, in apocalyptic vision according to Steiner the spiritual situation is rather a call to transformation, to crucial moral decisions that need to be made, and a visionary freedom—the call to be determined by the future, not by the past. It is the model of spiritual awareness today when, as Steiner says, our 'consciousness must become apocalyptic'; as individuals we must be able to go beyond the past and all it has so far made of us. And conceived as transformation, this apocalyptic struggle leads over into the Mystery-sphere—in the form of the 'initiation of all mankind', of individuals wrestling with their situation and destinies.[16] Here is another point at which on an esoteric level two spiritual spheres can speak to one another, though without blurring their own proper forms. The new Mysteries which Steiner envisaged would certainly also be open to the knowledge absorbed on the path of Michael.

The point of transition itself lies in that 'transformation' to be achieved. For at that point we are no longer closed up within ourselves, within our own consciousness, but taking part in the changing world. The fundamental direction of Steiner's philosophical thought leads to this point directly, for he argues that we are not merely onlookers at the world. We are a living part of the world we inhabit. Our freedom is indeed attained through detachment, but it is the precondition for the realization of greater involvement, a greater fulfilment which the world would not otherwise achieve. In the *Leading Thoughts* he deepens our understanding of our inwardness, our spiritual activity in thinking, feeling and willing, into awareness of the spiritual beings who underlie the reality of the world around us. In these lectures on the Mysteries, too, he leads over the knowledge drawn from our life of soul into a knowledge of the substance which we share with the cosmos. And here we touch the Mystery-sphere. We are no longer just active in ourselves, but engaging with other beings or substances and changing them. At first it seems as though we are only transforming ourselves. But Mystery-knowledge reveals that we are thereby taking part in the process of cosmic transformation, which will lead ultimately to the spiritualizing of the earth.

The new Mystery-science will thus be an alchemy, though a scientific one, contributing to science as it now stands the understanding of the transformation of substance, metamorphosis. That is the way the spirit can be found again in substance. And that is a major theme in the lectures in this book, where the understanding of the spirit at work in the substances of metals, of living plant-substance and in the earth itself is shown to lie at the foundation of the ancient Mystery-wisdom. Steiner's exposition of it is profound, and despite its wonderfully poetic character the reader will need to draw on many previous studies to comprehend it in its depths. Steiner's related courses *True and False Paths of Spiritual Investigation*,[17] *Man as Symphony of the Creative Word*,[18] and *The Four Seasons and the Archangels*[19] may stand him or her in especially good stead. Yet the lectures must finally be seen in their wider perspective of Rudolf Steiner's extraordinary achievement of providing the foundation for a renewal of the Mysteries in the present day—in the context, that is, of the Christmas Foundation Meeting, the building of the Second Goetheanum, and the understanding of how the spirit can work into the spheres of modern life that informs all his later thought. His early death prevented him from nurturing the plant he had started in its growth, and circumstances have brought us only now, perhaps, to the point of taking up together the challenge of the Christmas Foundation with all its implications.

The task is a great one, but these lectures help us to see the dynamic of the evolution of Mystery-knowledge that points to its form today and in the future. It will need to know, too, how to receive the help of the Michael-spirit that comes to meet the task from the evolution of all those individuals who collectively are the School of Michael. And it will need to know how in this task we also have to reach out in trust to the working of the Christ-impulse in humanity as a whole. The Anthroposophical Society must reach out esoterically to meet these tasks. For only with the help of these spiritual forces can humanity bring back to life Sophia, the divine Wisdom which luciferic abstract knowledge has killed and laid in her cosmic grave.[20] But with them, human beings can restore her Mysteries and, as human-divine wisdom—Anthropo-Sophia—she will live again.

LECTURE 1

The Life of the Human Soul

My dear friends, let us make use of the time available for lectures at the Goetheanum between now and Christmas to help those who have come for the Christmas Conference to absorb as much as possible of what the anthroposophical movement can bring to human hearts. What we can do at the last moment will then really stir the thoughts of those who are staying over Christmas. Not that I shall be speaking about the international Anthroposophical Society—that can be briefly covered at the Conference—but I shall try to formulate what I say in a way that will help prepare the right mood for the forthcoming event.[1] I shall therefore speak from a different point of view of a subject I have been dealing with in recent weeks, and will proceed from a description of the life of the human soul itself to speak of its entry into cosmic secrets.

Let us begin in the simplest possible way and consider what happens in the human soul if we practise self-reflection beyond the point I actually had in mind when I was writing the articles in the *Goetheanum Weekly*. These four articles can serve as an introduction to what we shall now look at together.[2]

If we begin practising self-reflection thoroughly and comprehensively we shall realize how the life of the soul can be enhanced and intensified. What happens in the first place is that we let the external world work upon us—we have been doing this since childhood—and then we have thoughts that are the product of our inner world. Indeed, what makes us human beings in the real sense is that we allow the effects produced in us by the external world to live on further in our thoughts and are able to experience ourselves inwardly in these thoughts. We create a world of mental pictures that in a certain way reflects the impressions made upon us from outside. It is possibly not very helpful to our inner life to ponder a great deal on how the external world is reflected in our soul. By doing so we do not get beyond a shadowy picture of the world of mental images in ourselves. A better form of self-reflection is to concentrate on the activity itself and try to experience ourselves in the actual element of thought without regard to the external world, pursuing in thought what came to us as impressions of the external world.

It will depend on a person's particular nature whether he or she tends more towards thinking abstract thoughts; one person may or may not devise philosophical world systems or sketch abstract plans for anything and everything. Another person who has reflected about things that have made an impression on him and then enlarges upon them in thought may go more in the direction of imaginative ideas. We will not go further into how this inner thinking, without any external impressions, takes its course according to a person's temperament, character or further disposition. We will rather make ourselves conscious of the fact that it is a special case when, as far as our senses are concerned, we withdraw from the external world and live for a change in our thoughts and mental images, enlarging upon them, often perhaps merely as possibilities.

Some people, of course, consider it unnecessary to pursue further possible thoughts about existence, and so on. Even in difficult times like the present you will often find people who are occupied with their business the whole day, providing all kinds of things required in the world, afterwards getting together in small groups to play cards and suchlike, in order—as people so often say—to pass the time. And it will not often happen that people get together in similar groups in order to exchange thoughts, for example, about what might have happened in connection with the day's business if things had gone slightly differently. That would not be as amusing as playing cards, but it would have been doing some further thinking. And if they also retained a sound feeling for reality there is no reason why such thinking need become mere fantasy.

This living in thoughts leads finally to what you will experience if you read *The Philosophy of Freedom* properly. If you read that book as it is meant to be read you will understand what it means to live in thoughts. *The Philosophy of Freedom* is based upon experience of reality, but at the same time it is entirely the product of real thinking. Thus you will see that *The Philosophy of Freedom* has its own special mood. I conceived it in the 1880s and wrote it down in the early 1890s. But I have to say that among the kind of people whose job it ought to have been to at least take note of what the root nerve of the book is, I found a total lack of understanding. There is a particular reason for this. Even those who are called thinkers today are unable to experience their thinking otherwise than as a picture of the outer physical world. And then they say: perhaps something belonging to a superphysical world might arise in a person's thinking. But just as a chair or a table are outside us yet our thinking assumes them to be inside, our thinking would have to be capable of experiencing a supersensible object outside us just as the chair and the table are outside. This was approximately Eduard von Hartmann's conception of the function of thinking.

Then he comes across *The Philosophy of Freedom*. In that book the argument is that to experience thinking in the real sense means that a person can come to no other realization than this: if you live in thinking in the real sense you are living in the cosmos, even if, to begin with, in a somewhat undefined way. This connection of the deepest experience of thinking with the secrets of the world process is the core of *The Philosophy of Freedom*. This is why the statement is made in the book that in thinking we grasp one corner of the whole world-mystery.[3]

This may be putting it simply, but what is meant is that when one experiences thinking in the real sense one no longer feels outside the mystery of universal existence but within it; one no longer feels outside the divine element but within it. If one grasps the reality of thinking within oneself, one grasps the divine element within oneself.

This was the point people could not comprehend. For if we really grasp it, if we make the effort to achieve this kind of thinking, we are no longer in the world in which we were but in the etheric world. It is a world of which we know that it is not conditioned by any part of the physical earth but by the whole cosmic sphere. We are within the etheric cosmos, and we can no longer have any doubts about the law and order of this cosmic sphere if we have grasped thinking as it is understood in *The Philosophy of Freedom*. We have achieved what may be called etheric experience, and we realize we have taken a specific step forward in life.

Let me characterize this step as follows. Our thinking in ordinary consciousness is concerned with tables, chairs, human beings of course, and so forth; we may think of other things too, but they all belong to the outside world. And as we grasp these outside things with our thinking we do so from the centre of our being. Everyone is aware that with his thinking he wants to comprehend the things of the world.

But once you achieve the experience of thinking I described just now, you are not grasping the world; nor are you merely confined within your ego centre. Something quite different happens. You get the feeling—and quite rightly—that with your thinking, which is not localized in any particular place, you grasp everything *inwardly*. You feel you are making contact with your inner being. Just as in ordinary thinking you stretch your spiritual 'feelers' outwards, so with this thinking, which experiences itself in itself, you are continually stretching inwards, into your own being. You become object, object to yourself.

It is a very significant experience to realize that whereas up till now it was always the world which you grasped, now, with this experience of thinking, it is your own self you have to grasp. In the course of this firm grasp of your own self you come to realize that you have broken out of your skin. You grasp yourself inwardly and in the same way you grasp the whole world-ether from within, not of course in all its details but you know with certainty that this ether spreads over the whole cosmic sphere in which you are, and in which are also the stars, sun and moon, and so forth.

Now a second thing a human being can develop in his inner soul life is that instead of being wholly occupied with thoughts that are prompted from outside he gives himself up to his memories. If he does this and makes the process an inner reality, he will again have a quite definite experience. The experience of thinking I have just described to you does actually lead a person initially to his own self; he grasps his own self, and this process gives him a certain satisfaction. But when he passes on to the experiencing of memories he will finally find, if he is inwardly active in the real sense, that the most striking feeling is *not* that of approaching his own self. That is what happens in the experiencing of thinking; and for that reason a human being will find freedom in the course of this thinking, a freedom which depends entirely upon the personal element in him. That is why a philosophy of freedom must set out from the experience of thinking, for it is through this experience of thinking that a human being discovers his own self, finds his bearings as an independent personality. This does not happen in the case of the memory experience. If you proceed with real earnestness and are able to immerse yourself entirely in the experience, you will finally have the feeling of being liberated from yourself, of getting away from yourself. That is why the most satisfying memories of all are those which enable you to forget the present. I will not say they are always the best, but in many cases the most satisfying.

You can certainly get an idea of the value of memory if your memories can carry you out into the world no matter how utterly dissatisfied you may be with the present and wish you could get away from it. If you can waken memories which, as you give yourself up to them, give you an enhanced feeling of life, this will be a preparation for what memory will be like when it becomes much more real.

You see, memory can become more real if you bring to life with the greatest possible exactness something you actually experienced years or even decades ago. I want to describe just what it is like. Suppose, for instance, you turn to a collection of old papers and take out letters you wrote on some particular occasion. You put these letters down in front of you and let them carry you back to the past. Or it is even better not to take letters you wrote yourself or which others wrote to you, because the subjective element would be too strong. Try to get hold of your old school books, and look at them as though you were still a schoolboy, actually bringing the past to life. The effect is remarkable. If you do as I suggest you will entirely transform your present state of mind. You must exercise a little ingenuity here. You can do this with anything. For instance a lady might come across a dress or something she has not worn for 20 years, and she puts it on and is transported back into the situation she was in at the time. Choose something which will bring the past into the present with the greatest possible reality. This enables you to separate yourself radically from your present experience.

With our ordinary consciousness we are too close to ourselves in our actual experience to get anything out of it. We must be able to get farther away from ourselves. Now a person is farther away from himself when he is asleep than when he is awake, for during sleep his astral body and his ego are outside his physical and etheric bodies. You get close to this astral body which, as I have said, is outside the physical body during sleep, if you summon up some past experience into the present as vividly as possible. To begin with you will probably not believe this because you will be reluctant to attribute such significance to something so trivial as the awakening of past experiences by means of an old dress. But just put it to the test, and if you succeed in conjuring up some past experience into the present so vividly that you are wholly engrossed in it and can completely forget the present, you will find that you come close to your astral body, your sleeping astral body.

But you will be mistaken if you expect that all you have to do is to look to your right or left and you will see a shadowy form that is your astral body; that is not how things work. You must pay attention to what actually happens, which may be for instance that after such an experience you gradually begin to see the dawn and the sunrise very differently from hitherto. On this path you will gradually begin to feel the warmth of the dawn as something that brings a message, as something which has an elemental, prophetic power. You will begin to sense that the dawn has spiritual strength, and you will be able to see an inner meaning in this prophetic force. Although you may possibly have believed it to be an illusion at first, you will eventually feel there is some relationship between the dawn and your own being. Through the experience I have described you will gradually come to sense, as you look at the dawn, 'This dawn will not leave me alone. It is not that the dawn is merely over there and I am over here. There is an inner connection between my own being and the dawn. The dawn is part of my own soul. At this moment I myself am the dawn.' If you have been able to unite yourself with the dawn in such a way that you experience the coloured radiance out of which the sun rises in your very heart as a lively feeling, then you will also feel that you are actually travelling across the heavens with the sun, that, as I put it just now, the sun will not leave you alone, that it is not a case of your being here and the sun there, but that in a sense your existence reaches right up to that of the sun—in fact that you journey through the day in company with the light.

If you develop a sense for this, not out of thinking, where you approach your own being, but arrive at these experiences out of memory in the way I have described or, to be more exact, out of the power of memory, then the things that you otherwise perceive with your physical senses begin to show a different face—they begin to become spiritually transparent. When you have acquired the feeling of travelling with the sun—when you have gained the strength from the dawn to travel with the sun—then all the flowers of the field will look different to you. The blossoms will not merely display the red or yellow colours on their surface; they begin to speak in a spiritual way to your soul. The blossoms become transparent; a spiritual element in the plant begins to stir, and the blossoming becomes a kind of speaking. In this way you are actually uniting your soul with external nature. You get the impression that behind natural existence the light with which you have united yourself is borne by spiritual beings. And in those spiritual beings you gradually recognize the characteristics described by anthroposophy.

Let us now compare the two stages of feelings which I have just been describing. The first feeling, which can be had by an inner experience of thinking, is one of expansion. The feeling of being in the confines of space ceases altogether. Your experience widens and you have a definite feeling that the core of your inner being extends into the cosmos and is of the same substance as the rest of the world. You feel one with the whole world, with the etheric element of the world. But as you stand here on the earth you feel that your feet and legs are drawn down by the earth's gravity; you feel that your whole being is bound firmly to the earth. The moment you have this experience of thinking you no longer feel bound to the earth; you feel dependent on the wide expanses of the cosmic sphere. Everything comes in from the expanses, not from below, as it were from the centre of the earth upwards, but from the cosmic expanses. And you feel that to understand the human being this feeling that there is a streaming in from the cosmic expanses must be present.

This applies even to a true understanding of the human form. If I want to give expression to the human form in sculpture or in painting, I must picture to myself that only the lower part of the head proceeds from the inner bodily and spatial nature of the human being. I shall not bring the right spirit to the work unless I am able to convey the impression that the upper part of the head has been brought there from outside. The lower part of the head is formed from inside outwards, but the upper part from outside inwards.

Our forehead, the top of our head, is actually always added from outside. If you looked with artistic understanding at the paintings in the small cupola of the Goetheanum which was destroyed, you will have seen that this principle was always observed: the lower part of the face was always represented as having grown from within the human being, and the upper part of the head as something given him from the cosmos. This played an important role in times when these things were known. You will never understand the form of the head of a genuine Greek sculpture unless you associate this feeling with it, for it was out of similar feelings that the Greeks created their works of art.[4]

Therefore in experiencing thinking one feels oneself united with the surrounding expanses.

Now it might be imagined that this process would simply continue in this manner and go further and further outwards, as you pass from the experience of thinking to that of memory. But it is not so. If you succeed in developing within yourself the experience of thinking, you will finally have the impression of the Third Hierarchy: angeloi, archangeloi, archai. Just as you can picture a human being's bodily experience here on earth in the working of gravity and in the process of the digestion of foodstuffs, you can picture the conditions under which the beings of the Third Hierarchy live if, through this thinking experience, instead of trudging around the earth you feel yourself borne by forces reaching you from the ultimate boundary of the cosmos.

Thinking Experience: Third Hierarchy

Now if you pass from the experience of thinking to that of memory it is not a matter of being able to reach this ultimate boundary of the cosmic expanses. You can, it is true, reach this boundary if you know the reality of the thinking experience. But you do not go farther out still, for something different presents itself. An object may be in front of you—a crystal, a flower or an animal. What happens when you pass from the experience of thinking to what the experience of memory can offer you is that you can see right into the object.

When your gaze, which had extended to the ultimate boundary of the cosmic expanse, continues farther as an experience of memory, it penetrates into the essence of things. You do not press on into indefinite abstract expanses but this extended gaze perceives the spiritual element in all things. For instance, in light it sees the active spiritual beings of light, and so on, and in darkness the spiritual beings who are active there. So we can say: the experience of memory leads us to the Second Hierarchy.

Memory Experience: Second Hierarchy

There is of course something in the life of the human soul that reaches beyond memory. Let us see what it is. Memory gives our soul its special colouring. Suppose we come across a person who criticises everything, who reacts with bitterness to everything we say to him, who, whenever we tell him about something that is really pleasing, at once speaks of something unpleasant. In such a case we may know with certainty that this characteristic is connected with his memory. Memory gives the soul its colouring.

But there is something further than this soul colouring. We may encounter a person who meets us with an ironic sneer particularly when we say something to him, or he wrinkles his forehead or puts on a tragic expression. Or on the other hand he may give us a friendly look, so that we are cheered not only by what he says but also by this look. When something important is said during a lecture it is interesting sometimes to have a quick look at the faces in the audience to see whether the expressions are cheerful or miserable, whether foreheads are wrinkled or not, and see the blankness in some faces and the mobility in others. What is being expressed there is not merely memory that has persisted in the soul and gives it its colouring, but something that has gone over from memory into a person's physiognomy, his gestures, his whole bearing. If a person takes in nothing, if his face betrays the fact that all the sufferings, sorrow and joy in his life have left him unimpressed, that too is characteristic. A face that has remained smooth and unlined is as characteristic as one that is deeply furrowed by the tragedy or the seriousness of life, or one that expresses much contentment. In such cases, what otherwise remains part of the life of soul and spirit as the outcome of the power of memory passes over into actual physical form. The effect is so strong that later on in life it is expressed outwardly in a person's gestures and physiognomy, while his temperament is inside. For in old age we do not always have the same temperament as we had in childhood. Our temperament in old age is often the result of what we have undergone in life and has become memory in the inner life of our soul. What enters into a person inwardly in this way can also become reality, though this is more difficult. It is comparatively easy to bring before the eyes of our soul something we experienced in childhood or many years ago, and to make the memory of it a fact. It is more difficult to transpose ourselves into the temperament we had in childhood or in our earlier years. But the practice of such an exercise can bring results of immense significance. And we actually achieve more if we can do this with inner perseverance than if it is merely an external act.

Something can certainly be achieved in a person if, say at the age of 40 or 50—naturally within the obvious limits in such circumstances—he plays the games he played in childhood, if he skips as he did then, or if he even tries to make the same kind of face he made when, as an eight-year-old, his aunt gave him a sweet! If he can transpose himself back into the actual gesture or posture of that moment, he will again find that something is brought into his life whereby he is led to the conviction that the outer world is the inner world and the inner world is the outer one.

We can then penetrate with our whole being into, say, a flower, and then, in addition to the thinking experience and the memory experience, we have what I will call a gesture experience in the best sense of the word. In this way we acquire an idea of how the spiritual element is directly at work within the physical.

You cannot with your full consciousness inwardly apprehend the gesture you made perhaps 20 years ago in response to some outer provocation without realizing, with the greatest inner depth and reverence, the union of the physical and the spiritual in all things. But then you will have arrived at the experience of the First Hierarchy.

Gesture Experience: First Hierarchy

The memory experience enables us, when we see the dawn, to identify ourselves with it, and to feel and experience in ourselves its glowing warmth. However, when we break through to the gesture experience, what we meet with in the dawn will unite with everything that helps us experience the objective qualities of colour, sound, and so on.

When we simply look at the objects around us that are illumined by the sun, we see them in the way the light presents them to us. But the dawn changes when we pass gradually from the memory experience to the gesture experience. The colour experience detaches itself entirely from the material part of it. It becomes living being, becomes soul, becomes spirit, abandons the space in which the outer, physical dawn appears to us, and the dawn begins to speak to us of the mystery of the connection of the sun with the earth. We experience how the beings of the First Hierarchy work.

If we still direct our gaze to the dawn, and it still appears almost as it did through experiencing memory, we learn to recognize the thrones. And then the dawn dissolves away; the element of colour changes into beings, becomes living, becomes soul, becomes spirit, and speaks to us of the relation of the sun to the earth as it was in the Ancient Sun period, speaks to us in such a way that we experience the cherubim. And finally, if with the enthusiasm and reverence aroused in us by this twofold revelation of the dawn—by the revelation of the thrones and the cherubim—we remain alive in our soul, there penetrates into us from the dawn, transformed now into living being, experience of the nature of the seraphim.

Thinking Experience: Third Hierarchy
Memory Experience: Second Hierarchy
Gesture Experience: First Hierarchy

In all that I have been describing to you today my aim has been to indicate how, by simply following the course of the soul from thinking to thought-filled, soul-imbued gesture, the human being can develop feelings—to begin with no more than feelings—of the spiritual foundations of the world right up to the sphere of the seraphim.

I wanted to present this to you as a kind of introduction to the lectures which will follow and which, proceeding from the life of the soul, shall take us into the far expanses of the spiritual cosmos.

LECTURE 2

The Working of the Soul on the Human Body

If we seek for a transition from the life of the soul itself, to which we devoted some attention yesterday, to the creative way the soul works on the human physical body, particularly in connection with the experiences then described, we are led in two different directions. Memory of course initially points the soul back to earlier experiences, and, as I told you yesterday, thinking leads the soul into the realm of etheric experience. That which affects a person even more strongly than memory, so strongly in fact that the inner impulses pass over into his bodily life, I called 'gesture'. And the study of gesture brings us to the subject of how the soul and spirit manifest in the physical body.

The entry of the human being into physical life on earth is a process in which the being of soul and spirit takes hold of the physical element. And remaining with memory for the moment, this consists of something experienced previously in earthly existence being carried over into later life.

The question now is: just as memory points back to earlier happenings confined to the course of earthly life, is it possible to look farther back to what preceded the entry of a human being into this life?

Here we come to two factors: on the one hand, there are the experiences a human being has undergone as a being of soul and spirit in pre-earthly existence. We shall leave this for later consideration. On the other hand, there is something that is connected with his physical bodily constitution which he, as an individual, carries over into that bodily constitution. It is what from a scientific point of view we call heredity. In the very traits of his temperament, which have a considerable effect on his life of soul, a person bears within him qualities and impulses that have an obvious connection with those of his physical ancestors.

Modern humanity approaches such matters somewhat superficially, with little real thought. Only this morning, while I was travelling, I read a book dealing with the head of a well-known, now extinct royal family, and the effect of heredity on the dynasty. The author mentions characteristics that can be traced right back to the seventh century and were repeatedly inherited. Then comes a strange passage to the effect that some members of this royal family have displayed a marked tendency towards freakish behaviour, eccentricity and the like, while others have no such tendencies. You will agree that this is a peculiar way of thinking, for surely a writer who makes such a statement ought to realize that no conclusions whatever can be drawn from it. But if you examine a lot of what at the present time is supposed to lead to so-called well-founded views, you will find plenty of similar examples.

However superficial prevailing views of heredity seem to be, it must be admitted that a person is indeed the bearer of inherited characteristics. This is the one aspect. He must often battle against these inherited traits and rid himself of them in order to bring to fulfilment the talents laid into him before he entered earthly existence.

The second aspect to be noted has to do with what a human being acquires through education, through his dealings with other people and also with outer nature. Customary study of the lower kingdoms of nature leads us to speak of this as the adaptation of human beings to their environment. As you know, modern natural science regards these two impulses, heredity and adaptation, as influences of supreme importance for a living being.

But if we go into these things with an open mind, we feel that we cannot reach any real explanation of them without taking the path into the spiritual world. And so today we shall consider in the light of spiritual knowledge these questions which meet us in life at every turn.

We must go back here to something with which we have been repeatedly concerned in earlier studies, namely, the separation of the moon from the earth. The moon separated from the earth at a particular time in order to influence it from a distance, but I have also spoken of the spiritual reality behind this separation of the moon. I have told you how at one time there lived on the earth superhuman beings who were the first great teachers of humanity and from whom originated what our human thinking may call the primeval wisdom; it is of deep significance and inspires reverence even in the fragmentary form in which it survives today. It was once actually the content of what was taught by those superhuman teachers at the time when the evolution of earthly humanity was beginning.

These beings found their way up to the moon-sphere and are now part of the moon population. Now when a human being has passed through the gate of death he journeys by a series of stages through the planetary world belonging to our earth. After his earthly existence he enters first of all into the sphere of the moon's activities, then into the spheres of Venus, Mercury, the sun, and so on. Today we are particularly concerned with how he passes into the moon's sphere of activities.

I have already indicated here that with imaginative vision the life of a human being can be followed beyond the gate of death, and that in actual fact after his physical body has been laid aside and returned to the elements of earth he is to be found in the world of the spirit. After his etheric body has been received into the etheric sphere connected with our earth, soul and spirit remain—that is to say, his ego and astral body and all that is part of them. But when we follow with imaginative vision this being who has passed through the gate of death, he still presents himself to us in a definite form: it is the form which gives shape to the physical matter which the person bears within him. Compared with the robust physical body this form is little more than a shadow but makes a very forceful impression on the soul. In this form the head makes only a weak impression, whereas a very powerful impression is made by what, in the course of the life between death and a new birth, is gradually transformed into the head of the new incarnation. But there is something important to say about this form that is visible to imaginative perception after a human being has passed through the gate of death. The form is a kind of physiognomical expression of his life on earth; it is a faithful portrayal of the manifestations of the good and evil for which he was responsible in his physical life on earth. In earthly life a person can conceal whether evil or good is active in his soul. After death this is no longer possible. The spirit form presents after death the physiognomical expression of what the person was on earth.

A human being who carries through the gate of death some moral evil inherent in his soul will bear a physiognomy in which there is an outer resemblance to ahrimanic forms. During the first period after death it is a fact that a person's feeling and perception are dependent on what he can reproduce in his own being. If he has a physiognomical resemblance to Ahriman because he has carried some moral evil with him through the gate of death, he can reproduce in himself—which means he can *perceive*—only things that resemble Ahriman, and he is as it were blind to those human souls who passed through the gate of death with a sound and good moral disposition. Indeed it is one of the sternest judgments confronting a human being after death that in so far as he is himself evil he can see only what resembles himself, because he can reproduce in his own being only the physiognomy of other evil people.

After death human beings enter into the sphere of the moon and there, if they bring evil with them, they come into the presence not only of supersensible, superphysical beings but also into that of others with a physiognomical resemblance to themselves—that is to say, to ahrimanic figures. This passage of certain individuals through an ahrimanic world has very definite significance in the whole nexus of cosmic happenings. And we shall grasp what actually happens if we bear in mind the purpose of those ancient teachers of humanity when they departed to establish the moon colony in the cosmos.[1]

Now as well as those beings of the higher Hierarchies whom we usually call angels, archangels, and so forth, other beings who belong to the ahrimanic and the luciferic realms are also bound up with the whole process just as are the normally developing beings. The luciferic beings work continuously with the aim of preventing anything that has the tendency to press on into physical materiality from achieving that end. In the human realm the luciferic beings use every opportunity to lift human beings away from their physical corporeality. Their endeavour is to make them into purely etheric beings possessed of soul and spirit. The endeavour of the ahrimanic beings is to separate human beings from everything that urges them towards the soul and spirit, which has to be developed in the human kingdom. They want to transform into spirit the subhuman elements, the instincts and urges, everything that comes to expression in the body. In their own way both the luciferic and the ahrimanic beings want to change humanity into spirit. But while the luciferic beings want to draw the soul and spirit out of human beings so that they would cease to concern themselves with their earthly incarnations but would prefer living as beings of soul and spirit only, the ahrimanic beings would like to disregard soul and spirit entirely and detach from human beings what has been given them as a sheath, a covering, an instrument in the physical and etheric realm, and bring it all into their own realm.

And so on the one hand humanity faces the beings of the normally developing Hierarchies, but because human beings are interwoven with the whole of existence they are also faced by the luciferic and ahrimanic beings. So whenever the luciferic beings endeavour to approach human beings their purpose is to estrange them from the earth, whereas on the other hand when the ahrimanic beings make efforts to dominate human beings their aim is to make their nature more and more earthly, changing the earth in the process into spirit consisting of dense spiritual substance and dense spiritual forces.

In speaking of spiritual matters one sometimes has to use expressions that may seem grotesque when applied to such matters, but one has, after all, to use human language. So you will allow me to use ordinary words even when I am speaking of something that takes place on the purely spiritual plane. You will understand me and will yourselves raise what I say onto a spiritual level.

Those beings who at the beginning of earth existence brought the primal wisdom to humanity withdrew to the moon in order, as far as lay in their power, to establish the right relationship of the luciferic and the ahrimanic beings to the life of human beings. Why was that necessary? Why was it necessary for beings as exalted as these primordial teachers to elect to leave the earth, which for a time had been their field of action, and proceed to the extraterrestial moon in order to create the possibility for the right relationship of the luciferic and ahrimanic beings to human beings?

When, in a soul-spiritual form, a human being descends from his pre-earthly existence into the earth-sphere, he traverses the path I described in the course of lectures entitled *Cosmology, Religion and Philosophy*.[2] As a being of soul and spirit he unites with the physical embryo provided for him in the direct line of heredity by father and mother. These two components, the physical embryo and the spiritual element, interpenetrate and unite, and in that way a human being enters into existence on earth. But in the line of heredity, in the inherited characteristics transmitted by ancestors to their descendants, there lie points of attack for the ahrimanic beings. The ahrimanic forces lie in the forces of heredity. And if a person has many of these inherited impulses in him, he will have a bodily make-up to which the ego cannot satisfactorily gain access. Indeed, the secret of many human beings is that they have within them too many inherited qualities. This is what is meant today by saying that a person is 'burdened by heredity'. The consequence is that the ego cannot fully penetrate that person's body, cannot adequately take possession of the various bodily organs. The body then develops an activity of its own independent of the impulse of the ego which should rightly be working in the body. Thus through their efforts to put as much as possible into heredity the ahrimanic powers succeed in ensuring that the ego is only very loosely connected with the human being. That is the one aspect.

But human beings have also to adapt themselves to external conditions. This is very evident when you think of the effect of climate and other geographical conditions on human beings. This effect of the purely natural environment is extraordinarily significant for us. There were even times when the wise leaders of humanity made use of it in particular ways.

When we consider a certain remarkable phenomenon in ancient Greek culture, namely, the difference between Spartans and Athenians, we shall realize that this difference, which is described very superficially in our history textbooks, is based ultimately on measures adopted in the ancient Mysteries, and the effect of these measures on the Spartans differed from that made on the Athenians.

In Greece, as you know, great value was attached to gymnastics. Gymnastics was regarded as the most essential part of a child's education, because through controlling and directing the body in a particular way an effect was made on the nature of spirit and soul by methods characteristic of the Greeks. But the method used by the Spartans was different from the one used by the Athenians. The Spartans were primarily concerned to ensure that by means of their gymnastic exercises the boys' development should depend as completely as possible on what the body, by itself alone, could achieve. Thus Spartan boys were obliged to carry out their exercises regardless of weather conditions.

Among the Athenians it was different. They attached great importance to the gymnastic exercises being adapted to weather conditions, and insisted that the boys doing the exercises should be exposed to the sunlight in the appropriate way. To the Spartans it was a matter of indifference whether the exercises were carried out in rain or sunshine. The Athenians demanded that there be a stimulus, particularly the stimulating effect of the sun.

The treatment given to a Spartan boy was intended to make his skin impervious, so that the whole effect should come from the body. The Athenian boy did not have his skin treated with sand and oil but he was exposed to the influence of the sun.

The Athenian boys received from outside all the effects the sun can have on human beings. They were encouraged to speak and to use beautiful language. The Spartan boys, on the other hand, were enclosed in themselves as the result of all kinds of massage with oil; indeed the purpose of massaging the skin with sand and oil was so that their development could take place entirely independently of outer nature. They were trained to drive whatever forces can be developed by human nature back into themselves, and not to allow them to emerge. Thus a Spartan boy, unlike an Athenian boy, did not become talkative. He was trained to be sparing with words, to say little, to remain silent. If he did say anything it had to be important, have real content. Speeches made by Spartans were rare but were renowned for their content; speeches made by Athenians were renowned for the beauty of their language. All this was connected with the adaptation of human beings to their environment by means of the appropriate system of education.

You can see this elsewhere in the relationship that is established between human beings and their environment. Southerners who are exposed to the maximum of sun influences gesticulate a great deal and are talkative; their speech is melodious because there is a connection between their own warmth and the warmth outside. Northerners, on the other hand, are not talkative because they have to hold on to the stimulus their bodily warmth gives them. Northerners are notorious for their silence; they will sit together evening after evening without feeling the urge to say much. One of them may ask a question, and not until two hours later or not until the following evening will he get a 'Yes' or a 'No' in reply. The reason for this is that it is necessary for Northerners to have a stronger impulse within them to produce warmth because warmth does not come to them from outside.

Here you have examples of what we can call human adaptation to external conditions of the natural world. Just think of the effects of all this in education and in other spheres of the life of soul and spirit. Just as the ahrimanic beings exercise a considerable influence on what lies in heredity, luciferic beings exert a considerable influence on adaptation to the environment. They can approach the human being when he is establishing a relationship to the external world. They entangle the human 'I' in the external world. But in so doing they often bring about confusion between this 'I' and karma. Whereas the ahrimanic beings bring the human 'I' into confusion in regard to his physical impulses, the luciferic beings bring the 'I' into confusion in regard to his karma. For what comes from the external world does not always lie in immediate karma but must first be woven into karma by means of many threads and bonds so that it can have a place in future karma.

Thus the ahrimanic and the luciferic powers are intimately connected with human life. This state of things must be regulated in the process of the whole of human evolution. This is why it became necessary for the primeval teachers of humanity to leave the earth where such regulation would not have been possible. It cannot be undertaken during a person's earthly life, and when that life is over he is obviously not on the earth. The primeval teachers were therefore obliged to withdraw from the earth and continue their existence on the moon. And then, when they had withdrawn to the moon—and here I must use ordinary language for something which one would prefer to clothe in different word-pictures—these wise teachers came to an arrangement with the ahrimanic and the luciferic powers. Now the effect of the ahrimanic beings on human existence after death would have been particularly harmful if they could have exercised a real influence on it. For when a human being goes through the gate of death bearing the after-effects of anything evil in his soul, he finds himself, as

I have told you, in an entirely ahrimanic environment; he will even hold ahrimanic views, and he himself has an ahrimanic physiognomy. He can perceive only those human beings who have a similar appearance. All this must remain purely an experience in the soul. If Ahriman could now intervene and influence the astral body, this would become a force which Ahriman could propel into humanity—a force that would not only gradually find its karmic balance but would make human beings very closely related to the earth, bringing them into too close a connection with it. That indeed is the endeavour of the ahrimanic beings. While a person, after death, in his spirit-form still resembles his earthly form, the ahrimanic powers strive to gain access to him by way of the evil impulses he carries with him through the gate of death. They want to permeate this spirit-form with forces, to draw as many of such beings as possible down to earthly existence and so to speak to establish there an ahrimanic earth humanity.

It was for this reason that the primeval teachers now inhabiting the moon-sphere made a contract with the ahrimanic powers, a contract which those powers were obliged to accept for reasons which I will explain later. Under the terms of this contract the ahrimanic powers were allowed to exercise their influence in the fullest sense of the word and within the limits of possibility on the lives of human beings before they descend to earthly existence. Thus in accordance with the agreement reached between the primeval teachers and the ahrimanic powers, when human beings are again passing through the moon-sphere on their way to earth these powers may have a certain influence on them. And this influence comes to expression in the fact that heredity has become possible. As against this, after the domain of heredity had been allotted to the ahrimanic beings as a result of the efforts of the primeval teachers, the ahrimanic beings were obliged to renounce all interference with processes taking place in human evolution after death.

Conversely, an agreement was also reached with the luciferic beings, to the effect that they might exercise their influence on human beings only when they have passed through the gate of death and not *before* they descend into earthly existence.

Thus the great primeval teachers were able to regulate the extra-earthly influences of Ahriman and Lucifer. But we have already heard, and a little reflection will at once make it obvious, that humanity is thereby brought into contact with nature. Because ahrimanic beings can exert their influence on human beings before they descend to the earth, human beings are exposed to the operations of the forces of heredity. And because the luciferic beings can work on them, human beings are exposed to factors in the physical environment such as climate and the like, also to factors in the social and cultural environment such as education, modes of behaviour and the like. Thus a relation is established between human beings and their natural environment, and the ahrimanic and luciferic beings can work into this environment.

I now want to say something from a quite different aspect about the existence these ahrimanic and luciferic beings lead particularly in this natural environment. I have already referred to this subject when dealing with the theme of Michael, and I now want to go into it in more detail. Picture to yourselves the change that occurs in nature in the phenomenon of rising mist. We may perhaps be living in an atmosphere that is saturated with watery vapours rising up from the earth. Someone who has developed spiritual vision discovers that in this phenomenon of nature there is something that carries an earthly element upwards in the centrifugal direction. It is not without reason that people who live in misty areas become melancholic, for there is something about the experiencing of mists that weighs down the will.

Now there are exercises whereby a person can manipulate his imagination so that he can himself weigh down his will. These exercises consist in concentrating on certain bodily organs, especially the muscles, whereby a kind of inner sensing, inner awareness of the muscles is produced. The tension arising through this concentration while standing still is different from becoming aware of the muscles while walking. If such exercises are practised consistently, like others described in the book *How to Know Higher Worlds*,[3] the will is weighed down through a person's own activity. And then he sees what it is in the rising mist that can make people morose and melancholy; he perceives with the eyes of the soul and spirit that certain ahrimanic beings live in the rising mists. Spiritual knowledge makes it clear that in rising mist ahrimanic beings rise up from the earth into cosmic space, thus expanding their sphere of action in the earthly realm.

It is quite different—and there are excellent opportunities for this here at the Goetheanum—if you gaze at the sky in the evening or the morning and see the clouds flooded with sunshine from above. A few days ago in the late afternoon you could have seen a kind of red-golden light becoming embodied in the clouds and calling forth an infinite variety of wonderful formations. And that same evening the moon shone with special intensity. Elsewhere too, of course, you can see the clouds illuminated from above in a brilliant play of colours. Such a spectacle can be seen anywhere. I am merely speaking of what can be seen especially well here in Dornach.

Just as ahrimanic beings live in the rising mists, luciferic beings live in the light that fills the atmosphere and floods down onto the clouds. If someone can look at this with conscious imagination and succeeds in getting his thinking to accompany the forms and colours of the changing clouds, so that instead of having sharp outlines his thoughts go through a metamorphosis, expanding and contracting together with the forms and colours of the clouds, then he will genuinely begin to see this play of colours above the clouds, especially in the evening and morning sky, as a sea of colours in which luciferic forms are moving. And whereas a mood of melancholy is produced in human beings by rising mist, his thoughts and also his heart learn to breathe with almost superhuman freedom at the sight of this luciferic sea of flowing light. This is a special relationship a human being can establish with the surrounding world, for then he can really rise to the feeling that his thinking is like an inhalation of the light. He feels his thinking to be a breathing, and what he is breathing is light. If this is actually experienced, the passage in the Mystery Plays about beings who breathe light will be better understood. Through this experience a person can have a premonition of the nature of the sort of beings who breathe light.

So we find that ahrimanic and luciferic beings are also part and parcel of the phenomena of external nature. In the realm of heredity and adaptation to his environment the human soul and spirit makes contact with nature. When we contemplate the rising mists and the clouds bathed in flowing light we see how ahrimanic and luciferic beings unite with the phenomena of nature. But when the human soul and spirit approach the facts of heredity and adaptation, this, as I have shown you today, is also simply approaching the forces of Lucifer and Ahriman. Thus in the part of the human being that belongs to nature we shall find Lucifer and Ahriman, and we find Lucifer and Ahriman again in certain natural phenomena containing something that need not concern the physicist. And this is the very point from which we have the chance of perceiving nature influencing human beings in a way that transcends the phenomena of earthly existence.

To begin with let us hold firmly in our minds that Ahriman and Lucifer are present in the sphere of human heredity and adaptation. We find them in the rising mists and in the light that floods down onto the clouds where it is caught and held. And we find in human beings an urge to establish a balance, a rhythm between heredity and adaptation. We also find in external nature the urge to create rhythm between the two powers working in nature—the ahrimanic and the luciferic powers.

If you follow the whole course of events in the world of nature you have a wonderful drama. Follow the rising mist and observe how ahrimanic beings are striving outwards into cosmic expanses. The moment the rising mists form themselves into a cloud they have to give up their efforts and return again to earth. The clouds are where Ahriman's arrogant striving finds its limits. Clouds do not have the quality of mist in which Ahriman feels at home. But the clouds enable the light to spread out over them. Lucifer is there, above the clouds!

Try to grasp this in its full significance. Picture the rising mists with the greyish-yellow ahrimanic forms concentrated in cloud masses, and in the light above the clouds the luciferic forms striving downwards. Then you have a picture of the ahrimanic and the luciferic elements in nature.

And then you will also realize that in times when people still had a feeling for what lies beyond the threshold, for what lives and weaves in the luminous clouds and in the rolling mist, the position of painters, for example, was quite different from later on. The spiritual powers they recognized carried the colours to the right place on the canvas. Poets, conscious that divinity, that spirituality was speaking in them, could say,

'Sing, O Muse, of the wrath of Peleus' son, Achilles,' or, 'Sing to me, O Muse, of the man, the much-travelled one.' These are the opening lines of Homer's epics. Klopstock, who lived in times when a feeling for the divine-spiritual was no longer present, substituted: 'Sing, Immortal Soul, of the redemption of sinful man.'[4] I have often spoken of this. Just as the poets of old would have said it—could put it into words and begin their poems with it—the painters of old too, even those living in the epoch of Leonardo and Raphael, would still have been able to say, and would have felt it in their own way: 'Paint for me, O Muse, paint for me, O Divine Power, direct my hands, bring my soul into my hands, so that the brush in my hands is guided by you.'

It is very important to understand this close union of human beings with the spirit in all situations of life, especially in the most significant ones.

So we have arrived at the fact that, on the one hand, in heredity and adaptation we bring the human element itself into relationship with Ahriman and Lucifer; and, on the other hand, through an intuitive observation of nature Lucifer and Ahriman can be brought into relationship with nature in its external manifestations.

We shall continue these studies in the lecture tomorrow.

LECTURE 3

The Path into the Inner Core of Nature through Thinking and the Will

Yesterday I was speaking to you of how human beings are subject to what natural science generally calls heredity, and also of how they are subject to the influences of the external world and adaptation to it. I also said that everything relating to heredity is connected with the ahrimanic forces, and adaptation in the widest sense with the luciferic forces. But I also told you how in the realm of the spiritual beings that form the basis of the cosmos provision has been made to enable the luciferic and ahrimanic forces to play a lawful part in human life. Something shall now be added to what was said yesterday, so we shall recall the content once again.

We turned our minds to how memory and everything related to it gives human beings their configuration as soul beings. To a far greater extent than we imagine, our configuration as beings of soul originates from our memories. Our soul has been shaped by the process whereby our experiences have become memories; we are the product of our life of memory to a greater extent than we think. And anyone who is capable of exercising even enough self-observation to enable him to penetrate into his store of memories will realize how particularly important a part is played throughout earthly life by the impressions of childhood. The kind of life we spent in childhood (which really does not loom large in our consciousness), the period in which we learnt to speak, to walk and in which we got our first inherited teeth, the impressions made on us during these periods of development—all these play an important part in the life of soul throughout our life on earth. And some of what arises in us as thoughts which have a characterological emphasis and are connected with memories (in fact everything that does not happen to come into our thoughts by way of outer impressions has of course to do with memories), things arising in this way and bringing us a gentle touch of joy or sadness—all this life of memory also accompanies our astral body when we pass into the state of sleep. If with imaginative vision we are able to observe the human being as a being of soul and spirit during sleep, the following picture presents itself. During sleep the etheric body and the physical body are still enclosed within the skin and the astral body is outside—I will speak of the ego later on. This astral body is seen virtually to consist of the person's memories. However, these memories in the astral body, which is now outside the physical body, are seen to be swirling in and through one another in a kind of eddy. Experiences that were widely separated in time and space are now in juxtaposition; parts of the content of certain experiences are eliminated, so that the whole life of memory is transformed during sleep. And when a person dreams he is becoming conscious of this transformed life of memory. And in the character and make-up of the dream he can be inwardly aware of the swirling eddy of memories which imaginative clairvoyance can perceive from outside.

But there is another aspect as well. These memories, which from the time of going to sleep until waking form the main content of the life of the human soul, unite during sleep with the forces behind the phenomena of nature. It may therefore be said that all that lives as astral body in our memories enters into connection with the forces that lie behind, or rather lie *within*, the minerals, within the plants, behind the clouds, and so on.

Those who recognize this truth find it horrifying when people come and say that material atoms are behind the phenomena of nature. The fact is that our memories do not unite with material atoms during sleep but with the spiritual forces behind the phenomena of nature. This is where our memories reside during sleep. So that we can truly say that during sleep our soul dips down with its memories into the inner being of nature, and we are not saying anything untrue or unreal when we assert that when we go to sleep we give our memories over to the powers that are spiritually active in the crystal, the plants and all the phenomena of nature.

You may go for a walk where you see by the wayside yellow and blue flowers, green grass, gleaming ears of corn promising well for the harvest, and you say to them: 'When I pass by you during the day I see you from outside, but while I am asleep I shall sink my memories into the spiritual core of your being. While I sleep you receive and harbour the memories into which I have transformed the experiences I had in life.' There is perhaps no more beautiful feeling for nature than to have not merely an external relation to a rose bush but to realize that you love it because a rose bush harbours the first memories of childhood. Space plays no part at all. However far away the rose bush may be, during sleep we find the way to it. The reason why people love roses—only they do not know it— is that roses receive and harbour the very first memories of childhood.

When we were children the love shown us by other human beings made us happy. We may have forgotten all about it, but we carry it in our feeling life, and when we are asleep at night the rose bush receives into its own inner being the memory we have ourselves forgotten. We are more closely united than we realize with the world of outer nature, that is, with the spirit which presides there. Memory of our earliest childhood is particularly remarkable in connection with sleep because in the first years of life and in the years up to the time of the change of teeth—up to about the seventh year—it is only the element of soul that is received and harboured during sleep. It is a fact of our life as human beings that the inner, spiritual core of nature harbours the element of soul belonging to our childhood. Other things can also happen: the element of soul developed in childhood when, for example, we may have been cruel, that too remains in us; the thistles harbour it! All this is said by way of comparison, but it points to a significant reality. The following will make it clear what it is that is *not* received from childhood into the innermost core of nature.

In the first seven years of life the child's whole bodily make-up is inherited, including, therefore, the first teeth; all the material substance we have in us during this period is, in essence, inherited. But after approximately seven years all the material substance has been thrust out and renewed. The form of the human being remains, his spirit form. His material components are gradually pushed out, and after seven or eight years everything that was previously there has gone. And so when we have reached the age of nine our whole bodily make-up has been renewed. We then shape it in accordance with external impressions.

It is very important indeed that in the early phases of life the child should be in a position to build his new body—not the inherited body but the one developed from within himself—in accordance with good impressions from the environment and by a healthy process of adaptation. Whereas the body the child has when he comes into the world depends on whether the inherited forces are given him in a good or not so good a way, the body he has between the seventh and the fourteenth year is very dependent indeed on the impressions he receives from his environment. Every seven years we build up our body anew.

Now we must realize that it is the 'I', the ego, that is responsible for this. Even though, in a seven-year-old child, the ego has not yet been born into the outer world—for it is born at a later age—nevertheless it is at work, for it is connected of course with the body and is responsible for its formation. It is the ego which forms the things I have been speaking about, all that comes to manifestation in the way of physiognomy and gesture, as the outer, material expression of the human soul and spirit. It is a fact that someone who takes an active part in affairs of the world, who has many interests and assimilates their substance and content will reveal this in his gestures and his very facial expression. In the later life of such a person, every wrinkle on his face will be indicative of his inner activity, and it will be possible to read a great deal there, because the ego comes to expression in human gesture and physiognomy. A person whose attitude to the world is one of boredom and lack of interest will retain the same facial expression all his life. Subtler experiences leave no impression on physiognomy and gestures. In many a face you can read a whole biography; in others there is not much more to read than that the individual was once a child, which does not tell you a great deal.

It is extremely significant that through the change of bodily substance after every seven or eight years a human being shapes his outer appearance from out of his own inner form. And this work on his outer appearance as revealed in physiognomy and gesture is again something that is carried, while he sleeps, into the innermost being of nature.

If, then, you look at the human being with imaginative clairvoyance, and observe the ego when it is outside in the sleeping condition, you will find that the ego actually consists of physiognomy and gesture. Thus those human beings who are able to put a great deal of their inner nature into their facial expression or their gestures have shining, radiant egos. This activity of shaping gesture and physiognomy again unites with certain forces in nature. If in life we often had the opportunity to be friendly and kind, nature is inclined, once this kindness has become a facial expression, to receive it into its own essential being. Nature takes our memories into its forces, our gestures into its very being. Human beings are so intimately connected with external nature that there is immense significance for the latter in the memories they experience in their souls and also in the way they express their inner life of soul in physiognomy and gesture. For these live on in the innermost being of nature.

As you know, I have often quoted in the abstract words of Goethe which were really a criticism of a saying by Haller: 'Into the inner core of nature no earthly creature can go. Happiness enough is yours, that she her outer trappings doth show!' Goethe retorted: 'O, you philistine! We are within her being wherever we look. Nothing is only inside or outside, for what is inside is outside, and what is outside is inside. Ask yourself first of all whether you are core or shell.'[1] Goethe said he had heard the remark in the sixties and had secretly cursed about it. He felt—naturally he could not then know anything of spiritual science—that if someone whom he could only regard as a philistine says, 'Into the inner core of nature no earthly creature can go,' he shows he knows nothing of the fact that human beings, simply because they are beings with a memory, beings with physiognomy and gestures, continually penetrate into the inner being of nature. We are not creatures who stand at nature's door and knock in vain. Through our own core of being we are connected by intimate ties with the innermost essence of nature. But because a child, until its seventh year, has a body that is wholly inherited, nothing of its ego, nothing of its physiognomy and gestures, passes over into nature. It is only at the time of the change of teeth that this begins to happen. Therefore it is only then—after the change of teeth—that we are mature enough to begin to reflect about any natural phenomenon. Until that time it is only arbitrary thoughts that arise in a child, thoughts that really have not very much to do with nature, and for that very reason are so full of charm. The best way to approach children is to be poetical and call the stars the eyes of heaven, and so on, and the things we speak about with children should be as remote as possible from outer physical reality.[2]

It is only after the change of teeth that children gradually 'grow into' nature, and then their thoughts can in course of time comprehend thoughts of nature. Fundamentally speaking life from the seventh to the fourteenth year is a period during which children 'grow into nature', for in this period, in addition to their memories, they also carry into the realm of nature their gestures and physiognomy. And this then continues throughout the whole of life. It is not until the change of teeth that, as far as the inner core of nature is concerned, we are 'born' as separate human individuals.

This is why the beings I have called elementals—the gnomes and undines—listen so eagerly when a person tells them something about childhood as it was before the age of seven. For as far as these nature beings are concerned human beings are really only born at the change of teeth. This is an extremely interesting phenomenon. Before that time human beings are to the gnomes and undines beings 'in the beyond'. Therefore it is for them something of an enigma that human beings should appear at this age in a certain state of completion. It would, however, be immensely stimulating for pedagogical imagination if, through absorbing spiritual knowledge, a human being could really participate in a dialogue with the nature spirits, if he could transport himself into the soul of the nature spirits in order to obtain their views about what he can tell them about children. This would produce the most wonderful fairy-tale imagination. And if in olden times fairy-tales were so wonderfully vivid and full of content it was because the story-tellers could actually converse with gnomes and undines and not merely hear something from them. These nature spirits are sometimes very egoistic. They become taciturn if they are not told things they are curious to know. Their favourite stories are those about the things babies do. Then one learns a great many things from them that can create the atmosphere of a fairy-tale. What seems utterly fantastic to people today can be very important for the practical application of spiritual life. It is an actual fact that because of the circumstances I have told you about, these dialogues with the nature spirits can be extremely instructive for both sides.

On the other hand, what I have said will of course give rise to a certain anxiety, for during sleep human beings are continually creating images of their inmost being. Behind the phenomena of nature, behind the flowers of the field, and extending into the etheric world, there are reproductions of our memories, good and futile alike. The earth teems with what lives in human souls. Human life is intimately connected with such things.

First of all, then, we encounter nature spirits as beings into whom we penetrate through our gestures. But we also find the world of the angeloi, archangeloi and archai. We grow our way into those beings too. Our memories carry us into the deeds of the angelic world, our physiognomy and gestures—for which we ourselves are responsible—carry us into the very substantiality of those beings themselves. The following sketch will give some indication of what happens when, during sleep, we penetrate into nature. Let this (lowest) curve represent our skin; as we move outwards in a radial direction we pass from the region of the angeloi into those of the archangeloi and the archai. We enter the sphere of the Third Hierarchy. And when, during sleep, we sink down with our memories and gestures into the flowing sea of angeloi, archangeloi and archai then, from one side, there comes another stream of spiritual beings [see diagram]. This is the Second Hierarchy: exousiai, kyriotetes and dynamis. If we want to find something in the physical world that bears a resemblance to this, we can say that the daily course of the sun from east to west expresses the path on which the Second Hierarchy cross the Third Hierarchy. The Third Hierarchy hover up and down, up and down, handing to one another the 'golden vessels'.[3] In this description we think of the Second Hierarchy following the path taken by the sun from east to west—not the apparent but the actual daily path of the sun, for the Copernican theory does not hold good here. So if a human being has the necessary vision he sees how during sleep he passes into the world of the Third Hierarchy. But this world of the Third Hierarchy is permeated ceaselessly by the grace of the Second Hierarchy flowing in from the side. And this Second Hierarchy also make their influence felt in our life of soul.

In the lecture the day before yesterday I pointed out to you the significance of vividly reliving experiences of youth. You may be deeply impressed if you turn again to the Mystery

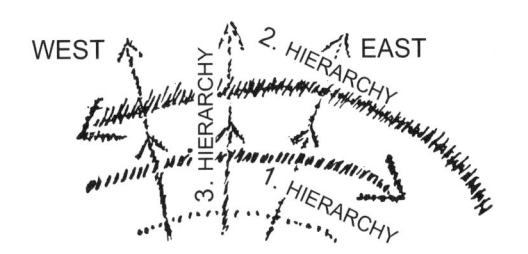

Plays and now, perhaps with greater understanding than before, read the passages about the appearance of the spirit of Johannes' youth.[4] It is doubtless the case that a person's own inner being can become vividly perceptible to him if, with an active effort of will, he relives his younger days. I suggested you might pick up old school books and steep yourself in what you either learnt or failed to learn from them. It does not matter whether you learnt anything or not. What matters is that you should relive what happened at the time. It was vitally important for me, a year or two ago, when I needed to strengthen my powers of spiritual understanding, to relive a situation of my youth. I was eleven years old at the time and had just been given a new schoolbook. The first thing that happened was that through carelessness I accidentally upset the inkpot and blotted two pages of the book so badly that they were illegible. That was also an action. And many years ago I relived this action many times—the textbook with the ruined pages and what I had to suffer in consequence, for the book had to be replaced by a family with very little money. I suffered dreadfully on account of this book with its enormous inkblot! As I said, it is not a matter of having behaved well in circumstances recalled in later years but of experiencing them with real intensity. If you recall such happenings as vividly as you possibly can, you will experience something else as well. While you are in bed, shut off from the day's impressions, you will experience a situation more than in a dream, in actual perception in fact. If during the day you have vividly recalled a scene once inwardly experienced, then when everything around you is dark and you are all by yourself at night you will see, as though displayed in space, a scene in which you once participated. Suppose you have recalled a scene where you were once present, say, at eleven o'clock. Afterwards you went somewhere else and found yourself sitting among a number of people. You have now summoned up something you experienced inwardly. What was around you outwardly at that time was entirely a spatial spectacle. If attention is paid to circumstances such as these, very significant discoveries can be made. Let us suppose that as a youngster of 17 you were accustomed to having your midday meal in a guest-house where the guests were continually coming and going. Now you recall some such scene which you had inwardly experienced; and you recall it vividly. Then, in the night, you have this experience. You are sitting at table with other people whom you did not see very often because the guests in a guest-house are perpetually changing. The face of one of these people makes you realize: this is something I actually lived through all those years ago. The external spatial element is added to the inner soul experience when you activate memories in this way.

This means you are actually living in the stream that flows from east to west [see diagram]. More and more the feeling grows in you that becoming absorbed by the spiritual element into which you pass in sleep is not the only thing that happens to you, but that in this spiritual element something more is happening that is reflected outwardly in the moment when you again see the people sitting around the table in the guest-house. You had forgotten about the episode, yet it is there. You see it as things can often be seen inscribed in the Akashic Record.[5] The moment you have this before you, you have made contact with the stream that flows from east to west—the stream of the Second Hierarchy. In this stream of the Second Hierarchy lives something of which the *day* is an image.

Now the day varies in length throughout the year. It gets longer in spring and shorter in autumn; it is longest in summer and shortest in winter. During the course of the year the day undergoes a metamorphosis. This is caused by a stream running from west to east, countering the east-west stream [diagram]. It is the stream of the First Hierarchy, of the seraphim, cherubim and thrones. Thus if you follow how the day changes in the course of the year, if you pass from the day to the year, then, my dear friends, you pass into the stream flowing in the opposite direction, and which meets you in sleep.

It is really the case that in sleep we grow into the spiritual world in a radial direction both in the direction going from west to east and the direction going from east to west. As I have told you, when we recall some experience vividly spatial images appear before us.

It is the same when we become conscious of our will. It is just this that becomes gesture and physiognomy—when we become conscious of our will. What I am now going to say will have a certain significance for eurythmists, although naturally it is not the purpose of eurythmy to vindicate what I am saying. It is a fact that when a person really begins to shape his external appearance according to his inner being, and his ego comes more and more to expression in his physiognomy and gestures, then he does not only have an impression of the day. An impression of the day comes from passing over from a vivid, inner experience of memory to a perception of things in the external world of space. To experience again what you learnt at the age of 17, and then to see the people who sat at table with you in the guest-house, in pictures, as in the Akashic Record—that is experiencing the day!

But you can also experience the year. This is possible if we pay attention to how the will works in us—if we notice that it is comparatively easy to assert our will when we are warm, whereas it is difficult to get the will to stream through our body when we are very cold. Whoever can inwardly experience a connection between the will and being warm or cold will gradually acquire the ability to speak of a winter will and a summer will in themselves.

We find that the best way to describe this will is to relate it to the seasons. Let us observe, for example, the kind of will that seems to carry our thoughts out into the cosmos and make it easy to handle the body, so that in its whole bearing and gestures the thoughts seem to be borne out into the cosmos; they just slip out of your fingertips. You are very aware of how easy it is to activate the will. We may be standing by a tree and something at the top of it pleases our eye. If our will is warm within us our thoughts are carried up to the top of the tree—in fact sometimes they even go up to the very stars in heaven, when on summer nights we feel ourselves in possession of a warm will.

On the other hand, if the will within us grows cold it is as though all our thoughts were only in our heads and none of them could reach into our arms or legs. Everything goes into the head. The head suffers the coldness of the will and, if the coldness of the will is not so overwhelming as to give rise to a feeling of iciness, the head will become warm as a result of its own inner reaction and then it develops thoughts.

Thus we can say that summer will leads us out into the wide expanses of the cosmos. Summer will, warm will, carries our thoughts here, there and everywhere. Winter will carries thoughts into our head. You can distinguish the two kinds of will. And we shall feel that the will that carries us out into the cosmos is related to the course of the summer, and the will that carries thoughts into the head, to the winter. In the same way as we experience day we now, through the will, experience the year.

You know, there is the actual possibility of experiencing as a reality what I am now going to write on the blackboard for you. Your experience of winter through the medium of the will can be expressed in these words:

> O cosmic likenesses!
> wafting towards me
> from wide widths of space
> you seek me out
> and enter with strength
> into the thought forces
> of my head.

These words have no merely abstract meaning. If you can feel your own will united with nature you will also feel, when winter comes, as though your own experiences, handed over to nature, were being brought to you from the expanses of space. And in the wavelike flow movement indicated here:

> O cosmic likenesses!
> wafting towards me
> from wide widths of space
> you seek me out,
> and enter with strength
> into the thought forces
> of my head...

you can be aware of your own experiences which had already passed over into nature. This is how winter will feels. But you can also feel the summer will which bears your thoughts out into the cosmos:

> You, of my head
> the soul-forces a-forming
> you fill my whole body...

which means that the thoughts which are at first experienced in the head pass over into and fill the whole body, but then wing their way forth from it:

> Then wing your way outward
> to cosmic expanses
> uniting my being
> with the might of creation.

These words express the nature of summer will, the will in us that is related to summer. And if I feel that I have called up out of my inner being the active memory of something experienced long ago, then the day followed by night brings it back to me again, supplemented by the spatial picture. This corresponds to the stream from east to west. Thus we may say: winter will changes in us into summer will, summer will into winter will. We are no longer related to the day with its alternating light and darkness, but through our will we are related to the year, and therewith to the stream flowing from west to east, the stream of the First Hierarchy—the seraphim, cherubim and thrones.

In our further meetings we shall see how human beings may be hindered or helped through heredity or adaptation to the external world through this association with the inmost life of nature. For what I have just been telling you refers to the fact that human beings, when hindered as little as possible by ahrimanic and luciferic forces, grow in this way, by means of thought forces and will, into the inmost life of nature and are received by the spirits of time, the spirits of day and the spirits of the year—Third Hierarchy, Second Hierarchy and First Hierarchy. But the ahrimanic forces manifesting in heredity and the luciferic forces in adaptation exert very deep influences. This big subject will occupy us next time.

Winter Will	*Summer Will*
O cosmic likenesses!	You, of my head
wafting towards me	the soul forces a-forming
from wide widths of space	you fill my whole body.
you seek me out,	Then wing your way outward
and enter with strength	to cosmic expanses
into the thought forces	uniting my being
of my head.	with the might of creation*

---

* For German text see Appendix 1.

LECTURE 4

The Relation of Human Beings to the Earth

A continuation of the themes we discussed last time will lead us today to things that will serve as a preparation for the two following lectures. It brings us to study the connection of the human being, the whole human being, with our planet earth. As I have often said, we are under a kind of illusion if we ascribe to ourselves as physical beings a full and individual existence separate from the earth. As beings of soul and spirit we are independent and individual; with regard to our physical bodies and to some extent also in respect of our etheric bodies, we belong to the organic totality of the earth.

I will begin today by describing how this connection between human beings and earth existence appears to supersensible vision. As a form of introduction I will use a more narrative style today. Let us suppose that someone with imaginative consciousness were to go on a journey through the primeval alps where the rocks consist of quartz, of siliceous minerals and similar formations. These primeval mountains are composed of the hardest rocks on earth, but as well as being the hardest, these rocks, when they appear in their original form, have an inherent purity about them, a quality untouched by the commonplace things of earth. We can well understand it when, in a beautiful essay which has actually been read here, Goethe speaks of his experiences among these primeval mountains, of the solitude he felt as he sat there, and the impression made upon him by these granite rocks, towering up from the earth. Goethe speaks of granite, composed as it is of silica, mica and felspar, as the 'enduring son of earth'.

When with ordinary consciousness a human being approaches these primeval mountains he can of course admire them from outside; he is deeply impressed by their forms, by their wonderful structure, primitive as it is, but extraordinarily eloquent. However, if he approaches this hardest of rocks of the earth with imaginative consciousness he penetrates beneath the surface of mineral nature and is then able, with his thinking, to grow together as it were with the rock. He reaches in soul into the depths of the rock and enters spiritually into a holy palace of the gods. The interior is revealed to imaginative vision as transparent, and the outer surface as the walls of this palace of the gods. At the same time the knowledge comes to him that within this rock there is a reflection of the cosmos outside the earth. The world of stars is mirrored here before our soul. We ultimately get the impression that all quartz rocks are like eyes through which the earth can see into the cosmos. We are reminded of the many-faceted eyes of insects, which divide into a number of parts whatever comes towards them from outside. We should, and indeed must, picture innumerable quartz and similar formations on the surface of the earth as being eyes enabling the earth to mirror within it and indeed inwardly to perceive the cosmic environment. And gradually the knowledge dawns on us that every crystal formation present in the earth is a sense organ for perceiving the cosmos.

The majesty of the earth's snow covering, but even more of the falling snowflakes lies in the fact that in each single snowflake there is a reflection of a large part of the cosmos; so that, with this crystallized water, reflections of parts of the starry heavens fall upon the earth.

I need not remind you that the starry heavens are there by day as well as by night, only they cannot be seen by day because the sunlight is too strong. If ever you have an opportunity to go into a deep cellar with a high tower above it open at the top, you can see the stars even in the daytime because you are looking out of the darkness and the sunlight does not obtrude. There is, for instance, such a tower in Jena through which the stars can be seen in the daytime. I mention this in passing to make it clear to you that this reflection of the stars in the snowflakes, and indeed in every crystal, is of course there in the daytime too. It is not a physical reflection; it is a spiritual reflection, and the impression a person can have of it must be communicated inwardly.

But that is not all. This spiritual sense impression, if I may call it that, gives rise to a feeling in the soul that if you enter imaginatively into the crystal covering of the earth you yourself are able to share in all the experiences coming from the cosmos to the earth through the crystals. You thereby extend your own being into the cosmos and feel yourself one with the cosmos. And, most important of all, it now becomes a deep truth to someone possessed of imaginative vision that what we call our planet earth, in every single part, has in the course of ages been born out of the cosmos. For here the kinship between the earth and the cosmos appears vividly to the inner eye. Thus by living our way into the millions of crystal eyes in the earth we are being prepared to feel and experience the inner kinship of the earth with the cosmos.

This experience, again, makes you realize how connected as a human being you are with the earth. For this birth of the earth out of the cosmos—and I shall describe this in far greater detail over the coming days—took place when human beings were still very primitive beings, not physical but spiritual beings. And in their own being humans shared in the processes undergone by the earth after its birth out of the cosmos. In actual fact the same inner connection once existed between the earth and the neighbouring cosmos as that between an unborn child and the body of its mother. Later, however, the child begins to become independent. Similarly, the earth developed independently after having been more completely a part of the cosmos during the earliest part of the Saturn epoch. Human beings accompanied this process towards independence until they were finally able to say: My finger is a finger only as long as it is part of my organism; the moment I have it amputated it is no longer a finger and withers away. And if human beings with regard to their physical part can be thought of as separated by only a few miles from the conditions of the earth organism they would wither away like the amputated finger. Because they can move by themselves over the face of the earth people are under the illusion that as physical beings they have an existence of their own independent of the earth, whereas a finger cannot run around by itself. If it could do so it would be succumbing to the same delusion human beings succumb to regarding their own physical existence and the earth. Higher knowledge makes clear to us this relationship of our physical nature to the earth.

So this is the first way in which imaginative consciousness helps us get to know the hardest component of the earth's surface.

A further way is possible by descending a little more deeply into the earth, to the veins or lodes of metal ores, in fact to any metallic substance in the earth's interior. Here you are penetrating beneath the surface of the earth. But metals have a very special character, a character which deviates from that of any other earthly substance. Metals have a certain independence which can be experienced, and this experience is of very great significance for human beings.[1]

Even someone who reaches a certain level of imaginative vision still does not have a full grasp of things when, through experiencing quartz and other primeval rocks as the million eyes of the earth, he expands his being into the cosmos. If, however, he penetrates farther into the interior of the earth, the first impulses he receives can arise from the wonderful stimuli that can be had in a metal mine. Once you have the momentum, however, all that is necessary to be able to experience the nature of metallic substance without going down the shaft of a mine is spiritual vision. But the first feeling of the experience I am talking about can be acquired with particular intensity in metal mines themselves. It is no longer the case today, but it was still true a few decades ago, that miners who are inwardly wedded to their work display something of this profound sense of the spiritual element in metals. For the metals not only 'see' the surrounding cosmos but they speak. Their speech is a spiritual kind, but speak they do, and tell their story. And the language they speak is very similar to the impressions received from a language spoken in a different domain.

You know, when we succeed in establishing an inner connection of soul with human beings who are in the stage of evolution between death and a new birth we shall need a special language to communicate with them. What the spiritualists say is puerile, for the simple reason that the dead do not speak the language of earthly human beings. Spiritualists believe that the dead speak in such a way that their words can be written down, just as though a letter were being received from a contemporary living person. In most cases the messages heard in seances sound high-flown and pompous of course, but even on earth some of our living contemporaries sometimes write the same sort of thing. This is not how it is at all. The fact of the matter is that we have first to find the right approach to the language which the dead speak and which bears no resemblance whatever to any earthly language, although it *does* have a vocal-consonantal character. But the same language, and this can be apprehended only by spiritual hearing, is spoken by the metals in the interior of the earth. And this same language, by means of which we can approach the souls of the dead living between death and a new birth, can also recount the memories of the earth, the experiences undergone by the earth in its course through the epochs of Saturn, Sun and Moon, and so on. The metals can tell us of the past history of the earth. The destinies of our whole planetary system are to be learnt from what Saturn has to communicate. It is of what the earth has undergone in the evolutionary process that the metals tell.

The language in which the metals speak about the earth can also take two forms. In its usual form it will reveal what the earth has undergone in the course of its evolution beginning with Saturn. What you find about this evolution in my *Occult Science: an Outline* arose largely in this way, as I have often described—by direct spiritual perception of the process concerned. That, however, is a somewhat different way of learning about the earth's history than the one I have in mind just now. The metals—if I may put it this way, although naturally it sounds rather strange—the metals tell us more about the 'personal' experiences of the earth, the earth as a specific entity in the cosmos. So if I wanted to lay particular emphasis on the stories told by the metals, stories learnt by spiritual penetration into the interior of the earth, I should have to add many details of the Saturn, Sun and Moon epochs, and so forth.

A first example would, for instance, be that in the conditions on Old Saturn described in my *Occult Science* as consisting of differentiations of warmth, there appear gigantic and mighty warmth beings which, even during the Saturn epoch, had reached a certain degree of density.[2] Roughly speaking I could say: if it were possible—which of course it is not—but if it were possible for an earthly human being to encounter these beings, he would notice them and even be able to touch them. Thus about the middle of the Saturn epoch these beings were not *purely* spiritual but displayed a certain physical quality. If you had touched them your fingers would have blistered. It would be wrong to assume that they had a temperature of millions of degrees, but their temperature was such that any contact would have caused blisters.

Then we should have to pass to the Sun epoch and relate, as I did in *Occult Science*, how other beings appeared, manifesting wonderful transformations, metamorphoses. Seeing these beings in process of metamorphosis we should get the impression that the metamorphoses described by classical authors such as Ovid have something to do, though of course not directly, with this experiencing of the communications of the metals. Ovid was certainly not himself capable of understanding the language of the metals directly, and what he describes in his *Metamorphoses* does not fully convey the impression we get, but what he says is derived in a way from this source.[3] And we can indicate the underlying process to a marked degree. You know, even Paracelsus, who lived at a much later time than the personality to whom I have just referred, did not go to college to learn the most important things he wanted to learn. I do not imply that he did not actually go to college, for as a matter of fact he did, and I have no objection whatever to such a course. But for knowledge of the greatest importance he went where more significant information could be obtained. He went, for example, to men such as metal-miners, and acquired a great deal of his knowledge this way.

Anyone familiar with the technique of acquiring knowledge is aware of how extraordinarily illuminating the simple words of a peasant engaged in the business of sowing and reaping can be. You will say that he does not know what he is talking about. You do not need to bother about that, as long as *you* understand what he tells you. Certainly it will be only very rarely that the speaker himself understands what he is saying—it is a matter of instinct. And even more fundamental knowledge can be acquired from creatures such as beetles, butterflies and birds, who understand nothing at all of what they say to us.

Pythagoras, on his travels, studied with great intensity what could be learnt by listening to the speech of the metals in the mines of the Near East, and a great deal of what he learnt made its way into what then became Graeco-Roman culture. In a weakened form it appears in a work such as Ovid's *Metamorphoses*. This is the one form of the speech of metals in the interior of the earth.

The other form—and grotesque as this seems, it is true—is revealed when the speech of the metals becomes poetical and begins to produce cosmic poetry. Cosmic fantasy actually manifests in the language of the metals. And then this cosmic poetry tells of the close relationship existing between the metals and human beings. These most close of relationships do indeed exist. The crude relationships known to physiology involve only a few metals. It is known that iron plays an important role in human blood, but iron is really the only metal of this kind. A few others—potassium, calcium, sodium and magnesium—also play a certain part. But a large number of metals, which are important for the structure and functioning of the earth, seem to crude observation to play no part in the human organism at all. But that is only apparently the case. If you penetrate into the earth and learn there to know the speech of the metals, you will also learn that the metals are truly not present only in the interior of the earth but everywhere in its environment as well, although in exceedingly fine distribution, in a hyper-homoeopathic solution, if I may so express it.

In the crude, material sense we cannot have lead within us; in the finer, more ethereal sense we cannot live without it. For what would become of us human beings if lead from the cosmos, from the atmosphere, did not have its effect upon us, if lead in an infinitely fine state of distribution did not penetrate with the rays of the sun through our eyes into our skin, if lead did not penetrate into us through the breathing process, and again in an infinitely fine state into the food we eat? In short, where would human beings be if lead did not work in them?

Without lead we would indeed have sense perceptions; we would be able to perceive colours and musical tones, but with every perception we would become slightly faint, slightly out of our body. We would never be able to stand back from our perceptions and reflect in thoughts and mental concepts about what we had perceived. If we did not absorb any lead in the infinitely fine homoeopathic potencies of which I spoke, into our nervous system and, above all, into our brain, we should be entirely given up to all our sense perceptions, as if they were something outside us. We should be unable to form any mental picture of our sense perceptions or retain any picture of them in our memory. It is the finely distributed lead in our brain that makes this possible.

If a considerable quantity of lead is introduced into the human organism the result is lead-poisoning—a dreadful condition. But those who are aware of the facts can realize from this power of lead to poison that just because it has a disastrous effect if introduced into the human organism in any considerable quantity, when it is administered in an extremely fine hyper-homoeopathic dilution it can at any given moment bring about the dampening down of the life forces to the extent necessary to enable a human being to be a conscious being and not to be perpetually in the grip of uncontrolled processes of growth, which cause faintness and loss of consciousness. For this is what happens if growth forces, by themselves, become overpowering.

Human beings have definite relationships to all the metals, including those of which crude physiology says nothing. Knowledge of these relationships is the foundation for a true therapy. 'Inside' information about the relationships of the metals to human beings can be given only by the poetic speech of the metals of the earth. So it may be said that whereas the ordinary speech of the metals gives information about the actual destiny of the earth, information about the therapeutic relationships of the metals to human beings is given by the metals when their speech becomes poetic.

There is a remarkable link here. From the cosmic aspect medicine is cosmic poetry, just as altogether many mysteries of existence lie in the fact that what at one level is pathological or leads in that direction is, at another level, something of the loftiest, most perfect and beautiful nature. This is what emerges when inspired consciousness finds access to the metallic element in the earth.

Now we can relate in another way too to metals, and this comes about when metals are subjected to natural forces, for example to fire. Just think of the remarkable formation of antimony ore. It is composed of single spear-shaped structures, showing by this formation that it follows certain lines of force that are active in the cosmos. If antimony is subjected to a process of combustion it becomes an antimony 'mirror'. When it is spread on glass it develops a special power of reflection. It has other peculiarities too, for example it readily explodes if handled electrically and connected to a cathode. All these characteristics of antimony indicate how a metallic substance of this kind relates to the forces of the earth and the earth's environment. The same can be seen with all metals; this can be observed when they are exposed to fire, and the temperature rises higher and higher, and they pass first of all into the super-homoeopathic condition which I told you about. At these temperatures they assume a quite different form. In regard to this our modern physicists have only the roughest idea. They imagine that when lead melts it becomes softer and softer, and so it does to begin with. The lead gets softer and softer as the temperature rises, and as it gets hotter and hotter it becomes more and more volatile, giving off lead fumes, and so on. What the physicists do not know is that all the time something that does not reach beyond a certain temperature is being deposited, separated off. Lead in this finest, super-homoeopathic state passes over continually into invisible life in general, and in this form it works upon human beings.

Actually it is always like this. In the earth itself there are metals of infinite kinds, but above the earth these metals are present everywhere in the finest possible state of distribution; they have vapourized. Down in the earth the metals have their sharp contours and definite structures; at a still greater depth they are of course in a molten condition. But in the environment of the earth, where they are in the finest possible state of distribution, they are continually radiating, and actually radiate out into cosmic space. Now in cosmic space there is inner elasticity. However, the forces do not radiate in a limitless fashion—as the physicists imagine to be the case with light rays—but these forces ray out to a certain boundary and then return. As they ray back, the metal forces can be pictured as returning from all sides, from the periphery of the universe. And we observe these returning forces at work where we witness one of the most wonderful, most beautiful of all sights in human life—a child, in its early years of life, learning to walk, speak and think.

One of the most wonderful sights in the whole of earthly life is to see a child, from the crawling stage, standing upright and orientating itself in space, coming to itself as a human being. The returning forces of the metals are working inwardly in the forces that give the child the power of orientation. As the child learns to raise itself from the horizontal position of crawling, it is permeated by the forces of the metals as they ray back. This is the force that actually raises the child into the upright position. If this connection is recognized, then at the same time you grasp another factor. It is that in the deeds, in the essential nature of the human being living here on earth, you recognize the connection with his previous incarnation. The faculties for perceiving the workings of the metals in the cosmos and the karmic connection between the successive lives on earth are the same. The one recognition comes with the other, and neither is possible without the other. That is why I said in an entirely different context that in this power of orientation, in the power that enables the child to rise from crawling to standing and walking, in the faculties of learning to speak and to think, lie the fruits coming from earlier lives on earth. On that occasion I said that anyone with an eye for these things perceives in the way children take their first steps, whether they tend to put their toes or heels down first, whether they bend their knees very much or not—in all this, a karmic disposition from an earlier incarnation can be perceived. It shows itself first of all in the gait. This is because together with the faculty enabling the metal forces as they ray back to be perceived comes the faculty to perceive the connection of the present life of a human being with his earlier lives.

The assertion that anthroposophy is not open to proof is

entirely unjustified. People who assert this are accustomed to bringing forward sense-perception as proof. But that is tantamount to saying: 'Are you actually telling me that the earth moves freely in space? It is simply not possible. Either there must be something to support it or it would fall!' In point of fact it does not fall because cosmic bodies mutually support one another. Only in the conditions prevailing on earth does everything need to be supported. So it is only for truths recognized by the everyday consciousness that proofs can rightly be offered if they are called for. Truths relating to the spirit are mutually confirmatory—but this must also be felt as an inner conviction.

I told you some weeks ago that from the way a child—or an adult—walks, whether he raises his toes or his heel first, treads firmly or lightly, bends his knees a great deal or is more inclined to stand stiffly—these things show that the karma from his previous earthly life is coming to realization. Today I am showing you how the forces of the metals as they ray back enable us to recognize the connection between earthly lives. Here you see two mutually confirmatory truths. But it happens all the time that we hear a truth, then after some time we hear the same truth from a different angle, and perhaps we hear it a third time. In this way the truths of anthroposophy confirm one another, just as in the cosmos the heavenly bodies uphold one another without needing outer support. It has to be like this when we rise from truths that are valid only for everyday consciousness to truths that are self-sustaining realities in the cosmos. And what anthroposophical knowledge comprises is indeed self-sustaining reality.

You must hold together in your mind statements made at different times, statements that mutually support, attract, or also repel each other, revealing thereby the inner life of anthroposophical knowledge. Other forms of knowledge, customary today, live by virtue of the supports on which they are based; anthroposophical knowledge is self-sustaining.

LECTURE 5

The Mineral, Vegetable and Animal Creations

On the basis of what I said yesterday it is possible to speak in greater detail of certain events in the course of the earth's evolution which have brought about its present form. As you will remember, I said that with clairvoyant consciousness a relationship can be established with the metallic substance of the earth, in fact with everything in the earth that acquires substantial reality by virtue of the veins of metal running through it. This relationship that can be established with the earth's metallic element enables us to look back over the earth's history.

It is particularly interesting to look back at what happened in the process of evolution in the times preceding the Atlantean epoch, to the period I rather loosely called the Lemurian age, and also to the epoch immediately before that, when the earth was recapitulating the Sun stage. It is interesting to look back at these happenings, for we can get an impression from them of the extent to which everything to do with earth's existence is capable of change.

We are accustomed today to regard the earth as having always existed in the form in which it appears to us now. We inhabit a continent where we are surrounded by plants, animals and birds of the air. We know that we ourselves are living in a kind of atmospheric ocean surrounding the earth, that we take oxygen out of this atmosphere into ourselves, and that our relation to nitrogen also plays a certain part. On the whole we simply think of ourselves as surrounded by air consisting of oxygen and nitrogen. We are also aware of the seas and oceans—further details need not be mentioned—and from all this we get a picture of the planet we inhabit in the universe. But the earth has not always been as it is today; it has undergone tremendous changes and, if we go back to the epochs I have just mentioned—perhaps only to the Lemurian epoch or a little earlier—we shall find an earth very different from that of today.[1]

Let us begin by thinking of the air we breathe today and which we regard as being devoid of life. Even this atmosphere proves to be quite different from anything to be found in early periods of the earth's evolution. Still farther in the past something resembling a solid core of the earth as we know it today is in evidence, surrounded by an atmosphere. But in those days there was nothing at all like the air we breathe today. In this air oxygen and nitrogen play the most prominent part, carbon and hydrogen a subsidiary role and sulphur and phosphorus a role of less importance still.

But it is really not possible to speak of oxygen, nitrogen, carbon, sulphur and the rest in those early times, simply because what the chemists call by these names today did not then exist. If a spirit being of those times were to have met a modern chemist who spoke to him about carbon, oxygen, nitrogen and the rest, he would have retorted that nothing of the kind exists. We can justifiably speak of carbon, oxygen and nitrogen today, but this could not have been done in those early times. Oxygen, nitrogen, carbon, as we speak of them today, became possible only when the earth had reached a certain density and had developed forces such as it contains today. Oxygen, nitrogen, potassium, sodium, and so on, all the so-called lighter metals, did not exist at all in those times. On the other hand, in the earth's environment which is filled today by our atmosphere there was something a little like albumen in consistency, a very fine fluid half-way between our present water and air. The earth at that time was entirely surrounded by an albuminous atmosphere. The albumen we know in eggs today is very much coarser, but a comparison is possible.

When, at a later time, the earth became denser, what we today call carbon, hydrogen, oxygen, nitrogen and so on were differentiated out of this atmosphere around the earth. But it would be erroneous to say that the then albuminous atmosphere was composed of these elements, for they were not specific ingredients of it. Nowadays we think of everything as composite, but that is nonsense. Certain substances of a higher nature are not always composed of what comes to light when they are analysed; the different ingredients cease to be there. Carbon does not appear as carbon nor oxygen as oxygen, for it is a substance of a higher nature. As I said, it can be described as extremely fluid albumen. And all this substance surrounding the earth in those days was permeated by the inpouring cosmic ether, which imbued it with life. Thus it was the cosmic ether pouring into it which gave this substance its life. However, it did not only have life, but in addition it was differentiated in a curious way. For instance in one area this substance was structured so that people would have suffocated in it had they been there, and in another area the structure of it would have invigorated them. Chemical elements in the modern sense did not then exist, but certain formations arose then which remind one of the effects of the chemical elements we know. The whole sphere teemed with sparkling, gleaming reflections of light, and it was warmed through and through by the cosmic ether.

Such were the properties, in that early period, of the earth atmosphere—if I may use the modern expression. The first things that formed from out of the cosmos on the earth, as I described yesterday, were the primeval mountains. The quartz to be found in those mountains, with its beautiful structure and relative transparency, was as it were poured into the earth from the cosmos. This is how it happens that when a seer endowed with imaginative vision enters into these primeval rocks, which are the hardest substance on earth, they become for him eyes with which to see the cosmos—the same cosmos which implanted these eyes into the earth. Only the quartz and siliceous substances, which permeated the whole atmosphere and were gradually deposited as primeval mountains, were not as hard as they are today. They hardened into the state we know because of the conditions that prevailed in later times. In the form in which they emerged from the cosmos their consistency was scarcely more solid than wax. A quartz crystal to be seen in the mountains today is so hard that if you were to hit your head against it your skull—not the quartz—would crack. But in the far distant past, because of the all-pervading life, this primeval stone was as pliable as wax when it emerged from the cosmos, and it was also transparent. Its consistency can be pictured only by thinking of it in connection with the sense of touch. If one could have touched it, it would have felt like wax. Thus the primeval mountains consisted of wax that showered down out of the cosmos and then hardened. Silicic acid also had wax form in those times.

I described yesterday how pictures of the cosmos arise in clairvoyant contemplation of this dense rock. These pictures represent a more spiritual aspect of the phenomenon that was once absolutely perceptible as a kind of plant form in portions of the transparent waxlike silica emerging from the cosmos. Any observer of nature will know that in the mineral kingdom today records of an earlier age are still to be found. When you look closely at certain stones you will see something like a plant form within them. But in that distant past a quite unusual phenomenon was that pictures were projected from the cosmos into the atmosphere, into this albuminous atmosphere, pictures that were not only seen but were reproduced, physically photographed, onto the inside of the wax substance.

And then there was a remarkable development. The fluid albumen filled these pictures and they became somewhat denser and harder, and were then no longer pictures. The siliceous substance fell away from them, dispersed into the atmosphere, and in the earliest Lemurian age there appeared gigantic floating plant formations which remind one of the algae of today. They were not rooted in the soil (there was as yet no soil), they floated in the fluid albumen, drawing their own substance from it. But they did not merely float in it, they began to shine, to shed light, and then vanished, appeared again, and vanished. They were capable of going through change to such an extent that this arising and disappearing was possible.

Try to picture this vividly. It is a vista very different from anything to be seen in our environment today. If as a modern person you could project yourself into that far-off time, set up a little observation hut and look out on that ancient world, you would see the following spectacle. A plant image appears, a gigantic plant image similar, as I said, to our present-day algae or even palms. It would not appear to grow out of the earth in springtime and die away in the autumn. It would shoot up in springtime it is true—but the spring was then much shorter—and reach an enormous size; then it would vanish again in the fluid albuminous element. As an observer, you would see a constant change between the greening process and the fading away. You would not speak of plants covering the earth but of plants appearing out of the cosmos like airy clouds, condensing and then dissolving, a greening in the albuminous atmosphere. Of the period which would correspond more or less to our summer, you would say that it was the time when the environment of the earth became green. But you would look upwards to the green rather than downwards. In this way we can picture how the siliceous element in the earth's atmosphere penetrates into the earth and draws to itself the force of the plants, which is actually out in the cosmos. This is indeed how the plant kingdom came down to the earth from the cosmos. In the period of which I am speaking, however, we must say of the plant world that it was something that came into being in the atmosphere and passed away again.

And there is also something else to be said. If as a human being today you project yourself, by means of a relationship with the metallic element of the earth, into those past times, you would feel as if all this belonged to you yourself, as if you had something to do with the process of greening and fading then taking place in the atmosphere. Now if you think back to your own childhood, that is simply a memory of a short span of time. If, however, you recall a pain suffered in your childhood, that is something which really belongs to you. Similarly, in the cosmic memory of the past kindled through the metallic element of the earth, this process of greening and fading in the far past seems to be something which belongs to you. As human beings we were at that time already connected with the earth, which was surrounded by this watery-albuminous atmosphere; although we were still entirely spiritual. It is correct to say—and this idea must be got hold of—that these plants seen in the atmosphere at that time were something pushed out, 'excreted' by the human entity. This happened at the time when the human entity was still one with the whole earth. And this same concept must also be extended to apply to something quite different which humanity also pushed out. I will tell you what happened. Everything that I have so far described is the result of the fact that the silica element had already, at an earlier time, been precipitated into the atmosphere as the waxlike substance of which I have spoken. But apart from this there was the albuminous atmosphere upon which the infinitely diverse forces of the cosmos were working, those forces which modern science chooses to ignore. This is why our modern knowledge is no real knowledge at all, because a great many happenings on earth simply would not take place if they were not brought about by cosmic forces and influences. Since our modern scientists do not speak of these cosmic forces they do not speak of reality at all. They take no account of what lives in things. Even in the tiniest section looked at through a microscope not only earthly forces but cosmic forces are at work. And if these cosmic forces are not taken into account you do not have reality.

Thus cosmic forces were working in that remote time upon the fluid albumen in the earth's environment, and these forces worked upon certain sections of it in such a way that it coagulated. Cosmic, coagulated albumen swam about in the atmosphere. However, these forms were not cloud masses but the definite forms of living creatures. In reality they were animals consisting of the coagulated albumen which had solidified into a gelatinous state, into a substance similar to gristle as it is today. Animal creatures of this kind were present in the fluid albuminous atmosphere. The forms of our present reptiles, lizards and the like resemble, on a small scale, the forms of those earlier animals, but the latter were not so solid; they existed as gelatinous masses and were inherently mobile. At one moment their limbs were extended, at another drawn in—comparable with what a snail does with its feelers today.

Now while these forms were coming into being above the earth, something further than silica was being deposited in the earth from out of the cosmos; it is what you find today as the calcium constituents of the earth. If you go not necessarily into the oldest mountains but only into the Jura Mountains, you will find limestone rocks. It came down to the earth at a later stage than the silica, but it too came from the cosmos. This chalk is to be found as a second substance in the earth.

This chalk deposit constantly oozed farther into the earth, and its actual effect was that at its core the earth became denser and denser. And in certain localities the chalk combined with the silica. But this chalk retained its cosmic forces and was altogether different from the crude substance which chemists consider it to be. Wherever it appears chalk contains relatively latent formative forces.

Now in an epoch rather later than the period I described to you when the greening appeared and then faded away, we find that within this albuminous atmosphere there is a constant rising and falling of the chalk; chalk mist is followed by chalk rain. There was a period in the history of the earth when what we know today as water vapour and falling rain was a chalky substance, rising and falling. Then comes a remarkable development. The chalk was particularly attracted to the gelatinous, gristly masses; it filled them, impregnated them. And thanks to the earth forces which, as I told you, it contains, it dissolved the whole gelatinous masses of coagulated albumen. The chalk took away from the heavens what the heavens had formed in the albuminous substance and brought it nearer the earth. And out of this the animals with calcareous bones gradually came into being. This development happened in the later Lemurian epoch.

We must therefore think of plants in their earliest form as pure gifts from heaven, and the animals and all animal-like formations we must regard as something which, after the heavens had presented the earth with chalk, the earth has taken—literally filched!—from the heavens and made into creatures of earth. The happenings of these ancient times affect us strangely, and we most certainly feel a connection to them, so that we feel this whole process, also, to be a process taking place in a dimension of our human nature that as it were reaches as far as the cosmos.

Such things of course sound paradoxical because they touch upon a reality of which a modern person usually has no conception; nevertheless they are absolutely true. It would correspond with reality today to speak from out of one's memory and say: 'When I was nine years old I sometimes gave my friend a sound bashing.' You may be pleased or sorry this happened, but nevertheless the memory of it rises up. Similarly there rises up in this human consciousness expanded through a relation to the metals, and which becomes an earth consciousness, the realization that in the process of forming your whole being as it came down from heaven onto the earth you pushed forth the plants from out of yourself. They are something you have secreted. You also pushed out animal nature; your desire, in the first place, was that in the form of coagulated gelatine or gristle it should become a secreted product of yours. But then you were compelled to realize that pre-existent earth forces took this task over from you and reshaped the animals in their different forms, which are products of the earth. You can feel these happenings, through cosmic memory, to be your own experience, just as the other incident I mentioned is an experience belonging to brief earthly life. As a human being you feel connected with these happenings.

But all this is connected with various other processes—I am speaking briefly of only the most important ones. Many other things were happening. For example, during the period when what I have been describing was taking place the whole atmosphere was also filled with sulphur in a highly rarified state. This rarified sulphur combined with other substances, and from this union there arose the ancestors of what is present in the ores today as pyrites, as galena, as zinc blende, and so forth. All these substances developed at that time in an earlier form, in a soft, still waxlike consistency, and the body of the earth became filled with them. Then, when these metallic ores emerged from the universal albuminous substance and formed the solid crust of the earth, there was really nothing much else for the metals to do, unless human beings made some use of them, than to reflect about the past. And we do indeed find that they conjure up for the inner vision everything that has happened in the earth's history. However, now the time has come for a human being who feels these things to be his own cosmic or at least terrestrial experience to say to himself: Through having cast away from yourself the primeval plant form—which has since developed into the later plant formations—through having cast from you the complicated processes of animal evolution, you have also rid yourself of everything that previously stood in the way of your having a *will* within your own human entity.

It was necessary for human beings to push all this out, just as today they must secrete sweat and other things. This had to be got rid of so that the human being ceased to be a being in whom only gods willed, but became an individual with his own will which, even if it was not yet free, was nevertheless a will of his own. All this was necessary as a preparation for the earthly nature of human beings.

In the course of further development, during which there were many other happenings, everything changed. Naturally, when the metallic ores had become separate in the earth, the whole atmosphere also changed. It became far less sulphurous. Oxygen gradually gained predominance over the sulphur, whereas in ancient times sulphur was a very significant factor in the earth's atmosphere.

In this changed environment humanity was able to cast away other elements from itself, and these are the successors of the earlier plants and animals. As these later plant forms gradually came into existence they took root, but in a substance that was still very soft. Out of the earlier reptilian and lizard-like creatures animals with a more complicated structure developed, traces of which modern geology is still discovering. Nothing at all of the earliest animal creation of which I spoke can be found. It was not until the later epoch, when—for a second time as it were—humanity cast out more complicated structures, that the conditions I have been describing were present: cloud formations continually forming and dissolving, greening appearing and then fading again, soft animal-like structures which, however, were real animals; at times they contracted and had a life of their own, and then they lost their identity in the general life of the earth. All these developments resulted in greater solidification.

Among animals of this kind was one which at that time looked more or less like this [diagram]. It had a very large eyelike organ surrounded by a sort of aura. Adjoining this organ a kind of snout protruded forwards. The body was lizard-like, with powerful fins; such structures were already more solid in themselves. It would be equally correct to speak of wings as of fins in the case of these animals, for they were not yet sea creatures—there was as yet no sea. There was only the soft earth mass and the still pliable elements in the surrounding atmosphere from which only the sulphur had to some extent gone. In this atmosphere such animals flew or swam—it was something between flying and swimmimg.

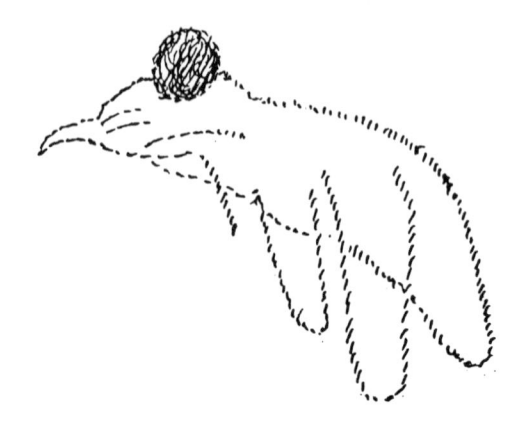

Besides these there were other animals whose limbs were not like this but which were formed more from out of the forces of the earth itself. These limbs were more reminiscent of the limbs of todays's lower species of mammals, and so on.

If someone living in the present were to travel, not in space but in time, and go back into the period connecting the Lemurian with the Atlantean age, he would be confronted by a strange spectacle: huge flying lizards with a lantern-like formation on their heads, radiating light and warmth; and down below a soft, marshy earth, but with something very familiar about it because it would seem to a visitor of today to be emitting an odour between that of decaying substance and green plants. The mud of this soft earth would emit an odour partly seductive and partly extremely pleasant. And in it, moving about like creatures of the swamp, there would be these other animals, with more in the way of limbs, reminiscent of the lower species of mammals today, but with powerful formations below—more powerful of course than the webbed feet of ducks—by means of which they propelled themselves through the swamp and also rocked up and down.

Humanity had to go through this whole process of secretion

so that independent *feeling* might be prepared in them for earthly existence.

Thus we have the first stage of vegetable-animal creation, consisting of the products secreted by the human being, and this prepared the way for him to become a being on earth possessed of *will*. If all these products had remained within him, they would have taken over the will, which would have become a wholly physical manifestation. By casting them off he got rid of physical matter, and his will became a quality of the soul. Similarly, it was through this second stage of creation that human feeling became a soul quality. Plants and mammals somewhat similar to those we know did not appear until the middle or later period of Atlantis. It was then that the earth acquired a structure definitely resembling that of today. During this phase, the substances known to modern chemists, such as carbon, oxygen, the heavy metals, and so on, gradually developed, and it was then possible for the third casting-off process to take place, and humanity secreted the plants and animals to be found in the environment today. As this environment came into existence the human race was being prepared to live on earth as *thinking* beings.

In those early times humanity was not so divided up as we are today into single individuals; there was one universal humanity, still of the nature of spirit and soul, descending into the ether. For as this ether streamed down from out of the cosmos onto the earth it brought humanity with it from the cosmos. The happenings I have described in *Occult Science* then took place: humanity came to earth, then departed to other planets, and subsequently returned during the Atlantean epoch. This went on concurrently with other events. For whenever it was a matter of casting something off, humanity could not remain with the earth, but had to depart from it in order that certain forces, now more of the nature of soul, might be strengthened. Humanity then came down again to the earth. These happenings add details to what you can read in *Occult Science*. Humanity in truth belongs to the cosmos, and it is human beings who prepare the earthly environment for themselves by casting off the kingdoms of nature and sending them forth into the earth realm. They are now here in the earthly kingdom and form our human environment. By sending these secretions into the earth realm human beings have equipped themselves bit by bit with the faculties of willing, feeling and thinking. It was only in the course of time that we evolved into what we are today: thinking, feeling and willing beings depending on an organic-physical bodily basis during our life between birth and death, with a connection, also, to the beings who, in order to further our evolution, have in the course of time separated from the human realm, and in this state of separation have metamorphosed into their present forms.

It is clear from what has been said that we cannot generalize in an abstract way about the relationship that can be established with the metals of the earth. For it is like this. When a relationship has been established with the metals, which hold within themselves the memory of past earth happenings, then one really can say something about what is remembered and discover for oneself what I have been describing to you today.

If we now go back to still earlier times we shall find that everything is even more transient, more evanescent. Think of the grandeur and the majesty of the vista I described to you: those appearing and disappearing waxlike silica formations in which were depicted images of the plant world that filled themselves with the soft albumen, thus producing in the earth environment up above the phenomenon of greening and fading. Think of all this, and you will realize that in contrast to the plants growing out of of the earth today, with their firmly formed roots and leaves, or even our present trees with their strong trunks, all this was as ephemeral as a cloud. How fleeting these earlier forms were compared to a present-day oak. The oak may not itself be proud of its strength but the people living near such trees are usually the ones who are guilty of pride, for they mistake their frequent weakness for the sturdiness of the oak! If you compare this sturdiness of our present oaks with those ancient ethereal plant formations appearing and passing away like shadowy mists in the atmosphere, condensing and then vanishing away, or, to take more glaring examples, if you compare a thick-skinned hippopotamus or elephant or any other heavily built animal with those earlier creatures that emerged from the universal albumen, and were laid hold of by the chalk and, becoming rather more solid as a result, developed the rudiments of bones and were drawn down into the 'animality' of the earth (using this expression more in an adjectival sense), if you picture all this and compare the earth's present density, should I say the elephantine density of the earth today with the conditions that once existed, you will no longer be able to doubt that the farther back you go into the past the more volatile and transient the phenomena become.

In even more remote times we come to conditions where there are only surging and weaving colour formations, appearing and disappearing. And if you turn to the descriptions of Old Sun or Old Saturn given in the book *Occult Science*,[2] you will realize how obvious it is that conditions were of that nature, knowing that they were in that remote past. At the later stage the transient plant formations filled themselves with the albuminous substance and were like cloud formations. At still earlier stages we can speak only of formations appearing as colour processes as I described in connection with Old Sun and Old Saturn.

If therefore we go back from physical conditions with the 'elephantine' quality through finer physical conditions, we finally come to a time when conditions were entirely of a spiritual nature. In this way, by paying attention to actual realities, we come to realize that everything belonging to the earth is of spiritual origin. The earth originated in the spiritual realm. This is a matter of actual vision. And I think it is a beautiful idea to be able to say to oneself: if you penetrate into the interior of the earth and let the hard metals tell you what they remember, they will tell you that once upon a time they were so widely diffused over the expanses of the cosmos that they were not physical substances at all but were colour, weaving, hovering undulating in the spiritual cosmos. The memories of the earth's metals go back to a condition when each metal was a cosmic colour permeating the others, when the cosmos was a kind of inner rainbow, a spectrum that differentiated out and only then became physical.

And it is at this point that the—I would like to call it—merely theoretical—impression communicated to us by the earth's metals becomes a moral impression. For every metal tells us: 'I come from the expanses of the cosmos far away from the earth. I come from the heavenly realms and have been compressed and am now under an enchantment in the interior of the earth. But I await my redemption, for in time to come my essential being will again fill the cosmos.' When we learn to understand the speech of the metals in this way, gold tells us of the sun, lead of Saturn, copper of Venus. And then these metals say to us: 'Just as truly as there was a time when we were spread out in the vast expanses—copper reaching Venus and lead Saturn—we are now under a spell down here, and will again stretch far out when the earth's mission is fulfilled and humanity will have achieved on the earth what they can achieve only on the earth. We accepted this enchantment in order that humanity might become free beings on earth. When human beings have won their freedom then our disenchantment can begin.

This disenchantment has already been in the process of preparation for a long time. We have only to understand it. We must understand how the earth's development, together with that of human beings, will proceed in the future.

LECTURE 6

The Mysteries of Ephesian Artemis

When people speak about the word today they usually only mean the weak human word, which has so little significance in comparison with the majesty of the universe indicated at the beginning of St John's Gospel with the momentous words: 'In the beginning was the Word, the Logos, and the Word was with God, and a God was the Word.' And anyone who reflects on this most significant opening of St John's Gospel must ask himself: What does it mean when the Word is placed at the primal beginning of all things? What is actually meant by the Logos, the Word? And what connection does it have with our trivial human words?

Now the name of John is also connected with the city of Ephesus, and if someone who is equipped with imaginative perception of the world's history contemplates the momentous words, 'In the primal beginning was the Logos, and the Logos was with God, and a God was the Logos,' he will be directed time and again, by an inner path, to the ancient Temple of Diana at Ephesus. For anyone who has attained a certain degree of initiation the enigma presented in the first verses of St John's Gospel points to the Mysteries of the Temple of Artemis or Diana at Ephesus. And so it must seem to him that knowledge of the Mysteries of Ephesus will help him to understand the beginning of the St John's Gospel.

Prepared by what we have heard in the last two days, let us think of the Mysteries of the Temple of Diana at Ephesus as they were six or seven centuries before the birth of Christianity

THE MYSTERIES OF EPHESIAN ARTEMIS 103

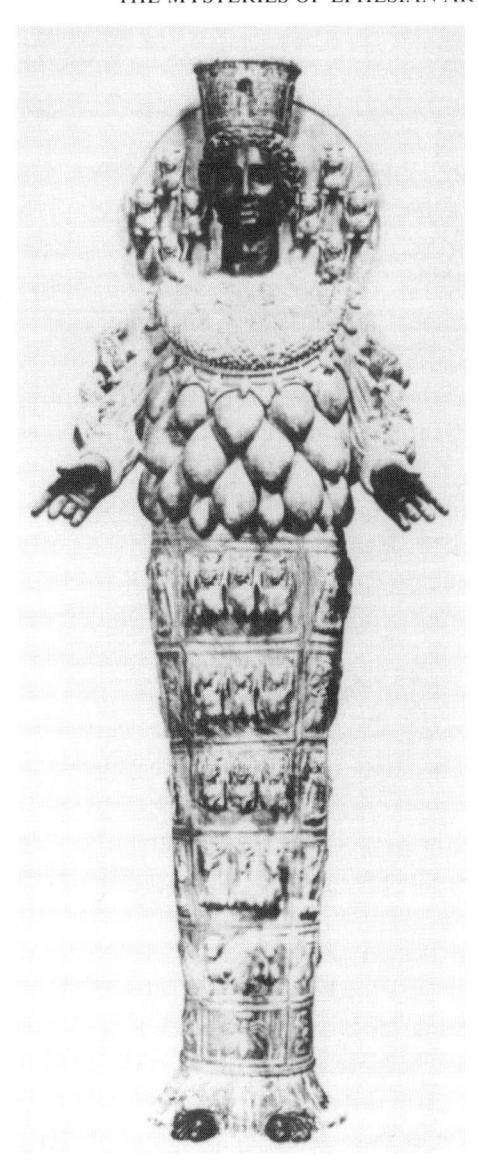

The Ephesian Artemis: the virgin Mystery-goddess in her special cultic form at Ephesus, perhaps representing her as a queen bee surrounded by ova.

or even earlier, and of what was done in this sanctuary which was held to be so holy by the people of old.[1] Then we find that the instruction given in the Mysteries at Ephesus did indeed begin with drawing attention to the sounds of human speech. We can learn not from any historical account, for the barbarism of humanity took good care that such records were destroyed, but from the Akashic Record, that thought-record in the ether where the events of world history are inscribed and which is accessible to spiritual sight—it is from this record that we can learn about what went on in these Ephesian Mysteries. And the Akashic Record reveals again and again how the teacher first of all directed the attention of his pupils to human speech. Again and again the pupil was urged to learn to feel in his own speech organs what actually took place when he spoke. The processes at work in speech elude crude perception, for they are delicate and intimate. But let us consider first of all the external aspect of speech, for it was from this that the instruction given in these Mysteries took its start. The attention of the pupil was first directed to the way in which the word sounds forth from the mouth. He was told over and over again: 'Mark well what you feel when the word sounds forth from your mouth!' He was then taught to notice how something of the spoken word turns upwards in order to receive the thought in the head, while something from the same word turns downwards in order that the feeling content may be inwardly experienced.

Again and again the pupil was instructed to push through his throat the utmost extremes of speech, and thereby to perceive the ebb and flow manifest in the word as it is uttered. 'I am, I am not'—a positive and a negative assertion—these he had to utter as articulately as possible, and then observe how, in the words 'I am' the upward ascent is felt, while in the 'I am not' there is more the feeling of pressing downwards.

Then the attention of the pupil was turned more towards the intimate feelings and experiences connected with the word. He became aware that from the word something like warmth rises up towards the head and this warmth, this fire, intercepts thought. And something like a watery element flows downwards, in the same way as a glandular secretion is discharged into the organism. Thus it was made clear to the pupils in the Ephesian Mysteries that human beings make use of the air in order for the word to sound forth, but in the act of speaking the air changes into the next element, into fire, warmth, drawing the thought down from the heights of the head, embodying it in itself. And there occurs as alternating conditions first a sending upwards of fire, then a sending downwards, as the air in the word trickles down like a glandular secretion in the form of water, of fluid. By means of this latter process human beings can feel the word inwardly.

The pupil was then led into the real secret of speech. This secret is connected, however, with the mystery of the human being. Nowadays this secret of the human being is hidden from scientists inasmuch as science places at the summit of all thought the incredible caricature of truth, the so-called law of the conservation of energy and matter.

Within the human being matter is continually being transformed. It does not endure. The air that is pushed out of the throat is transformed in the process alternately into the next higher element, warmth or fire, or into the element of water—fire, water; fire, water.

Thus the pupil at Ephesus came to understand that when he spoke a wave movement issued from his mouth: fire, water; fire, water. What this actually means is a striving up of the word into the realm of thought and a trickling down of the word into the realm of feeling. Thus thought and feeling interweave in speech inasmuch as the living wave movement of speech, beginning as air, first rarifies to fire, then densifies to water, and so on, again and again.

>   thought
>   ↑
> fire water fire water
>   ↓
>   feeling

And this was what the pupil had to feel when the great truth arising in his own speaking was brought home to him in the Mysteries of Ephesus:

> Speak, O Man, and you
> reveal through yourself
> world genesis.

This is really how things were in Ephesus, that when the pupil entered the portal of the Mysteries he was always reminded of the words:

> Speak, O Man, and you
> reveal through yourself
> world genesis.

And when he departed the words were said to him in the other form:

> World genesis is revealed
> through you, O Man,
> when you speak.

Then the pupil gradually began to feel that he with his own body was a kind of sheath for the cosmic mystery that sounded from his rhythmic system and lived in his speech.

All this was brought to the pupil to prepare him for the much deeper mystery. For this preparation enabled him to know that his own human nature was inwardly connected with the mystery of the cosmos. The saying 'know yourself!' acquired holy meaning inasmuch as it was not only spoken of as a theory but could be inwardly and solemnly felt and experienced.

Then, after the pupil had so to speak ennobled his being in this way, and was able to feel it to be as a sheath enveloping the cosmic mystery, he could be led still farther and come to know the power that spread the mystery over the wide spaces of the cosmos. And in this connection let us remember what we were looking at yesterday.

I described a condition in the evolution of the earth when the following occurred. The earth was in the condition when it contained as a substance essential for that stage of evolution what we now know as common chalk, such as is found in the Jura Mountains. In the chalk mountains, in the chalk of the earth today, we find the substance we want to study with regard to its function in those ancient times, when the earth was surrounded by what I called fluid albumen. We know that cosmic forces worked into the fluid albumen, causing it to coagulate into certain definite forms; and while the earth was in this condition a process took place resembling in a higher degree and in a denser substance what we know today as the rising of the mist and the falling of the rain. The chalky element rose upwards and permeated what had hardened in the fluid albumen, so that these forms acquired a bony content and the animal kingdom began to evolve. Through the spirituality contained in the chalk the animals were drawn down as it were, out of the atmosphere which was still albuminous.

I also said something else. I said that a human being is aware of all these happenings in his feelings; if he unites himself with the metallic element, the 'metallity' of the earth, he feels all these things as though it were his own being, as a memory within himself. And with regard to that stage of evolution he felt he was not yet a small human being enclosed in his skin but that he encompassed the whole of planet earth. To put it grotesquely I might say that to begin with the human being felt that chiefly his head encompassed the whole earth planet.

The processes described in the last lecture were felt by the human being to be taking place *in himself*. But how? Everything I have described to you here as the rising of the chalk, the uniting of this chalk with the coagulated albumen and then the descent of animality onto the earth—all this was experienced by the human being of that time in such a way that he *heard* it. You must try to imagine this. He experienced it inwardly, and in so doing he *heard* it. The forms that arose when the chalk filled out the coagulated albumen and made it bony and gristly, all that then took shape, was 'felt' in the ear—it was audible. The cosmic mystery was *heard*.

And it is the same today. When human beings learn in memory about the past of the earth, the memory that is kindled by the metals comes to them as though they heard it sounding. And in this sound the stream of cosmic happenings lives and weaves.

What is it that human beings hear? What is revealed. What is disclosed to them? The stream of cosmic happenings manifests as the cosmic Word, as the Logos. It is the Logos, the cosmic Word, that resounds in the rising and falling of the chalk. And if human beings are able to hear this language within themselves they will become aware of something else besides. The following will actually enter the bounds of possibility.

My dear friends, imagine yourselves standing in front of a human or an animal skeleton. What modern anatomy says about the skeleton is dreadfully superficial. But when, with inner mindfulness of the reality of nature and of spirit we look at a skeleton, what do we feel? We say to ourselves: 'Do not merely look at it.' It is terrible merely to look at it as it presents itself with its forms—the spinal column with its wonderfully shaped, intersecting vertebrae, with the ribs bending and curving forwards, with all the wonderful articulation as the vertebrae are metamorphosed into the bones of the skull, and that even more mysterious articulation where the ribs, bending to embrace the chest from either side, then, with a sharp turn form themselves into the arm bones and the leg bones. Confronted with this mystery of the skeleton we can do no other than say to ourselves: 'Do not merely look but *listen*. Listen how one bone transforms itself into another. Listen—for it speaks!'

At this point let me make a personal remark. When, with a feeling for these things, we go into a natural history museum we are confronted by something really miraculous. For there we have a collection of what are really musical instruments forming a mighty orchestra and resounding in the most wonderful way. I experienced this very deeply when I once visited the museum in Trieste. There, due to a particular way the animal skeletons were arranged—this was quite instinctive—one could hear resound, one after the other, at one end of the animal the secrets of the moon and at the other end the secrets of the sun. And the whole hall was as though filled with resounding suns and planets. One could certainly feel the connection between the skeleton—the bony system living in the chalk—and that which once upon a time spoke to the human being out of the flowing forces of the cosmos, when he himself was one with the cosmos, with the secret of the cosmos, which is at the same time the secret of the human being himself.

The beings which arose first of all, the animals, sounded forth in this way what they are. For, after all, animal nature lived in the Logos, in the sounding cosmic mystery. One did not perceive two separate phenomena. One did not perceive the animals, and then in some way or other the inner being of the animals. The actual genesis and development of the animal and its whole being—that was what spoke.

The pupil of the Ephesian Mysteries could receive, heart and soul, in the right way for that ancient time, what could then be revealed concerning the primal beginning, when the Word, the Logos, lived and moved as the inner essence of all things. The pupil could take it in, because he had been prepared by the ennobling and sublimating of his human nature to feel himself to be a vessel for the faint reflection of the cosmic mystery contained in the sounding forth of his own speech.

And now let us feel how the evolutionary process has passed as it were from one level to the other. Let us take a look at it. In the chalk element we still have something which was then fluid. It rose as vapour and fell again as rain. As it rose it was transmuted into air; as it descended it was changed into earth. So there was water, air and earth there, which was a level lower than in the human copy of it, where we have air, warmth and water. In those primeval times the still fluid chalk rarefied to air and condensed to earth, just as in our throat today the air rarefies to warmth and condenses to water. The element which lived in the world has risen from water to air. In former times it lived in water, condensed to earth and rarefied to air. This rose to the level of air, where it rarefied to warmth and condensed to water. And this makes it possible for us human beings to encompass the cosmic memory in miniature. While it was still on a large scale and was the great maya of the world it was one level lower. The earth densified everything. The chalk became denser, and so on. We human beings would not have been able to contain the cosmic mystery in this form, even if it had approached us on a miniature scale. We could contain it only when it rose one stage higher, from water to air, and surged up and down into warmth and into water, which is now the denser element.

Thus what was of universal dimension, the macrocosmic mystery, became the microcosmic mystery of human speech. And it is to this macrocosmic mystery—the translation into maya, into the big world—that the beginning of St John's Gospel refers: 'In the beginning was the Word, and the Word was with God, and the Word was God.' For that was still a living tradition in Ephesus at the time when the evangelist, the writer of St John's Gospel, could read there in the Akashic Record that for which his heart yearned, namely, the right form in which to clothe what he had to say to mankind concerning the secret of cosmic evolution.

But we can go a step farther. We can remind ourselves of what we said yesterday, namely, that prior to chalk there was silica, which appears today in quartz. In this the plant forms appeared like greening and fading cloud formations. And if, as I said, human beings had at that time been able to look out into the wide spaces of the cosmos, they would have seen this evolution of animal nature and would have seen too those primeval plants greening and fading away. But all this was of course an inner perception. The human being perceived it as belonging to his own being. Besides hearing as a living inner experience the 'sounding' of animal nature coming into being he could also in a certain sense accompany inwardly what he heard; in the same way as in his own head, in his chest and head, he ascends with his words by way of warmth to grasp thoughts; and he could proceed from what he heard resounding from the evolution of the animals to an experiencing of the evolution of the plants. This was the remarkable thing, my dear friends. The human being could experience the living being of animal creation in the rarefying and descending chalk. And when he then directed his attention to what was happening in the silica element, the greening and fading of plant nature, then the cosmic Word became cosmic Thought, for the plants in the silica element added Thought to the resounding Word. An ascending step was taken, and cosmic Thought was added to the sounding Logos, just as today *thought* is grasped in the element of fire and comes to meet the word of speech, as speech surges between fire and water.

My dear friends, if you study today how those particular pathological conditions connected with the sense organs of the head and with the sense organs in general are treated, you will hear of the healing effects of silica. Whereas here, in the context of world secrets, silica shows itself to be specifically the thought element in the greening and fading plant forms. Was I not able to say of it that it was the perception, the medium for perceiving the whole structure of the cosmos? In a wonderful way there actually comes to expression microcosmically in present-day human beings what has occurred in the evolution of life in the macrocosm.

Just think for a moment how human beings lived then, lived still at one with the cosmos, in unity with the cosmos. When a human being thinks today he has to think of himself as being isolated in his head. The thoughts are inside and the words come out. The cosmos is outside. Words can only point to the cosmos, thoughts can only mirror it. This was not so when the human being was still one with the macrocosm; he then experienced the cosmos as though it were within himself. The Word was at the same time the environment; and Thought was the element that permeated this environment. The human being listened, and what he heard was world. When he looked away from what he heard he looked into himself. The Word was first of all sound. The Word was first of all something struggling to be deciphered. The creation of the animals was a manifestation of something struggling to be deciphered. The animal kingdom arose in the chalk element as a question. Human beings looked into the silica element and the being of the plants gave the answer out of what it had received as a sense organ of the earth, and solved the riddle set it by the animal kingdom. The beings themselves solved each other's riddles. One being, in this case the animal, put the question, and the other being, in this case the plant, gave the answer. And the whole world became speech.

We may venture to say that this is the reality in the beginning of St John's Gospel. For in the first place we are taken back to a primal beginning of everything that exists. In this primal beginning, in this principle, was the Word. And the Word was with God. And the Word was God, because it was the creative essence in everything.

It is really and truly so, that the teaching given to the pupils of the Mysteries at Ephesus contains what led to the beginning of the St John's Gospel. And here let me say that the time is fully ripe for anthroposophists to turn to these secrets lying hidden in the past.

For you see, in a very particular and special sense, the building which stood here on the Dornach hill, the Goetheanum, had become the central point of anthroposophical striving. The pain in us today must live on further as pain, and will do so in everyone who was able to feel what the Goetheanum was intended to be. But whatever takes place in the physical world around us, that, my dear friends, for one who is striving upwards in his knowledge towards the spiritual realm, must be at the same time an external revelation, a picture of something deeper, something spiritual. If, on the one hand, we have to accept this pain, then we, as human beings striving for spiritual knowledge, must nevertheless be able to turn what has happened into an opportunity for looking into an ever-deepening revelation.

This Goetheanum was truly a place in which human beings endeavoured to speak, in fact did speak, again and again of the things connected with the beginning of St John's Gospel: 'In the beginning was the Word, and the Word was with God, and the Word was God.'

And then this Goetheanum went up in flames, and we can have this terrible picture of the burning Goetheanum. And out of the pain can be born the urge to look ever more deeply into this image which is still there in our thought, the image of the Goetheanum burning down on New Year's Eve. Although this was such a painful event it was nevertheless one that can lead into greater and greater depths of knowledge. Something was to have been founded there, something that had a connection with the Gospel of St John. In a certain sense we may say that this placed itself into the consuming flames. And we can form a most important resolution to allow these flames to prompt us to look through them to other flames which in past times consumed the Temple of Ephesus. Let that be a challenge to us to acquire a sense and purpose for enquiring into what is contained in the beginning of St John's Gospel. Urged on by these painful but holy demands let us look back from that Gospel to the Temple of Ephesus, which was also burnt down long ago; and then the Goetheanum flames, speaking to us so painfully and eloquently, will serve to remind us of what streamed into the Akashic Record together with the flames of the burning Temple of Ephesus.

Having beheld, on that tragic night, the consuming flames of the burning Goetheanum, do we not still see the molten metals of the musical instruments? And do we not have in the flames these metals of the musical instruments uttering in clear tones their holy speech, introducing magically into the flames the most remarkable colours? Auspicious colours, colours akin to the metals! And through this connection with the metallic element there rises up within us something that is like memory in the earthly sphere. And what it reminds us of is what went up in flames with the Temple of Ephesus. Then, even as there is a connection between those two fires, so the longing to probe further into something of the nature of 'In the beginning was the Word, and the Word was with God, and the Word was God' can link us to what was brought home again and again to the pupil at Ephesus: 'Study the mystery of man in the small word, the micrologos, in order to make yourself ripe to experience within yourself the mystery of the macrologos!'

Human beings are microcosms in relation to the world which is the macrocosm, but they also bear within themselves cosmic mysteries. And we shall penetrate more deeply into the cosmic mystery contained in the first three verses of St John's Gospel if we look in the right way at what was spoken of, among many other things, by the flames of the Goetheanum, densified as it were to a kind of script:

Behold the Logos
In the consuming fire;
Interpret it
In Diana's House.*

The fiery Akasha of New Year's Eve speaks these and many other words very clearly. And it presents us with the challenge to discover in the microcosm the micrologos so that we human

---

* For German text see Appendix 1.

beings may gain an understanding for that from which our own being proceeds, namely, for the macrocosm through the macrologos.

LECTURE 7

The Mystery Centres of Hibernia

In the previous lecture I needed to tell you about the Ephesian Mysteries of Artemis in order to draw your attention to certain connections between knowledge that has come to light during the course of human evolution and knowledge that can be acquired today through clairvoyant insight into the spiritual world. To further illuminate themes we have already studied, I want to speak today of another Mystery Centre which can also be said to stand at the starting-point of modern spiritual life. Although these Mysteries had taken over a great deal from earlier spiritual movements in which the primeval wisdom of humanity was still contained, they were nevertheless an effective impulse in the spiritual movement of the modern age. So today I propose to speak to you about the influential Mysteries once centred in the troubled island of Ireland, to the west of England, the Mysteries of Hibernia, to which I also referred in my Mystery Plays.[1]

Speaking comparatively, it is much more difficult than in other cases to approach these ancient Hibernian Mysteries in what I have called in many of my writings the Akashic Record. It is much more difficult for subsequent vision to find in that eternal record the pictures remaining there of these Mysteries than it is to find those of other Mystery Centres, for in trying to approach the Hibernian Mysteries the impression is that the pictures contain extraordinarily powerful forces that repel one and thrust one back. Even if the pictures are approached with a certain courage of vision—a courage which in other cases meets with less resistance than is experienced here—the opposition is so intense that it even gives rise to a kind of numbness. Knowledge of what I am about to describe to you is therefore fraught with hindrances, and in the next few days you will see why this is so.

In the Hibernian Mysteries too, of course, there were initiates who had preserved much of the ancient wisdom of humanity and who, stimulated and inspired by this wisdom, were able to achieve a degree of seership themselves. There were also pupils, candidates for initiation who, by the special methods applied there, were to be prepared to approach the secrets of the cosmic Word. Now the preparation given to those who were to be initiated in Hibernia was twofold. Firstly, all the difficulties involved in the acquisition of knowledge were brought home to the pupils; they were made inwardly aware of everything that can be torment on the path of the kind of knowledge which does not yet penetrate into the depths of existence but which consists of exerting to the utmost possible extent all the powers of the soul belonging to everyday consciousness. These pupils had to experience in their souls all the difficulties occurring on the path of knowledge of ordinary consciousness. They were compelled to experience every doubt, every torment, every inner struggle with its frequent aberrations, being deceived by no matter how excellent a logic or dialectic—all this they had to endure, and to experience the difficulties which make themselves felt when one has actually attained knowledge and then wishes to bring it to expression.

You will feel that there are two aspects here: to have struggled to attain a truth, and then to bring it to expression—to formulate it in words. Indeed, when the path of knowledge has been earnestly followed there is always the feeling that what can be compressed into words is something which is no longer absolute truth, something which surrounds the truth with all kinds of stumbling blocks and pitfalls.

The pupils were made acquainted with experience undergone only by someone who has valiantly and genuinely struggled to attain knowledge.

Secondly, the pupil was led to experience in his life of soul how little the knowledge acquired on the ordinary path of consciousness can, in the last resort, contribute to human happiness, how little human happiness can be promoted by logic, dialectic or rhetoric. On the other hand, it was also made clear to the pupil that if, as a human being, he wanted to keep his bearings in life, he would have to involve himself with those things which can to a certain extent bring him joy and happiness. Thus they were driven in the one direction to the verge of an abyss, and in the other direction too, to the verge of an abyss, and always made to wonder whether they should wait until they were supplied with a bridge to cross each one. And they were so deeply initiated into the doubts and difficulties connected with the attainment of knowledge that when at last they were led from these preparatory stages to the actual approach to the cosmic secrets they came to the decision that, if it had to be, they would even renounce knowledge; they would deny themselves everything that cannot make a person happy.

In these ancient Mysteries the pupils were subjected to such severe tests that they came to the point where, in the most natural and elementary way, they developed feelings which ordinary pedantic reason regards as baseless. But it is easy to say, 'Nobody would wish to forgo knowledge; it goes without saying that one wants to gain knowledge, however great the difficulties may be.' That, of course, is the attitude of people who do not know what the difficulties are, and who have not been deliberately led to experience them, as was the case with the pupils in the Mysteries of Hibernia. On the other hand it is also easy to say, 'We will deny ourselves both inner and outer happiness and tread a path of knowledge only.' But to someone who knows the truth of these things, both declarations, so often made, appear utterly superficial.

When the pupils had been prepared to the degree indicated, they were brought before two gigantic statues, enormous and majestic. One of them was majestic by reason of its external, spatial dimensions, while the other, of equal size, was impressive because of its special character. One statue was a male figure, the other female. By means of these two statues the pupils were to experience the approach of the cosmic Word. In a way they were the external letters with which the pupils were to begin to decipher the cosmic secret facing humanity.

The one statue, the male one, was of a thoroughly elastic material. Any part of it could be indented by pressure. And the pupils were told to push it in, all over. This showed it to be hollow inside. It was really only the 'skin' of a statue but made of a thoroughly elastic material so that, when a pupil pressed it, it returned immediately to its original form. Above the head of this statue—and its head was particularly distinctive—was something that resembled the sun. The whole head was of such a nature that one could see that it was meant to be just like an eye of the soul, portraying the content of the whole macrocosm on a microcosmic scale. It was through the sun that this manifestation of the whole macrocosm was to come to expression in this gigantic head.

I cannot, of course, draw a picture of the two statues at great speed, so I will just make a sketch. This is the one statue, and the immediate impression it gave was this: the macrocosm works through the sun and fashions the human head which knows what macrocosmic impulses are like, and forms itself inwardly and outwardly according to these impulses.

Coming to the other statue, the pupil's eyes fell first of all on something that seemed to be composed of luminous bodies radiating inwards, and in this framework the pupil saw a female figure which was lit up at every point. And he had the feeling that the head was being created out of these rays. The head had something indistinct about it. This statue was made of a different substance. It was a pliable substance which was easily moulded, as distinct from elastic, and it was extremely soft. The pupil was told to press this statue also. Wherever he pressed, the indentation remained. However, by the time the pupil returned to be tested again on these statues, the pressure marks he had made the previous time had been repaired. So that whenever the pupils were brought to this statue for this ceremony it had been made whole again. The statue made of elastic substance always returned by itself to its original form.[2]

With the second statue one had the impression that it was completely under the influence of moon forces which permeated the organism, and it was out of this that the head arose. These experiences made a most profound impression on the pupils. As I said, the form of the female statue was always restored. From time to time, at not very long intervals, a group of pupils would be brought to this statue, and to begin with, on these first visits, absolute silence reigned. They were taken there by those who were already initiated, left there, and the door at the back of the temple was closed, leaving them on their own.

Then came a time when each pupil was taken in separately, told, to begin with, to study the statues and feel the elasticity of the one and the plasticity of the other in which the indentations remained. He was then left quite alone with the impressions which, as I indicated, had a tremendous effect on him. And because of everything he had previously undergone along the path I described to you, he experienced all the difficulties of knowledge and all the difficulties of bliss, as I will call it. Such experiences mean far more than can be expressed in a mere description such as I am giving now. Such experiences meant that the pupil passed through a whole gamut of feelings. And standing there in front of the statues, these feelings gave the pupil the most intense longing to find some way of solving in himself what appeared to him as a tremendous riddle. He longed to get to the bottom of why, on the one hand, he was being compelled to undergo such experiences and, on the other hand, what was the nature of the riddle contained in the statues themselves and in the whole way in which it was possible for him to relate to the figures. All this made a tremendously deep impression on the pupils. And with regard to these statues their whole soul and spirit became like one big question. Their whole being questioned. Their reason questioned, their hearts questioned, their will questioned, absolutely everything questioned. There is still something a modern person can learn from these experiences which in earlier times were presented in a perceptible form but no longer can or need be so presented for the purpose of initiation. He can learn how wide a gamut of feelings must be passed through in order to approach the truth which then leads to cosmic mysteries. For although it is right for the pupil of today to develop along an inner path that is not dependent on outer perception, nevertheless he must still pass through the same gamut of feelings, must experience them through intense meditative effort. So the scale of feelings to be lived through today can be ascertained from knowledge of the experiences undergone in the ancient rites by those who were undergoing initiation.

After this, the Hibernian pupils were put through a kind of probation during which their experiences on the path of ordinary knowledge and of bliss were to be combined with what had now arisen in them as a great question filling their whole being.

And now, when the effects of these two aspects were inwardly present in the pupils, cosmic secrets relating to the microcosm and the macrocosm were expounded to them as far as was possible in those days, something of what had formed the content of the Artemis Mysteries of Ephesus, and already touched on in these lectures. Part of this was presented to the pupils during their time of probation. But this only intensified the great question that had arisen in their souls. So that the individual pupil, through the colossal inner deepening experienced and endured with regard to this questioning, was led thereby to the threshold of the spiritual world. He actually entered the region experienced by the soul when it feels: 'I am now standing in the presence of the forces that guard the Threshold.'

In ancient times there were all kinds of different Mysteries, and human beings were led in a variety of ways to the experience arising when the feelings are compressed into the words: 'Now I am standing at the Threshold to the spiritual world. I know why this spiritual world is guarded from everyday consciousness, and I realize the essential nature of its protecting might, of the Guardian of the Threshold.'[3]

When the pupils had passed this period of probation they were taken once more to the statues. And then they received a most remarkable impression, an impression that stirred them to the very depths of their being. I can give you an idea of this impression only by rendering in our modern language the utterances which it was customary to make in the language of that ancient time.

When the pupils had reached the stage I have described, each one was brought on his own to the statues. But now the initiating priest remained in the temple with him. And after the pupil had been able to listen in deep silence to what his own soul could tell him after all his preparations and trials—and this lasted for a considerable time—he saw the initiating priest as it were rising above the head of the one figure. The sun seemed to have receded and, in the space now intervening between the statue and the sun, the priest appeared, as though covering the sun. The statues were of an enormous size, so that the priest appeared small in comparison; his head alone showed above the statue and covered the sun. Then as though sounding forth from a background of musical harmony, with which the ceremony began, came the voice of the initiator. In the condition in which the pupil was at this stage, it seemed to him as though the words that sounded from the lips of the initiator were spoken by the statue itself. And the words were these:

> Of the world I am but an image,
> Behold, how I lack existence.
> I live within your knowledge,
> Your acknowledgment will give me existence.*

This too, as you may imagine, made a profound impression on the pupil, for he had been prepared to experience the power confronting him in this statue's image, which said of itself: 'Behold, how I lack existence. Of the world I am but an image. I live within your knowledge.'

The difficulties accompanying the ordinary path of knowledge had prepared the pupil to see in this image something that released him from these difficulties, although he could not conquer his doubts in regard to knowledge itself. In fact he had reached the point of feeling that he was incapable of conquering them. The experiences he had undergone made

---

* For German text see Appendix 1.

him inwardly prepared to cling to this image with his whole soul, to live with the cosmic power symbolized by it, to surrender himself to it. He was ready to do this because what came from the lips of the priest made the statue seem to be the lettering which conveyed to him the meaning conveyed in these four lines.

When the priest had withdrawn, the pupil was once again left alone in absolute silence, and after a while another initiator entered. He then appeared above the second statue. And again, resounding as though in musical harmony, there came the voice of this priest-initiator, speaking the words I can render somewhat as follows:

> Of the world I am but an image,
> Behold, how I lack truth.
> If you will dare to live with me,
> I will make you content.

And now, after the pupil had been brought to the point of longing for, even feeling the necessity for joyful inner fulfilment, when he heard these words sounding from the second statue he was absolutely ready to regard the cosmic power that spoke through this second statue as the one to which he wanted to devote his whole being.

Again the initiator disappeared, and again the pupil was left alone. And during this lonely silence, each one of the pupils—at least it seems to be so—each one felt something which may perhaps be expressed in the following words: 'I stand at the Threshold to the spiritual world. Here, in the physical world, we speak of something called "knowledge", but it has no value in the spiritual world. And the fact that here, in the physical world, we have difficulties with it is only the physical reflection of the worthlessness of the knowledge that can be acquired in this world concerning the supersensible, spiritual world.' And in the same way the pupils felt: 'Many a thing in the physical world tells us that we must forgo joyful inner fulfilment and take an ascetic path in order to enter the spiritual world. But that is an illusion, a deception. For what this statue expresses says emphatically of itself, "Behold, how I lack truth."'

Thus, on the threshold of knowledge, the pupil almost came to the point of feeling that the joyful inner fulfilment of soul and mind must be achieved by doing without the truth we endeavour to find here, in the physical world, with our feeble human striving fettered to the physical body. The pupil was already aware that the world on yonder side of the Threshold was bound to look different from the world on this side, and that a great deal which has value this side of the Threshold becomes worthless over yonder; that even knowledge and truth show a quite different face beyond the Threshold.

All such feelings and perceptions to some extent called forth in the pupil an awareness that he had left behind him many of the deceptions and disenchantments of the physical world. But there were also feelings which from time to time had the effect of fiery flames, so that the pupil felt as though he were being consumed by inner fire, were being inwardly destroyed. His soul vacillated from one feeling to the other. The pupil was so to speak being tested on the scales of knowledge and joy. And during these experiences it seemed to him as though the statues themselves were speaking. He had himself now achieved something like perception of the inner word, and this was as though the statues themselves spoke. What the first statue said was:

I am Knowledge.
But what I am is not real being.

And then the pupil had a feeling that rayed out sheer fright: 'The ideas we have are only ideas and there is no real being in them.' The pupil felt that if the human head is strenuously exerted, ideas will certainly come, but none of them have any real being. Ideas are only appearance, they have no being.

And then the other statue seemed to speak, saying:

I am Fantasy.
But what I am has no truth.

This is how the two statues presented themselves to the pupil, the one impressing upon him that ideas have no being, and the other that the images of imagination have no truth.

Please understand this rightly. There is no question of presenting dogmas or of looking for suitable phrases to give you some idea of facts and findings. The sole purpose is to present to you what the pupils experienced in the sacred sanctuaries of Hibernia. It is not the mere description itself that shall be set up as truth, but the object is to place on record what the pupils of the Hibernian Mysteries actually experienced at that moment of their initiation.

All these experiences were lived through by each individual pupil in absolute isolation. The experience became so intense that the pupil's power of sight ceased to function, and after a time he no longer saw the statues. But in the direction where he had been looking he read as though written in flames something which was not physically there but which he nevertheless perceived with utmost clarity. Where he had previously seen the head of the statue of knowledge he read the word SCIENCE and where he had seen the head of the other statue he read the word ART.

After this he was taken out of the temple again, and beside the exit stood the two initiators. One of them took the pupil's head in his hands and turned it towards something to which the other initiator was pointing: the figure of Christ. And this second initiator impressed upon him the following words:

> Open your heart
> To the Word and the Power of this Being.

And the other priest said:

> And receive from Him
> What the two statues wished to give you:
> Science and art.

These were the first two acts as it were in the Hibernian initiation, the special way in which the pupils in Hibernia were guided to a real feeling for the innermost nature of Christianity. This experience impressed itself deeply on the minds and hearts of these pupils, and now they could start on their further path of knowledge. What can be said about this we shall be studying in connection with other matters during the next few days.

LECTURE 8

The Nature of the Hibernian Mysteries

You will have seen that initiation in the Hibernian Mysteries, as I described them yesterday, aimed to give real insight into the secrets of cosmic and human existence, for the inner experiences I had to tell you about had a very powerful effect on the life of the soul. Everything leading along the path into the spiritual world depends on whether a human being makes certain conquests as a result of particularly drastic inner experiences, and in so doing increases his forces to such an extent that in one way or another he succeeds in penetrating into that world.

We heard that in the process of initiation in Hibernia the pupil confronted two symbolic statues—but the word 'symbolic' must not be misunderstood. I described to you how these statues were constructed and also what feelings and inner experiences were undergone by the pupils while contemplating them.

You must realize that the direct impression made by such majestic statues under the conditions I described had an infinitely more powerful effect on the inner being of the pupils than one receives from mere description. Therefore, after the pupils had lived through everything of which I spoke yesterday, it became possible for the initiators to produce in them echoes of what they had experienced in connection with each of the statues, and these echoes continued to resound for weeks or even longer, or in some cases shorter, the time span varying according to the karma of the individual concerned.

Having done the test on both statues—for what went forth from both statues together was intended to work on in the further soul life of the pupil as a combined impression—the pupil was nevertheless now urged to let the impression from the *male* statue reverberate very powerfully within him. And I will now describe to you the way this impression reverberated, but one has of course to use words that are not really suitable for depicting initiation experiences and the inner meaning of some of the things I am putting into words will have to be felt intuitively. What the pupil now experienced when he gave himself up to the impression of the male statue was a kind of soul rigidity, a rigid numbness of the soul which set in with greater and greater intensity the more he was bidden to let the echo persist; it was a soul rigidity which felt also like a bodily rigidity. In the intervening periods the pupil was able to attend to all the necessities of life, but time and again his soul was transported back to this echo and he again experienced rigidity. This was a type of initiation which was very strongly, even if not totally, reminiscent of the old style of the original Mysteries—and now this rigidity caused a change in the pupil's consciousness. One could not say that the consciousness was in any way dulled, but the pupil had the feeling: 'This state of consciousness in which I find myself is totally unfamiliar to me. At the moment, I cannot handle it; I do not know how to deal with it.' So that all the pupil felt was that his whole consciousness was entirely filled with the sensation of rigidity. At that point it was as though the pupil felt that what was rigid in him—namely, he himself—was being taken up into the cosmos. He felt as if he were being transported into the far spaces of the cosmos. And he could say to himself: 'The cosmos is receiving me.'

Then something very special happened—his consciousness was not extinguished but it became somewhat different. When this experience of numbness and of being received by the cosmos had lasted for a sufficient length of time—and this was ensured by the initiators—the pupil said something like this to himself: 'The rays of the sun and the stars are drawing me out into the cosmos, but nevertheless I am remaining within myself.' When this experience had lasted long enough, a remarkable vista presented itself. Now for the first time the pupil realized the purpose of this state of consciousness which had set in during the numbness, for now, all according to his experiences and their echoes, there came to him all manner of impressions of winter landscapes. Winter landscapes were there in the spirit before him, landscapes in which he saw whirling snowflakes filling the air—as I said, he saw all this in the spirit—or landscapes in which he looked at things such as forests with snow weighing down the branches of the trees, things which absolutely reminded him of what he had seen here or there in his everyday life but which always gave the impression of reality. So that after being transported into the cosmos he felt as though his own consciousness was conjuring up before him whole excursions in time through winter landscapes. And during this experience he felt as if he were not actually in his body, but certainly in his sense organs; he felt that he was living with the whole of his being in his eyes, in his ears, also on the surface of his skin. And then, when his whole sense of feeling and of touch seemed to be spread out over his skin, he also felt: 'I have become like the statue that is elastic but hollow.' And he felt, for instance, that his eyes had an inner connection with these landscapes. He felt as though this whole landscape he was looking at was active in each eye, as though the eye were an inner mirror reflecting everything outside him.

And further, he did not feel himself as a unity, but felt his ego multiplied to the number of his senses, namely, twelvefold.

And from the feeling that his ego had become twelvefold a remarkable experience caused him to say to himself: 'There is an ego which looks through my eyes, there is an ego which works in my sense of thought, in my sense of speech, in my sense of touch, in my sense of life. I am actually scattered over the world.' From this experience there arose an intense longing for union with the being of the Hierarchy of the angeloi in order that from this union strength and power might be acquired for mastering the splitting of the ego into the single sense experiences. And out of all this the question arose in the ego: 'Why do I have my senses?'

And this led to the quite remarkable result that the pupil now felt that everything connected with the senses, and with their continuation inwards towards the inner organism, was related to the real environment around him on earth. The senses belong to the winter—that is what the pupil felt. And this whole life through which he was passing, in which the changing winter landscapes tallied, as I said, with what he had seen in everyday life, yet which, because they were spiritual, shone for him in great splendour—all these experiences led the pupil to an overall soul response consisting more or less of the following: 'In my Mystery winter experiences I have passed through aspects of the cosmos that now really belong to the past. The snow and ice of my enchanted winter have shown me what death-dealing forces there are in the cosmos. I now know of the destructive impulses there. And my numbness prior to my Mystery winter experiences was the intimation that I was to behold those forces in the cosmos which come over from the past into the present, but in the present are dead cosmic forces.' This realization was what the reverberation of his experiences with the male statue conveyed to the pupil.

Then he was brought to the point where his experiences with the pliable—not the elastic—statue could echo within him.

And now he did not succumb to an inner rigidity but to an inner heat, a feverish condition of the soul, which began with bodily symptoms. It felt like intense pressure inside him, as though everything was under pressure—his breathing, and also the blood throughout his body. He felt extreme anxiety, in fact he was in deep mental distress. And this state brought home to him the second thing he would have to go through. Out of his mental distress there arose in him the realization which can be described more or less as follows: 'I have within me something that my bodily nature demands in my ordinary earthly life. This must be overcome. My earth ego must be overcome!' This conviction lived strongly in the pupil's consciousness.

Then, when the experience of this inner fever, this mental distress, this feeling that the earthly ego had to be overcome, had lasted for the necessary length of time, something arose in the pupil which he knew was not his previous state of consciousness but a state well known to him, namely, dream consciousness. Whereas from the earlier numbness had come the distinct feeling that he was in a state of consciousness unknown to him in ordinary life, he knew now that his consciousness was a kind of dreaming. He dreamed but in contrast to what he had dreamt before—although in harmony with what he had experienced—this time it was of the most wonderful summer landscapes. However, now he knew that these were dreams, dreams which filled him with intense joy or intense sadness, depending on whether what came to him from the being of summer was sad or joyful, but in either case with the intensity of feeling accompanying dreams. You need only remind yourselves of how a dream can affect you. It takes the form of pictures, but you may wake up out of it with a palpitating heart, hot and frightened. The pupil interpreted this intensity of feeling in an elementary and straightforward way, saying to himself: 'My inner being has brought the summer to my consciousness as a dream; the summer has come to me as a dream.'

At the same time the pupil knew that what appeared to his consciousness in a state of continual change, like an enchanted summer, was indicative of impulses leading into the far future of the cosmos. But now he did not, as he previously did, feel as though he were divided up into his separate senses and multiplied. On the contrary, he now felt himself to be completely gathered together inside himself as an individual being; he felt as though pulled together in his heart. And the culmination, the supreme climax of what he was experiencing was this sense of being held together in his heart, this being in full possession of himself and of being inwardly united with the dream of summer—not with the summer as outwardly seen, but with the dream of it. And the pupil said to himself, rightly: 'In what the dream of summer reveals, and I experience in my own being, lies the future.'

The next experience arising in the pupil was of these two conditions following one another. He was looking, shall we say, into a landscape of meadows and ponds and little lakes. Then came a vista of ice and snow which changed into whirling, falling snow, into a mist of falling snowflakes. Then this mist became more and more evanescent, and finally faded into nothingness. And the moment this happened, when he felt himself as it were in empty space, at that moment the summer dreams replaced the winter scenes and he realized in full consciousness: 'Now past and future are encountering one another in my own life of soul.'

From then onwards the pupil had learnt to look at the outer world and to be able to say of it, as of a truth that was to remain with him for all future time: 'In this world which surrounds us, in this world from which we derive our corporeality, something is perpetually dying. And the snow crystals of winter are the outer signs of the spirit that is perpetually dying in matter. As human beings we are not yet capable of feeling completely this dying spirit, which in external nature is correctly symbolized in snow and ice, unless initiation has been achieved. But through initiation we know that the spirit is constantly dying in matter, announcing this in the process of rigidification in nature. A void is continually being produced. And what is born out of this void is, to begin with, something resembling the dreams of nature. And the dreams of nature contain the seeds for the future of worlds. But the death of worlds and the birth of worlds would not have a meeting-point if the human being were not midway between them.' For if the human being were not there in the middle—as I said, I am simply relating to you the experiences inwardly undergone by the pupils of the Hibernian initiation—if no *human being* were there between them, the real processes revealed through the new consciousness born of the state of numbness would be an actual death of worlds, with no dream to follow. No future would arise to complement the past. Saturn, Sun, Moon and Earth would be there, but no Jupiter, Venus and Vulcan. For this cosmic future to unite with the past the *human being* had to be there between the past and the future. The pupil knew this simply through what he experienced.

All that the pupil had just experienced was then summarized by his initiators. The first condition, that of rigidity, when the pupil had felt himself as though sucked up into the cosmos, was summarized for him by his initiators in words which I can render to you in the following way.

In the wide expanses learn
How in the breadths of ether blue

World being has to disappear
To find itself again in you.*

These words were a summary of the actual feelings the pupil had experienced. The feelings accompanying the conditions brought about by the second statue were summarized as follows:

In your inmost depths discover
How true wisdom must be found
Out of evil's fevered heat
And through yourself its being ground.

Remember, my dear friends, that at the stage I spoke about at the end of the lecture yesterday, as the pupil was being released, the words SCIENCE and ART appeared in the place of the two statues. The word *science* appeared in the place of the statue that had said: 'I am Knowledge, but what I am is not real being.' And the word *art* stood in the place of the statue that had said: 'I am Fantasy, but what I am has no truth.' The pupil had known all the terrible heaviness of heart resulting from his soul having greedily desired something other than real knowledge. For he now clearly realized that the knowledge acquired on earth consists only of ideas, it is only of a picture nature, and has no actual existence. Now he lived through the reverberations of this experience, and had come to realize that the human being himself must find being for the content of his knowledge by losing himself in the expanses of the cosmos:

In the wide expanses learn
How in the breadths of ether blue
World being has to disappear
To find itself again in you.

---

* For German texts see Appendix 1.

For this was indeed the feeling. A human being rushes out as it were into the breadths of ether which are bounded by the blue of the wide expanses and ultimately unites himself with this blue of the far distances. But out there, what used to be earth is scattered to such an extent over the infinite expanses that it is as though transformed into nothingness. And he had learnt to experience this nothingness by beholding the magical winter landscapes. And now he knows that it is only the human being who can stand firm in the infinite expanse leading to the blue of ether distances.

Through the second experience the human being realizes that he finds in the depths of his own being what he must overcome, what he must recognize as evil, rooted and surging within him, and which has to be overcome through the impulse of good in human nature so that the world may have a future.

> In your inmost depths discover
> How true wisdom must be found
> Out of evil's fevered heat
> And through yourself its being ground.

The pupil had experienced that imagination has an inclination to avoid truth, to be satisfied with a relation to the world consisting of arbitrary, subjective pictures. But now, out of the dreamlike magical summer experience, he had acquired insight that enabled him to say: 'Whatever arises in me as creative imagination I can carry out into the world. Out of my inner being, fantasy-pictures, grow the true Imaginations of the plants. If I have the pictures of fantasy only, then I am a stranger to what is around me. But if I have Imaginations, then there grows out of my own inner self the things I can find in this plant and that one, in this and that animal, in one human being and another.[1] Whatever I find in my own being coincides with something outside. And for everything I meet with in the outer world I can find something connected with it rising up out of the depths of my own soul being.'

This sense of a twofold union with the world was an experience which, accompanied by a feeling of inner triumph, came to the pupil as an echo of the experiences connected with the two statues. And the pupil had in this way really learnt on the one side, may I say, to expand his soul spiritually into the cosmos, and on the other side to penetrate deeply into a region of his inner being where the forces are not working in the feeble way customary in everyday consciousness but as though they were being stirred to their very depths by the half-reality of magical dreams. The pupil had now learnt to balance this intensity of inner impulses with the intensity of outer impulses. Out of his relationship to the winter landscape on the one hand and the summer landscape on the other, enlightenment had come to him concerning external nature and his own self. And he had become deeply and intimately related to both.

He was then well prepared to go through a kind of recapitulation. In this recapitulation his initiators put it very clearly to him: 'While you are experiencing numbness you must make a deliberate pause, and you must do this again in the course of going out into cosmic expanses, and for a third time while you are feeling as though you are being poured into your senses and multiplied. You must become inwardly conscious of what each condition is like, and be able to distinguish clearly between them. You must have an inner, etheric experience of each of these three conditions.' And when the pupil, now with full consciousness, called up again before his soul the state of numbness, there appeared before him the kind of experience he had had before he came down to the earth out of spiritual worlds, before the earthly conception of his body, when he was drawing together out of the cosmos etheric impulses and forces in order to clothe himself with an etheric body. In this way the pupil of the Hibernian Mysteries was brought to experience the final stage preceding his descent into a physical body.

He had then to become fully aware of the inner experience of being transported out into the world expanses. This time, in the recapitulation, he did not feel as though he were being drawn up by the rays of the sun and the stars, but as though something were coming towards him, as though from all sides the Hierarchies were coming towards him from the wide expanses, and as though other experiences were also coming towards him. And he became aware of conditions lying farther back in his pre-earthly life. Then he had consciously to recapitulate the experience of being poured out into his senses and dispersed in fragments in the world of the senses. This brought him to the middle point of his existence between death and a new life.

You can see from these indications that the entry of the initiated one into these hidden worlds—worlds to which humanity, even so, belongs—can come about in the most diverse ways. And from the indications given yesterday and on many other occasions, you will realize too that vision of the supersensible world was achieved by methods differing widely in the several Mysteries. In later lectures we shall speak of why it was that such differences were considered appropriate, and why a uniform spiritual path was not adopted in all the Mysteries. Today I will merely mention the fact. But the purpose of all these different paths was to unveil the hidden aspects of world existence and human existence, which have been indicated again and again in our present studies as well as in other lectures and writings.

The pupil was then told that he must also recapitulate clearly and get a feeling knowledge of the separate stages of the other conditions he had experienced as after-effects of the other statue, and each condition was to be evoked in full consciousness. He carried out these instructions and, in recapitulating the state I described as a kind of soul distress, he had a direct feeling of the after-death experiences in the life of the soul.

Then, in his further experiences, he saw a vista of outer nature appearing as a summer landscape, yet as in a dream. As he recapitulated this experience and consciously distinguished it from the other, knowledge came to him of the further course of his life after death. And when he was able to make really alive and present the experience of contracting in his heart nature, he was able to reach as far as the middle point of existence between death and a new life.

Then the initiator could say to him:

Learn, in the spirit, to perceive the winter,
And you will behold pre-earthly life.

Learn, in the spirit, to dream the summer,
And you will experience life after death.

Please note carefully the words I have used, for in the relationship between 'beholding' pre-earthly life and 'experiencing' life after death, and between 'dreaming' and 'perceiving', lies the tremendous difference between the two experiences had by the candidate for initiation in the Mysteries of Hibernia.

The place of this initiation in the whole historic setting of human evolution, its significance in the evolutionary process and in what way a deeper meaning was indicated when, at that stage of initiation which I described yesterday, something like a vision of the Christ came to the pupil of the Hibernian Mysteries—of these things I shall speak tomorrow.

LECTURE 9

The Great Mysteries of Hibernia

There were various things I had to tell you about the character of the Hibernian Mysteries, in fact you heard yesterday that this remarkable path of development, which people could go through in Ireland, led in the first place to an insight into all that human souls can experience through their own inner activity. All the preparations undergone by the candidates for initiation made it possible for pictures of landscapes to be conjured up before their senses as though by magic—landscapes which in other circumstances were seen in the ordinary way. The impressions received in the Mysteries were not fantastic or hallucinatory. What the pupil had been in the habit of seeing now seemed to have been like a veil which he well knew was concealing something behind it. And the same applied when looking into his own being, as the enchanted picture of the dreamlike summer landscape was conjured up before him. He was being made ready to have Imaginations which, to begin with, were linked with what in other circumstances he perceived with his outer senses. But he knew that these Imaginations would lead him to something altogether different.

I showed you how the pupil reached the stage where he was able to have a vision of both the period before his earthly existence and the period after it to the point midway between death and rebirth; and he also had a vision of the time immediately preceding the descent to earth, again to the point midway between death and rebirth. But something else happened as well. In that the pupil was led to become totally absorbed in the experiences he had undergone, and his soul had been strengthened by the vision of life before birth and after death, and he had acquired insight into the perpetual dying and rebirth of nature, now, with ever greater inner strength and energy, he was able to enter again into the experience of numbness, then of being taken up into the cosmic expanses, winging his way as it were out into the blue ether distances, and then, once again of feeling himself altogether only as a personality existing in his senses, unaware of the rest of his being, aware only of what went on in the eye, in the whole tract of hearing, of feeling, and so on—when he was as it were entirely sense organ.

With strong inner effort the pupil had learnt to bring these conditions to life again within himself and then to be receptive to what was to lead to a further stage. When he had undergone the experiences I have described he was told to recapture the condition of inner numbness deliberately, with the result that he felt his own organism to be a kind of mineral, actually as something quite foreign to him, and his soul as though it were merely hovering over and surrounding this mineral entity. Then, in the resulting state of consciousness, he had a clear vision of the Old Moon existence preceding the Earth embodiment.

At this point, my dear friends, you will remember how I described this Old Moon existence in my *Occult Science*[1] and in numbers of lectures. What is described there came to life in the pupil's consciousness and was actual reality to him. The Old Moon appeared to him as a planetary body that actually, to begin with, was entirely in a watery, fluid state—not like today's water, but gelatinous, coagulated. And he felt himself to be an organism within this semi-soft mass. And he felt the structure of the whole planet streaming out from his organism.

You must realize how greatly experiences differed at that time from those familiar today. Today we feel bounded by our skin, and we consider ourselves as consisting only of what is inside our skin. This is of course a tremendous error, for directly we consider the volume of air in a human being it is obviously nonsensical to feel enclosed within one's skin. The air I now have inside me was not in me a short while ago, and the air that will soon be inside me is at the moment outside. In respect of the air therefore we cannot rightly think of ourselves, even today, as cut off from the external world. We are everywhere where there is outer air. Fundamentally speaking there is no difference if at one moment you have a lump of sugar in your mouth and the next moment it has gone on a certain path and is in your stomach, or whether at one moment a certain volume of air is outside and the next moment in your lungs. The piece of sugar goes one way, the air goes another—through the organs of air and respiration. And anyone who does not consider these part of himself should not maintain that his mouth is part of himself but insist that his body begins with his stomach! Therefore it is nonsense, even in this modern age, for a human being to imagine himself enclosed within his skin.

During the Old Moon period it was utterly impossible to imagine any such limitation. Objects such as the pieces of furniture here, which you can touch and take hold of, did not exist then; everything was part of nature. And when one stretched out the organ that can be compared in a certain respect with today's fingers, it could also be drawn in so that it completely disappeared. The arm could be drawn in, and one could make oneself very slender, and so on. Today, if you touch the blackboard, you do not feel that it belongs to you, but at that time you felt that whatever you touched actually belonged to you in the same way as the inbreathed air is part of you today. So that one's own organism was in fact felt to be just one part of the whole organism of planet Moon.

All this entered the consciousness of the pupil of the Hibernian Mysteries. He also received the impression that the gelatinous fluidity was a temporary condition of the Old Moon existence, and that there were certain periods when in this gelatinous fluidity something appeared that was much harder, physically, than our solids today. It was not a 'mineral' in the sense in which emerald, corundum or diamond are mineral today, but was hard and horny. There was no crystalline mineral substance as we ourselves know it but the forms taken by the hard substances, the horny and the mineral-like kind, were quite obviously the product of organic secretion, in the sense that we do not speak today of the crystalline structure of a cow's horn because we know that the horn only exists because it has been projected from an organism—and the same is true of a deer's antlers and similar formations. Fundamentally, the same is true of bones—yet they are mineral. And so at the time of the Old Moon evolution a mineral-like substance was produced out of organic material.

And those beings who were partly going through their human stage at that time, and who had only some aspects of this human stage to complete during Earth existence, are the individualities I have spoken of as the great and wise primeval teachers of humanity on earth and who now have their abode in the moon-sphere.

All this became known to the pupil during this state of numbness. And when he had passed through these experiences in the way that satisfied his initiators, it was impressed upon him that he must advance still further, and recapitulate the stage where he could let his benumbed being stream out to the ether distances, to the point where he could feel that the paths to the heights brought him to the far distances of the blue ether, to the very boundaries of spatial existence.

And then, in going through a repetition of this, the pupil became aware that all his feeling was in a certain way tending to move outwards towards the far distances of the ether. But as he moved towards the ether distances, after the heights had taken him up and brought him there, he felt as though at the very end of the spatial world something penetrated into and vitalized him. It is what we today would call the astral element. It was an element that was experienced in an inward way and at that time was united with the human being in a far more significant and energetic way than is the case today, although it could not then be perceived with equal intensity. It united with the human soul, but even more forcefully and livingly than, for example, a feeling that might arise within a human being today if he were to expose himself to the instreaming, revivifying light of the sun to the point where he becomes sensitively aware of each of his organs. If you will only pay a little more attention you will be able to feel, if you expose yourself freely to the sun, letting it stream through you, but not to the point of discomfort—if you expose yourself to the sun so that you let its instreaming light and warmth bring comfort to your body, then you will feel each organ in a subtly different way than before. You come unmistakably into a condition where you can describe the very make-up of your organism.

That such things are so little known today is merely due to a lack in the capacity of modern people to be genuinely attentive. If this capacity were not lacking today, people would actually be able to give at least dreamlike indications of what is revealed to them in the instreaming light. In earlier times the pupil actually was instructed about the inner constitution of the human organism quite differently from the way it is done today. Corpses are now dissected and anatomical atlases made. This does not require much attentiveness, and it must be admitted that even this is not forthcoming from many students—although not much attentiveness is required! Once upon a time the pupil of the Mysteries was taught by being exposed to the sun and then trained to become sensitive to the way his inner constitution reacted to the pleasant instreaming light, and after this experience he was well able to describe his liver, stomach, and so on. This inner connection of the human being with the macrocosm can become a reality provided that right conditions are established. It is quite possible to be blind and yet to feel the form of an object by touching it. So too, if one organ in your organism is made sensitive to another through attentiveness to the light, you can describe them—at any rate so that at least you can have a shadowy picture of them in your consciousness.

It was particularly important that the pupil should have implanted into him, and to a high degree, that when he was being transported out into the ether distances and the astral light was flooding into him he should not be conscious of his own identity but should feel in his consciousness the existence of a great and mighty world, a world of which he said: 'I am living entirely in an element with other beings. This element is basically pure nature-goodness. For out of this element in which I am swimming'—forgive me for using an expression possible only in a much later terminology—'out of this planetary element in which I am swimming like a fish in water, although it consists of light, volatile components, I feel a force streaming into me from all sides bringing me ease and contentment.' The pupil felt the astral light pouring into him on all sides, forming and building him. 'This element is pure nature-goodness,' he could have said, 'for I am being given something in every direction. I am actually surrounded by pure goodness. Goodness is everywhere, but it is a nature-goodness. It is also creative, for its forces enable me to exist, give me my form, and sustain me in so far as I swim and move about in this element.' Thus the impressions received were those of innate, nature-born morality.

A modern comparison with this experience might be expressed as follows. Suppose a person had a rose in front of him and in smelling its scent was able to say with inner sincerity: 'Divine goodness, which extends through the whole of planet Earth, also streams into this rose; and when the rose communicates its own essence to my organ of smell I become aware of that divine goodness.' Anyone saying this honestly and sincerely today would be experiencing something like a faint shadow of what in those ancient times was felt inwardly as the very life element of the individual human being. And that, my dear friends, was the experience of the Old Sun existence which preceded our earth. Thus the pupil of the Hibernian Mysteries could experience the Old Sun existence and Old Moon existence—the predecessors of the Earth.

And further, when the pupil had been led to be aware of himself in his senses only, had experienced something like a discarding of his whole organism, so that he was living only in his eyes, in the auditory tract, in the whole range of his feeling, then he became aware of what I have called in my *Occult Science* the Saturn existence[2]—an existence in which humanity existed and moved about in the element of warmth, in the differentiations of warmth. Human beings felt themselves then not as beings of flesh and blood, not as having bones and nerves, but solely as an organism of warmth—warmth of another kind—the planetary warmth of Saturn. They were aware of warmth when the outer warmth differed in degree from the inner warmth. Saturn existence was a weaving in warmth, being alive through warmth, a feeling of inner warmth as distinct from outer warmth.

This was experienced by the pupil when his whole being had moved out into his senses. These senses were not so highly differentiated as they are today. This perception of warmth by means of warmth, living by virtue of warmth, was the all-important experience. But there were moments when the pupil, aware of himself as an organism of warmth, approached a different degree of warmth and felt something in himself like a burst of flames; he now seemed to be in an element not merely of streaming, weaving, billowing warmth but at moments he seemed to be something akin to flame or something that was like a moving sensation of taste, not only like tasting with the tongue, for naturally it could not have been so at that time, but taste which he felt to be himself yet which was kindled through contact with something outside himself and to which he also gave something. Thus the Saturn existence came alive in the pupil.

So you see that in the Hibernian Mysteries the pupil was actually led into the past of the Earth's planetary existence. He learnt about the Saturn, Sun and Moon existence as the successive metamorphoses of Earth existence.

Then he was told to pass once again through the experience which led him into his inner being and which I described to you as a feeling of inner pressure, as though he were being prevented from feeling his own centre, as though the air inside him were being compressed; the corresponding condition experienced by a person today would be the feeling of not being able to breathe out, the feeling of pressure on all sides. This was the first condition that the pupil had now deliberately to call up in his soul. And when he did this, when he actually reached the dream state in which previously he had had a waking dream of nature as a series of summer landscapes—when he had induced this condition, then he suddenly had a remarkable experience. In order to give you any idea at all of this experience I must characterize it to you the other way round by putting it this way. Imagine that as a human being living on the earth today you enter a warm room. After feeling the warmth you go outside where the temperature is several degrees below zero, and feel the cold. You feel the difference between warmth and cold, but you feel it in your body. It does not affect your soul. For as an earthly human being, when you come into a warm room you do not exactly have the feeling that something like a great spirit is spreading out and enveloping you with love. This warmth is comforting to the body but you do not feel that it is of the nature of soul. It is similar with regard to the cold. You shiver, your body gets frozen, but you do not have the feeling that because of the particular climatic conditions demons are coming at you on all sides, blowing such bitter cold over you that your very soul feels cold. Physical warmth does not at one and the same time affect your soul, because as an earthly human being you do not in your everyday consciousness feel the soul element in nature with any intensity. As an earthly human being you can feel warmed by another person's friendship and love, and you can feel chilled by his coldness, perhaps also by his pedantry, but these are understood to be soul qualities. Just think how little inclined a modern person would be, on going out into the warm, summery air, to say: 'The gods love me a great deal just now!' Or, when going out into wintry cold: 'Now only those sylphs who are the pedants in their world are out flying today!' We do not hear expressions such as these nowadays!

This awareness, which I have endeavoured to characterize from another side, was something that came naturally to the pupil after he had experienced this feeling of pressure. He felt warmth as a physical quality and simultaneously as a quality of soul, and this was possible because his consciousness was projected into the Jupiter existence which will follow the

Earth. For we shall only become Jupiter citizens in that we combine physical warmth with soul warmth, so that as Jupiter people, when we lovingly caress another person, maybe a child, we shall at the same time actually be transmitting warmth. Loving and the streaming out of warmth will no longer be separate activities. We shall actually reach a point where, when we feel warm, we shall also be able to send this warmth out as a soul quality into our environment.

The pupil of the Hibernian Mysteries was led to this experience—not, of course, in the physical world but while he was transported to another world—and thus the Jupiter experience was revealed to him not in physical reality but in a picture.

The next intensification of consciousness was that the pupil was to feel deeply the inner distress of which I spoke yesterday, for now he realized the stern necessity to overcome his own ego, which could otherwise become the source of evil. When he had brought about this inner mood of soul, something arose within him so that he not only felt soul warmth and physical warmth as one and the same but this soul-physical warmth began to *shine*. The secret of the radiance of soul light dawned upon him, and he was thereby transported into that future time when the Earth will be metamorphosed into the Venus embodiment.

And when the pupil felt all that he had experienced up till then gathered up in his heart, as many streams coming together, as I described yesterday, then all this was revealed to him as being at the same time the experience of the whole planet. The picture that arose in the pupil was this. You have a thought; this thought does not at all remain inside your skin but begins to *sound*—the thought becomes word. What you bring alive forms itself into word. The word reaches out throughout the planet Vulcan. Everything on the Vulcan planet is articulate, living reality: word sounds towards word; word is clarified by word; word speaks to word; word learns to understand word. The human being feels himself to be the world-comprehending word, the word that comprehends the world of the Word. When this experience arose as a picture before the candidate for Hibernian initiation, he knew he had been transported to the Vulcan existence, the last metamorphosis of planet Earth.

Thus you see that the Hibernian Mysteries belong to what spiritual science calls the Great Mysteries.[3] For the initiation through which the pupils passed gave them a vista both of pre-earthly life and of life after death. At the same time it gave them a vista of cosmic life, life in which the human being is interwoven and out of which in the course of time he is being born. The pupil was learning to know the microcosm, that is to say, himself as a being of spirit, soul and body in connection with the macrocosm. But he also came to know how the macrocosm itself evolves, arises and passes away and undergoes metamorphoses. The Hibernian Mysteries were undoubtedly the Great Mysteries.

They were in their prime during the era preceding the Mystery of Golgotha. But the essential feature of these Great Mysteries was that the Christ was spoken of in these Mysteries as a Being belonging to the future, just as later on human beings spoke of the Christ as a Being who had figured in events of the past. And when, after the first initiation, the image of the Christ had been shown to the pupil as he was leaving the temple, the purpose was to bring home to him that the whole evolutionary course of the Earth in cosmic existence is orientated to the event of Golgotha, which at that time was presented as an event of the future.

On the island which later endured so many sore trials there was a centre of the Great Mysteries, a centre of 'Christian' Mysteries before the event of Golgotha—where the spiritual vision of human beings living prior to that mighty event were directed in a rightful manner to the Mystery of Golgotha.

And when the Mystery of Golgotha actually occurred, when in Palestine those remarkable occurrences took place which we include in the term the Mystery of Golgotha, at that very time, solemn festivals were being celebrated within the Hibernian Mysteries themselves and the community associated with them, that is to say, by people who belonged in some way to the Mysteries. And what was actually happening in Palestine was revealed in Hibernia in a hundred different ways in pictures that were not memories of anything in the past. On the island of Hibernia human beings experienced the Mystery of Golgotha in pictures simultaneously with the historical occurrence in Palestine. When, later on, the Mystery of Golgotha was shown in pictures to people in temples and churches, the pictures were reminders of something that already belonged to the past and was therefore a historical fact which ordinary consciousness could recollect. On the island of Hibernia these pictures were already in existence at a time when they could not have been memories of past history but could only be reached as spiritual revelation. The events that took place in Palestine at the beginning of our era and were visible there to physical eyes were beheld spiritually in Hibernia. On Hibernia humanity actually experienced the Mystery of Golgotha in the spirit. And this was the basis of the greatness inherent in everything that subsequently went out from Hibernia into the rest of the civilized world but disappeared as time went on.

I now beg you to pay attention to the following. Anyone who studies purely external history can find much that is splendid and beautiful, a great deal that is uplifting and enlightening when he looks back to the ancient East or to ancient Greece or Rome. Again, he can learn a great deal when he comes, let us say, to the time of Charlemagne and on through the Middle Ages. But just look at how scanty the historical accounts become in the period that begins a few centuries after the birth of Christianity and ends approximately in the ninth or tenth century of the Christian era. If you examine the records that exist, in all the earlier and more honest historical works you will find only very few and very meagre accounts of events in those centuries. It is only after that period that records begin to be more detailed.

Admittedly, later historians feel a certain professional shame at having to deal with the available material so unsatisfactorily. They cannot describe matters of which they have no knowledge, and so they think out all kinds of fantastic interpretations, which are inserted into the history of those centuries. But it is all so much nonsense. If external history is presented honestly, accounts of the period during which the downfall of Rome took place are very meagre, and the same applies to the migrations of the peoples—which as a matter of fact were outwardly not nearly so striking as people today suppose but were striking only because of their contrast with the previous and subsequent periods of tranquillity. If you were to calculate today—or rather, if you had calculated in the pre-war period—how many people, let us say, leave Russia for Switzerland every year, you would find that the numbers would be greater than they were during the time of the migrations over the same area of Europe. All these things are relative. So that if one were to continue talking in the style adopted when trying to describe the migrations of the peoples, one would have to say that up to the beginning of the war migrations were taking place all over Europe and also across to America. And the emigrations to America were more numerous than the streams of migrations of the peoples. But this is not realized.

It is nevertheless a fact that records of the period described as that of the migrations of the peoples and their aftermath are very scanty. Little is known about what was actually happening; little is said, for example, about what was going on in this neighbourhood, or in France, or in Germany. But it was precisely in these regions that faint echoes of what had been revealed in the Hibernian Mysteries swept over Europe; it was here that the effects and impulses of the Great Mysteries of Hibernia penetrated into civilization, even if only in faint echoes.

But then two great streams met. What I am now saying must not be taken as casting even the faintest shade of sympathy or antipathy upon anything, but merely to describe a historical necessity. Two streams met. The one which came over from the East by way of Greece and Rome depended on the increasingly prevalent faculty connected with the intellect and the senses and worked with what was available as a historic memory of outwardly visible, outwardly experienced events. From Palestine, by way of Greece and Rome, came the tidings of something that had taken place in Palestine in the physical world through Christ, the God, and people received this into their religious life to the extent to which they were capable of understanding it on the basis of a form of consciousness tied to reason and the senses. These tidings spread far and wide, and finally superseded what came over from the West, from Hibernia and, as a last echo of the ancient, instinctive earthly wisdom, took account of the fact that the traditional wisdom of humanity was now shedding its light into a new kind of consciousness. From Hibernia there spread across Europe an impulse which in the matter of spiritual illumination did not depend upon physical vision or 'proof' based upon evidence of any actual historical event. This impulse spread in the form of Hibernian cult and wisdom. It was concerned with illumination that comes to human beings from the spiritual world, even in the case of an event which, like the Mystery of Golgotha, had taken place simultaneously in physical reality in another part of the world. In Hibernia the physical reality of the event in Palestine was seen spiritually.

But the mentality that could grasp only physical reality overshadowed the impulse that relied upon the spiritual upliftment and deepening of the life of the human soul. And gradually, because of an inevitable necessity of which we have spoken regarding other aspects, the impulse connected principally with physical existence gained the upper hand over the impulse associated with spiritual vision. The tidings of the Redeemer present in a physical body on earth obscured the wonderful imaginations coming over from Hibernia and which could be presented in cult and ritual—those magnificent imaginations portraying the Redeemer as a spiritual Being and which took no account, either in the corresponding rituals or descriptions, of the fact that what had come to pass was also a historical event. Still less could this aspect have been taken into account before the actual event, for the cults had been instituted in the pre-Christian era.

And the time came when human beings became steadily more immune to everything that was not physically perceptible, when they came to the point of no longer accepting as truth anything that was not physically perceptible. Thus the substance of the wisdom coming over from Hibernia was no longer understood; nor was the art which came from there felt to be an expression of cosmic truth. The consequence was the ever-increasing growth of a science that was not a Hibernian science but one concerned only with what the senses perceive, and also of a form of art that was not Hibernian art but one—

including even the art of Raphael—using sense-perceptible objects as models, whereas Hibernian art set out to give a direct presentation of spiritual reality itself.

So the time came when a certain darkness came over spiritual life, when people put their sole trust in reason and the senses, and founded philosophies that were intended to show that in some way or other reason and the senses were able to discover the secret of existence and actually to reach truth.

Finally there came the remarkable phase when human consciousness was no longer accessible to spiritual influences. And where can one see this more precisely than in what was given to humanity in a work such as *The Chymical Wedding of Christian Rosenkreutz*.[4] I wrote about it recently in the journal *Das Reich*. I called attention there to the strange circumstances connected with this work. Valentin Andreae was the physical author; he wrote it down immediately before the outbreak of the Thirty Years' War. But nobody who has read the biography of Valentin Andreae will have any doubt about the fact that the man who afterwards became a pedantic cleric and wrote several unctious books did not write *The Chymical Wedding*. It is utter nonsense to believe that he wrote it. Just compare *The Chymical Wedding* or *The Reformation of the Whole World* or Valentin Andreae's other writings—physically he was of course the same personality—with the sanctimonious stuff written by Pastor Valentin Andreae in his later life. It is a really remarkable phenomenon. Here is a youth, hardly out of school, writing works such as *The Reformation of the Whole World* or *The Chymical Wedding of Christian Rosenkreutz*, and we have to make strenuous efforts to find any meaning in them at all. He himself understood nothing of their real content, as is shown in his later life, for he became a sanctimonious pastor. And yet it is the same man! This fact alone makes it plausible to state, as I did in my article, that *The*

Chymical Wedding was not written in the ordinary sense by a human being, or at least only in so far as for instance Napoleon's ever-nervous undercover secretary wrote his letters for him. But after all Napoleon was a man who stood firmly on the ground, who was a very physical personality. The one who wrote *The Chymical Wedding* was not a physical personality, and he simply made use of this 'secretary' who subsequently became the unctuous Pastor Valentin Andreae.

Picture to yourselves this wonderful event immediately preceding the Thirty Years' War. A young man, a very young man, lends his hand to a spiritual being who writes down, through him, a work such as *The Chymical Wedding*! This was only a specially striking example of what often happened in those days, but was not readily recognized, or preserved. The important things given to humanity at that time were given in such a way that the intellect was incapable of grasping them. The onward flowing spirituality was still revealing itself, but human beings were no longer capable of experiencing it within themselves, even though it came into the world through them.

And so it was the case that in regard to this period history books—however voluminous they may be—inevitably contained many blank pages, for human beings were living at that time in two currents: the one current was taking its course in the physical world below, where people were becoming more and more inclined to believe only in what their reason and their senses told them, but above there was an onflowing spiritual revelation which could be announced *through* human beings but which they could not themselves experience. And one of the most characteristic examples of this spiritual revelation is a work such as *The Chymical Wedding of Christian Rosenkreutz*.

What was revealed passed through human heads even though it was not understood, and it became weaker and also distorted. Magnificent, truly poetic material degenerated into the kind of gibberish of which verses in *The Chymical Wedding* are sometimes examples. And yet they are revelations of something truly great: tremendous macrocosmic pictures, powerful, majestic happenings between the human level and the macrocosm. If with the vision that is possible today we read *The Chymical Wedding* we learn to understand its imagery. The pictures melt away, for they have been coloured by the brain through which they have passed and sublime realities are apparent behind them.

Such things are a proof that what humanity once experienced actually did remain alive in the subconscious. It only dried up altogether in the early period of the devastating Thirty Years' War. In the first half of the seventeenth century there was an influx of what had once been great and impressive spiritual truth. The mystics alone preserved its impress in their souls, but the real substance, the spiritual substance, was totally lost. It was the time for reason to be victorious and to prepare the epoch of freedom.

And today we look back at these things and find our gaze directed with a very great and deep interest to the Hibernian Mysteries, for they are, in very truth, the last great Mysteries through which the secrets of human and cosmic life could be revealed. Today, when we delve into them again, we realize for the first time how great these Hibernian Mysteries are. But our vision cannot really penetrate into their depths if we have not first fathomed them through our own independent efforts. And even when this has been achieved, a strange thing happens.

When one approaches the pictures of the Hibernian Mysteries in the Akashic Record one feels that something is repelling one. It is as though some force were holding one back, as though one's soul could not reach them. The nearer one approaches the more one's goal seems to be eclipsed, and a kind of stupefaction comes over one's soul. One has to work one's way through this stupefaction, and the only possible way of doing so is to rekindle one's own independently acquired knowledge of similar matters. And then one understands why it is so difficult to approach the Hibernian Mysteries. It becomes evident that they were the final echo of an age-old gift to humanity from the divine-spiritual powers, but that when these Mysteries withdrew into a shadowy existence they were at the same time surrounded by a stout defence so that human beings cannot find their way to them if they maintain a passive attitude of soul. They can approach these Mysteries only by kindling their own spiritual activity—in other words, by becoming modern human beings in the true sense. Access to the Hibernian Mysteries was barred so that people could not approach them in that way, but are compelled to experience with the full activity of consciousness that which must be discovered *inwardly* in this age of freedom. Neither by a scrutiny of history nor by clairvoyant vision of great and wonderful ancient secrets can these Mysteries be discovered, but only by the exercise of a human being's own conscious, inner activity.

The Great Mysteries of Hibernia thus provide the very strongest indication of the fact that a new age begins at the time when they faded into the realm of shadows. But they can be seen again today in all their glory and majesty by a soul sustained by inner freedom. For through true inner activity they can indeed be seen again when the opposing forces, with their menace of stupefaction, are overcome and the way is opened to behold the revelations that were once accessible to those who were to be initiated, revelations of the ancient secrets of the spiritual wisdom—instinctive it is true, but none the less sublime—that once poured over earthly humanity as a primal power of the soul. The most beautiful and significant memorials in later times to the primal wisdom of humanity, to the sublime grace of divine-spiritual beings manifesting in the earliest stages of humanity, the most beautiful soul-spiritual tokens of that epoch, are the pictures that can be revealed to us when we direct our spiritual gaze to the Mysteries of Hibernia.

LECTURE 10

The Chthonic and the Eleusinian Mysteries

Let us once again recall the deeply significant fact that the knowledge and truths contained in the Mysteries of Hibernia gradually lost power and influence as they moved from the West towards Central Europe and the East; and in place of a knowledge of spiritual things—even in matters pertaining to religion—physical perception, or at any rate a tradition based on physical perception, made its appearance. You will remember the picture we arrived at at the end of the last lecture. We were speaking of the part the Christ Being played in the Mysteries of Hibernia, also with reference to the time when the Mystery of Golgotha was actually taking place. Over in Hibernia were the initiates with their pupils, and there, without any means of physical perception of the Mystery of Golgotha, and without any possibility of receiving information of the event, the Mystery was nonetheless celebrated simultaneously with all solemnity, because the initiates knew from their own insight that the Mystery of Golgotha was happening—out there—at that very time.

The initiates and their pupils in the Mysteries of Hibernia therefore had no choice but to experience in a *spiritual* way an actual physical reality, an event in the world of the senses. With their particular disposition of soul and with the orientation of knowledge then customary in Hibernia, there was no need to have anything more in the physical world than the spiritual element alone.

Thus it is clear that in Hibernia the spiritual element was

always predominant. Indeed, by all manner of secret streams in the spiritual life, what had been inaugurated in Hibernia was transplanted to the British Isles, to Brittany, to the lands that are now Holland and Belgium, and finally by way of the present Alsace to Central Europe. Though not recognizable in the general civilization of the first centuries of Christian evolution it can nevertheless be discovered in all these regions; here and there we find single individuals who were able to understand what had come from the Mysteries of Hibernia. In order to find these individuals we must set out with a deep and heartfelt longing for knowledge. In the first Christian centuries they are still fairly numerous, but later on, from the eighth and ninth to the fifteenth and sixteenth centuries, they become fewer and fewer. Yet in these centuries too, individuals are still to be found who gather around them in quiet places far removed from the great world and its civilization, little groups of pupils to whom what had been inaugurated in Hibernia in the West of Europe could be passed on.

In general a knowledge of these events, of a kind for which no direct spiritual perception was required, spread over Europe. People turned to historical tradition, which simply told of the physical events that took place in Palestine at the beginning of our era. And from this stream proceeded that attitude to history which takes account only of what happens in physical life. Humanity in general was less and less able to perceive the colossal contradiction that lies in the fact that the Mystery of Golgotha, an event which is comprehensible only by means of the deepest spiritual activity, should be referred only to an external phenomenon, perceptible to the physical senses. But this was, after all, the path which cultural development in Europe had to take.

Fundamentally speaking it had been gradually prepared over a long period, but it could be realized only because a very great deal of the old Mystery wisdom, even such as existed in Greece, had been forgotten. For these Mysteries of Greece fell into two categories. One was engaged in directing the human mind towards the spiritual world, towards the actual guidance and ordering of the world in the spirit; while the other investigated the secrets of nature, all that rules in nature, especially the forces and beings connected with the forces of the earth.[1] Candidates receiving a full initiation were initiated into both types of Mystery. And then one described them as having received the Mysteries of the Father, the Mysteries of Zeus, and also the Mysteries of the Mother, the Mysteries of Demeter. When we look back into those times we find a spiritual perception which, though somewhat abstract, could extend into the highest regions, and side by side with this, a conception of nature capable of descending into the depths. And most important of all, we find a union of the two.

Now in this union of the two a fact was perceived which today is but little noticed. It is the fact that a human being has certain external substances of nature within himself, but not certain others. This fact was observed and studied in its deepest meaning in the chthonic Mysteries in Greece. You know that iron is part of a human being's make-up. There are also other metals in him, calcium, sodium, magnesium, and so on, but there are many more metals which are not in him. If we were to try to find these other metals in the human body by using ordinary scientific methods, that is to say, by analysing its substances, then by means of this external investigation we should find no lead, no copper, no quicksilver, no tin, no silver and no gold.

That was the great riddle which occupied the initiator in the Greek Mysteries, eventually finding expression in the question: Why does it happen that the human being has iron in him, and also sodium, magnesium and other substances which

Triptolemus, legendary founder of the Eleusinian Mysteries, between the 'two Goddesses', the earth-mother Demeter and her daughter Persephone.

can also be found in external nature, but does not have, for instance, lead or tin in him? They were deeply convinced that the human being was a 'little world', a microcosm, and yet it would appear that he does not have in his make-up these other metals—lead, tin, quicksilver, silver and gold.

Now we may truly say that the students for initiation in earlier times in Greece were of the opinion that this was only *apparently* the case; for they were steeped in the knowledge that the human being is a real microcosm, which means that *everything* manifested in the world is also in *him*.

Let us for a moment look into the heart and mind of a human being about to be initiated in Greece. He would be instructed somewhat as follows—and here I must gather together into a few sentences things that were brought throughout long periods of training, but you will understand. He would be told the following. All over the earth there is iron hidden in its depths, and there is also iron in the human being. Similarly, when the Earth had not yet become earth but was in a previous planetary condition, when it was Moon, or perhaps even Sun, it had lead, tin, and so on, within it, and all the beings taking part in these earlier formation processes of the Earth had a share in these metals and their forces—just as human beings today have a share in the forces of iron. But because of the various changes which the ancient form of the Earth underwent, iron alone persisted in such strength and density that it could be part of the human make-up. The other metals enumerated are also still contained in the earth, but they are no longer of such a nature that human beings can take them directly into their constitution. They are, however, contained in an infinitely rarefied condition, in the whole of that part of cosmic space which concerns human beings.

If I examine a little piece of lead I see a well-known greyish-white metal with a definite density, and I can take hold of it.

But this same lead, which occurs in the earth as lead ores, exists in infinitely fine dilution in the whole of cosmic space surrounding humanity, and plays a significant part. For it radiates its forces everywhere, even where there is apparently no lead. And human beings do have a contact with these lead forces, not, however, by way of the physical body but by way of the etheric body—because beyond the lead ores in the earth lead exists in such a rarefied condition that it can now work only on the human etheric body. But this is where it does work, in this condition of infinite dilution spread out over the whole of cosmic space.

The pupil of the Greek chthonic Mysteries then learnt that just as today the earth is rich in iron—for it is a planet of which the inhabitants of another planet could say, 'That is a planet rich in iron,' the only other planet rich in iron being Mars. And just as the earth is rich in iron, Saturn is rich in lead. What iron is for the earth lead is for Saturn. And we have to imagine, as the pupils in the Greek chthonic Mysteries learnt, that once upon a time when Saturn separated from the general planetary form which the Earth once had (as described in my *Occult Science*) this fine dilution of lead took place. One could say that Saturn took the lead away with it and, by means of its own planetary life-force and its own planetary warmth, retained it in such a condition that it can permeate with this finely diluted lead the whole planetary system to which our Earth also belongs.

So you must picture to yourself the Earth, and in the distance Saturn filling the whole planetary system with rarefied lead, and this fine lead substance working upon human beings. And you can still find evidence that those who were being initiated in Greece learnt about how this lead works. They knew that if it were not for the activity of lead our sense organs, especially our eyes, would claim the whole of our being, and not allow us to come to self-dependence. A human being would be able only to see and not *to think about what he had seen.* He would be unable to detach himself from what he saw and say: 'I see.' He would be totally overpowered by seeing. It is this activity of lead that enables a human being to be self-dependent, so that as an ego he can withstand the receptivity to the outside world which lives in him. It is these lead forces which, entering first into the human etheric body and then impregnating the physical body in a certain way, endow him with the faculty of memory.

It was always a great moment when a pupil, such as a Greek pupil of the chthonic Mysteries, after having learnt all this was led to what follows. With the greatest possible solemnity and ceremony he was shown the substance lead, after which his whole mind was directed to Saturn. Then he was shown the relationship between Saturn and earthly lead. He was told: 'This lead which you see is harboured in the earth. But in its present condition the earth is not capable of directly giving the lead a form in which it could be active in human beings. But Saturn, with its very different condition of warmth and inner life-forces, scatters lead over cosmic space, making you an independent human being possessing the power of memory. Realize that you are a human being only by virtue of the fact that you can remember what you knew 10 or 20 years ago. Think how your humanity would suffer if you did not contain within you what you experienced 10 or 20 years ago. Your ego-force would be shattered unless this power of memory were present in full measure. You owe this to what rays to you from far-away Saturn. It is the force that has come to rest in earthly lead and, in this static condition, can no longer work on you. The Saturn lead forces enable you to collect your thoughts so that after a time they can arise again out of the depths of your soul, and you can have continuity in your life in

Heracles sacrificing his pig at Eleusis, from the 'Lovatelli urn': the preliminary act to initiation proper, of which Heracles' descent to Hell forms the archetypal instance in mythology.

Unfolded photograph of the Lovatelli urn, showing scenes of initiation at Eleusis with veiled initiate and the Goddess with her sacred symbols.

the outer world and not live merely in a transitory way. You owe it to these Saturn forces of lead that you will not have forgotten by tomorrow the objects you see around you today, but that you can retain them, and that you can recall to mind what you experienced years ago—that whatever you experienced throughout your whole life on earth can reappear to your inner eye as it was before.

It was a deep and powerful impression that the pupil received, and this knowledge was brought to him with great and solemn ceremony. And now he also came to understand that if these Saturn lead forces alone were active—giving him the power of the ego, the power of memory—he would be completely estranged from the cosmos. If the Saturn forces were the only ones affecting him the human being would be able to retain for his whole lifetime what he sees with his physical eyes, but he would become alienated from the cosmos; inspired by Saturn with the power of memory, he would become a kind of hermit on earth.

And then the pupil was told that there had to be another force working in the opposite direction from Saturn, namely, the moon force. Let us suppose that these two forces are positioned so that they work onto the earth and onto humanity from opposite sides yet flow into one another. What Saturn takes away from human beings they are given by the moon, and what the moon takes away from us we are given by Saturn. Just as in iron the Earth has a force which human beings can inwardly transmute, and Saturn has this force in lead, the moon has this same force in *silver*.

Now silver, in the form in which it exists in the earth, has arrived at a condition in which it cannot enter directly into the human being, yet the whole sphere embraced by the moon is actually permeated by finely distributed silver. And the moon, especially when its light comes from the direction of the constellation of Leo, works in such a way that human beings receive from these silver forces of the moon the opposite influence from the lead forces of Saturn, and they are therefore not estranged from the cosmos in spite of the fact that they are endowed by the cosmos with the force of memory. It was a deeply solemn moment when the Greek pupil was led to see this opposition of Saturn and the moon. In the holy solemnity of night he was told: 'Look up to Saturn surrounded by its rings. To Saturn you owe the fact that you are an independent being. Look in the other direction, to the silver rays of the moon. To the moon you owe the fact that you are able to bear the Saturn force without being cut off from the cosmos.'

In this way—with direct reference to the connection between human beings and the cosmos—teaching was given in Greece which we find caricatured later on in astrology. In those days it was a true wisdom, for people saw in the stars not merely the points or specks of light above them in the sky; in the stars they beheld living spiritual beings, and they saw humanity on earth to be in union with these living spiritual beings. Thus they had a natural science that reached up into the heavens and extended right out into cosmic space. And then when the pupil had received such an insight, when this vision of light had been deeply inscribed into his soul, he was led into the real Mysteries of Eleusis. (You have heard how these things took place in my descriptions of other Mysteries, for instance, the Mysteries of Hibernia). The pupil was brought before two statues. The first of these statues represented a fatherly god, the fatherly god who was surrounded by the signs of the planetary spheres and the sun. It showed Saturn raying out in a way that reminded the pupil, 'Yes, that is the lead radiating from the cosmos,' just as the moon reminded him, 'Yes, that is the silver radiating from the moon,' and so on with each single planet. Thus in the statue that represented the Father nature there appeared all the secrets which ray down from the planetary environment of the earth and are connected with the several metals of the earth, and which human beings are no longer able to make use of in their inner make-up.[2]

The pupil was being told: 'In front of you stands the Father of the world. In Saturn He holds lead, in Jupiter tin, in Mars iron—iron which is related to earthly existence—but here it is in a quite different condition. In the sun He holds shining gold, in Venus shining, flowing copper, in Mercury shining quicksilver and in the moon shining silver. You contain within you only so much of the metals as you were able to assimilate from the planetary conditions through which the earth passed in earlier aeons. In its present condition you can assimilate only iron. But as earth being you are not whole. The Father who stands before you shows you in the metals what cannot come to you today from the earth but which you have to receive from the cosmos, for in the Father you have another part of your being. Only when you look upon yourself as a human being who has lived through the planetary transformations of the earth—only then are you really a complete human being. You stand here on earth as a part of a human being. The other part of you the Father bears around His head and in His arms. What stands in front of you together with what He holds forms the real 'you'. You stand on the earth. But the earth was not always as it is today. If it had always been as it is today you could not live on it as a human being. For the earth holds within it, even though in a dead condition, the lead of Saturn, the tin of Jupiter, the iron of Mars (in that other state), the gold of the sun, the silver of the moon, the copper of Venus and the quicksilver of Mercury; it holds all these things within it. But the condition in which the earth holds these metals within it today is no more than a memory of the way in which, once upon a time, silver lived in the earth during the Moon existence, or gold during the Sun existence, or lead during the Saturn existence. And what you see today as the dense metallic ores of lead, tin, iron, gold, copper, quicksilver and silver—with the exception of the iron as you know it, which is not essentially earthly but belongs to Mars—all these metals, which you see today in such a dense and compact form, once poured down from the cosmos into the earth while they were in quite a different condition. The metals as you know them today on the earth are the corpses of the former essential being of the metals. Lead is the corpse of the metal being which played a part during the Saturn epoch and later on to a different extent during the Moon epoch. Tin played a part, together with gold, during the Sun epoch of the Earth, in an altogether different condition. And when you behold this condition in spirit, then this statue becomes for you, in respect of what it brings you today, a true "Father statue".' And in the spirit, as it were in a real vision, the Father statue of the true Mysteries of Eleusis became alive, and handed to the female figure standing beside it the metals in the state in which they then were. In the vision seen by the pupil the female figure received this ancient form of the metals and surrounded it with what the Earth could give from out of its own being when it became earth.

And the pupil now beheld this wonderful process. Once upon a time what the pupil now saw in a symbolic way had actually happened. The mass of metal streamed or rayed forth from the hand of the Father statue; and the earth, with its limestone and other rocks, came to meet it and surrounded these instreaming metals with earthly substance. And now the Mother statue's hand, outstretched in love, received the metal forces coming from the Father statue.[3] This made a deep and powerful impression on the pupil, for he saw the cosmic element working together with the earthly element in the course of the aeons. And he began to get a right perception and understanding of the offering made by the earth.

Look at the metal substance in the earth today in all its variety! You find it crystallized and surrounded by a kind of crust which is of the earth. The essence of the metals comes from the cosmos, and that which is of the earth receives in a kind of loving gesture what comes from the cosmos. You may see this all around you if you move about in those parts of the earth where metals are to be found, and interest yourself in them. And the essence of what came to meet the metal was called 'Mother', i.e. matrix. And the most important of these earthly substances that checked the flow of the heavenly form of the metals in order to receive them was called the Mothers.

This is also one aspect of the 'Mothers' to whom Faust descends. He is at the same time descending into those pre-earthly aeons of the earth in order to see how the mother-like earth takes into herself what is given, father-like, by the cosmos. Through all this a deep inner sympathy with the cosmos was aroused in the pupil of the Eleusinian Mysteries; he knew, with a knowledge that is of the heart, what the earth's natural products and nature processes really are.

My dear friends, when a present-day human being observes the products and processes of nature, it is all dead, it is nothing but a corpse. And when we occupy ourselves with physics or chemistry, are we really doing anything else with nature than what the anatomist does when he dissects the dead body? The anatomist handles the dead remains of what is made and intended for life. In the same way we with our chemistry and physics dissect living nature! A very different natural science was given to a Greek pupil—science of what is living, which enabled him to see our present lead as the corpse of lead. He had to go back into the times when lead was *alive*. And he became aware of the mysterious relation of humanity to the cosmos, the mysterious relation of human beings to all that is around them on the earth. And then, after the pupil had experienced these things and his whole soul had connected itself with the Father and the Mother statue, bringing alive in him the two opposite forces—the forces of the cosmos and the forces of the earth—he was led into the holiest place of all in Greece. There he saw in front of him the picture of the female figure suckling the Child at her breast. Then he was brought to an understanding of the words: 'That is the God Iacchos who will one day come.' Thus did the Greek pupil acquire, before the event, an understanding of the Christ Mystery.[4]

On a spiritual level the Christ was also placed before the pupils seeking initiation in Eleusis. At that time, however, human beings could only come to know the Christ as the One who was to come *in the future*, as the One who was as yet a child, a cosmic child, who had still to grow up in the cosmos. Those who were being initiated were called tellists, that is to say, those who should be looking towards the *end*[5] and the *goals* of Earth evolution.

And now came the great turning-point, the turning-point which comes to such keen and even historic expression in the transition from Plato to Aristotle.

It was a remarkable thing, my dear friends. As the fourth century approached in the evolution of Greek civilization, human thought had its first turning-point in the direction of becoming abstract. And it happened in the following way. At the time when Plato was already a very old man, at the end of his life in fact, the following scene took place between him and Aristotle, Plato speaking roughly like this (I have to clothe it in words, but of course the whole event took place in a much more complicated way): 'Many things that I have said in my lectures to you and the other students have not seemed to you

176 MYSTERY KNOWLEDGE AND MYSTERY CENTRES

Persephone with divine child, from the sanctuary of Persephone at Selinus in Sicily (left), and a parallel in less Greek style from nearby Monte Bubbonia.

to be quite correct. However, all that I have taught you and the other students is nothing else than an extract of the ancient holy Mystery wisdom. But a time will come in the course of evolution when human beings will adopt a form, an inner organization which, although it will gradually lead them to a higher stage than we now see in human beings, will make it impossible for them to accept natural science as is current among the Greeks. Therefore I intend to withdraw for a while and leave you to yourself. In the world of thought for which you are especially endowed and which is destined to be humanity's world of *thought* for many centuries to come—in this world of thought, try to develop in *thoughts* what you have received here in my school.'

Aristotle and Plato then remained apart, and in this way Plato carried out, through Aristotle, a great spiritual mission.

I am obliged, my dear friends, to describe the scene as I have done. If you look in history books you will also find the scene described, but I will tell you how it is given there, in the books from which people acquire their knowledge. Aristotle, so runs the story, was in reality always a headstrong pupil of Plato's, and Plato once said that Aristotle was indeed a gifted pupil but like a horse that has been trained and then turns and kicks its master. As time went on the trouble between them led at last to Plato getting angry, withdrawing from Aristotle and never again going into the Academy to teach. This is the account given in history books.

The one story is in history books and the other, which I have related to you, is the truth, and contains the seeds for something very significant. For the writings of Aristotle were of two kinds. One set of writings contained an important natural science which was the natural science of Eleusis, and which came to Aristotle indirectly through Plato. 'And the other kind of writings contained the abstract thoughts which it was

Aristotle's task to develop in pursuance of Plato's instructions—as the fulfilment, that is, of the mission which Plato had in his turn received from the Eleusinian Mysteries.

And what Aristotle actually had to give also followed a twofold path. There were his so-called logical writings, which owe their most productive thoughts to the ancient Eleusinian wisdom. These writings, which contained only a little natural science, Aristotle entrusted to his pupil Theophrastus, through whom, as well as through other channels, they came by way of Greece and Rome to form, throughout the Middle Ages, the whole wisdom and learning of the teachers of philosophy in Central Europe, who in those days also participated actively in the civilization of their time and in the teaching of world views.

The development which I described in the last lecture came about because human beings were destined to reject and turn away from the Mystery wisdom of Hibernia, and there was left for them only the tradition of the Event that had taken place in the physical world of the senses at the beginning of our era. With this was now united what had become separated out from the wisdom of Plato, that wisdom which still existed in Aristotle (in thought form) and which was in reality the wisdom of the Eleusinian Mysteries. True natural science bearing within it still the spirit of the Chthonic Mysteries of which the Eleusinian Mysteries were only a continuation, this natural science which, in order to find an explanation for earthly things, reached out to the heavens and soared aloft into the wide expanses of the cosmos—for this the time was passed in Greece. Only so much of it was saved as could be saved by Aristotle becoming the teacher of Alexander, who made his campaigns into Asia and did everything possible to introduce Aristotelian natural science to the East. In this way it passed into Jewish and Arabian schools, and from there by way of Africa to Spain, and there, in a diluted form, had a certain influence upon those isolated individuals in central Europe who, as I explained to you in the last lecture, still possessed something of the impulse of the Hibernian Mysteries. Theophrastus had given *his* Aristotle to the medieval teachers and fathers of the Church. Alexander the Great had carried the *other* Aristotle over to Asia, that Eleusinian wisdom which, in a very much weakened and diluted form, had made its way through Africa into Spain, and lights up in the Middle Ages where, despite the general character of the current civilization, it was cultivated in certain monasteries—for example by Basil Valentine, who has come down to posterity in mythical form. It lived on under the surface so to speak, while on the surface that particular culture prevailed of which I spoke in the last lecture, a culture which had no room for such truth as could still be taught at the time of Aristotle, that the Christ really has to be recognized.

The third picture, the female figure who carried at her breast the Child, the Iacchos Child, must also be understood, but what would be needed to bring an understanding of this third figure is still to come in the evolution of humanity. This truth Aristotle made clear again and again to Alexander the Great, although he was not able to write it down.

So we see how there lies in the bosom of time the call to understand in its pristine reality what has been so beautifully placed before the world by the Christian painters—the Mother with the Child at her breast. It has not yet been fully understood, neither in the Madonnas of Raphael nor in the Eastern ikons. It still awaits understanding.

Something of what is necessary in order to acquire such understanding will be spoken of in the coming lectures. Tomorrow I will describe the path along which many occult secrets travelled on their way from Arabia into Europe, and this will give you a clear picture of a certain historical phenomenon. And in the course of lectures[6] that will be given to the delegates at Christmas and are intended to show the occult foundation of the historical evolution of humanity I shall have occasion to explain to you the full significance of the campaigns of Alexander the Great in their connection with Aristotelianism.

LECTURE 11

The Secret of Plants, Metals and Human Beings

From what I told you yesterday, you will perhaps understand me when I say of Aristotle—who in the fourth century BC brought together all the knowledge of ancient times—that although we find what was spread over Europe through his influence to be no more than a kind of system of logic, he nevertheless based himself on the foundations of the Greek Mysteries, and indeed of all the Mysteries of his time. I can go further and say that anyone who is in a position to receive a world conception not merely with his intellect but with his heartfelt understanding will be able to feel, even in the logical and philosophical writings of Aristotle, that they have implicit within them a close and intimate connection with the secrets of nature. To spread over Europe a system of logic was the *destiny* of Aristotle rather than, if I may so express it, his proper path of development. For after all—to give an illustration of this fact—it would be almost unthinkable that Plato could have become Alexander's teacher, whereas Aristotle was able to be.

Plato, it is true, continued the teachings of the old Mysteries, but he did so in his own way, in the form of 'ideas'. And for this very reason he was the one who led humanity away from the secrets of nature, while Aristotle led back to them— as you will have gathered from the short account of him in my *Riddles of Philosophy*.[1] We can come to realize this in more detail and completeness when we are able to form an idea of the content of the seven years of instruction given by Aristotle to Alexander. Let me give you a brief summary of the content of this teaching, which was drawn from the ancient Mysteries.

In those times it was the case that whenever one spoke in an authentic way about nature the word did not convey what natural science understands by it today, namely, the purely earthly phenomena, from which one then goes on to infer in an external manner the phenomena of the heavens beyond the earth. No, the human being was thought of always as a member and part of nature in the widest sense; and this necessitated looking also for the spirit in nature—for to regard human beings as devoid of soul or devoid of spirit was quite impossible in those olden times.

And so, in the Mystery teaching about nature, we find that nature was thought of as extending far out into the cosmos, as far indeed as the cosmos was in any way accessible to human beings through their relationship to it.

Now you must understand that all teaching that was seriously undertaken in those olden times did not make an appeal primarily to the intellect or to the faculty of observation. What we think of today as 'knowledge' was really of very little account in those ancient times, even as late as the days of Aristotle. And if a modern historian of some particular science wants to give an account of the progress in thought in his domain he should really begin with Copernicus or Galileo, for anything he may add to his account by going further back is beside the point. And if he goes back as far as the knowledge of Greek times, what he says is mere fantasy. It is a continuation of the present back into earlier times, and it is utterly unreal. For even in the time of Aristotle any education that was taken seriously involved a complete change in the very nature of the pupil, for it made an appeal not merely to thought and observation but to the whole life of the human being. The acquisition of knowledge was meant to bring about a change, the essential thing in the Mysteries being that the human being should become through his education an altogether different being from what he was before. And in Aristotle's time in particular, the endeavour was made to bring about this transformation by subjecting the soul to two diametrically opposite impressions.

The pupil, who was to attain knowledge step by step, was exhorted to feel his way into his natural surroundings with as much of his humanity as he was able, and his instruction was worded something like this: 'Look, you breathe the air. In summer the air you breathe is warm, while in winter it is cold. In winter you can perceive your own breath in the form of vapour, but it is invisible when you breathe the warm air in summertime.'

A phenomenon like this was taken as a starting-point. A teacher of those olden times did not try to make the connection with nature by saying: 'Here is a body which has such and such a temperature. I heat it in a retort and it undergoes such and such a change.' No, he brought nature into direct contact with the human being himself, by making him attentive to the feeling he experienced in connection with the breathing process. And the pupil learnt to develop a true feeling on the one hand of the warmed air. 'Picture to yourself,' said the teacher, 'what it really means—warmed air. It wants to rise; and you must feel, when the warmed air comes towards you, that something is trying to carry you out into far spaces. And now feel, in contrast to this, cold water in some form or other. Just feel it. You actually do not feel at home in it. In the warm air you feel at home, so much at home that the warm air tries to carry you out into far spaces. In cold water you feel unnatural and not at home. And you feel that if you go away from the cold water and leave it to do what it wants to do out of its own nature, it will do something that has meaning for you and turn into snow crystals which fall to earth. You feel in your right place *outside* the snow crystals, watching them from outside. The warm air you can only feel *inside* you, and you would gladly let yourself be carried by the warm, ascending air into the far spaces of the cosmos. You can actually only feel the cold water outside you, and in order to have a relationship to it you would prefer observing what it does by means of your senses.'

These were the two opposite experiences to which the pupil was brought. If we describe it as 'learning to feel the difference between what is outside and what is inside a human being'— that is an empty expression! It really does not say very much. But 'warm air' and 'cold water' mean a great deal! Through these opposite experiences a human being is placed into the world with his whole inner being. 'Outside' begins to have meaning and reality when we think of it as *cold and damp* and 'inside' when we think of it as *warm and gaseous*. The contrast was experienced as having a *qualitative* character; a human being came to feel how he is placed *qualitatively* in the world.

Then the teacher ceased speaking of things and spoke of the human being himself. He spoke about the warm air leading to the gods in the heights, and the damp cold to the subterranean demons. But this journey to the subterranean demons is at the same time connected with the knowledge of nature. Only the pupil must take with him into the lower regions the knowledge and experience he has acquired from the warm air in the heights, so that the lower regions cannot harm him. And when, with this inner experience of the contrast between what was warm and gaseous and what was cold and damp the pupil approached nature, he was able in his further experiences of the objects and processes in nature to see altogether more deeply into the real being of the cosmos. Nowadays a chemist examines hydrogen and attributes to it certain properties.

Then he observes space, finds something there which manifests the same properties as hydrogen does in the laboratory, and draws the conclusion that hydrogen also exists in space. Such a method of instruction would have seemed sheer nonsense even in Aristotle's time. One went to work then in quite a different way.

When the inner experience of the pupil had been deepened in the way I have indicated the teacher led him to observe what actually lives in flowers as they strive upwards and open themselves to the expanses of cosmic space. He was being led in this way to a knowledge of the plants. Botany took the form of, 'Look into the opening petals of the flower and notice what kind of impression it makes on you to see what is there raying out into cosmic space.'

And when the pupil, whose feelings had been deepened in the way I explained, gazed out over the opening blossoms, an inner knowledge, an inner illumination, dawned within him. The flowers became the proclaimers on earth of cosmic secrets. The flowers told him about the cosmos. And in an impressive way, though always only in the way of gentle hints and intimations, the teacher then led the pupil to find, out of himself, the secret that streams from cosmic spaces into the being of the flower. The teacher asked him: 'What do you really perceive when you look into the blossom as it opens, and see the stamens raying out towards you? What do you actually perceive?' And the pupil was gradually brought to the point when he could answer: 'The plants tell me that the cold and heavy earth has compelled them to dwell upon the earth. But they really have not come from the solid earth but have only been planted and made secure in it; in reality they are born of water, and they had their proper existence in all its vitality as water-born beings in the earth's previous existence' (the Moon existence, as I described in my book *Occult Science*). The pupil was brought to perceive that in the flowers he could see a reflection of the secrets and mysteries of the moon, which has taken its departure from the earth and still preserves something of the pre-earthly Moon quality. For the flowers did not tell him the same thing every night! What the flowers said when the moon stood in front of Leo was different from what they said when it stood in front of Virgo or Scorpio. For the flowers of the earth told of what the moon experienced as it revolved around the zodiac. The secrets and mysteries of the cosmos out there—it was of these that the flowers of earth told. It was indeed true that through these things brought to the pupil he was able to say out of the depths of his heart:

> I look into the flowers.
> They reveal to me their kinship with the moon.
> Captives on earth are they,
> For they are beings born of water.*

The pupil was able to have this feeling because he had previously experienced the impression made on him by the chilling water. That experience enabled him now to acquire this knowledge from the flowers.

And when the pupil was sufficiently familiar with the secret of the moon disclosed to him by the plants which sprout forth out of the earth, he was led a step further to contemplate the metals of the earth, the principal metals: lead, tin, iron, gold, copper, quicksilver and silver.[2] We spoke of them in another connection yesterday. And when he approached the metals with his feeling and understanding deepened in the way I have indicated, then he gradually made himself familiar with the secrets they told him, the secrets of the whole planetary

---

* For German texts see Appendix 1.

system. Lead told him about Saturn, tin about Jupiter, iron about Mars, gold about the sun, copper about Venus, quicksilver about Mercury and silver about the moon, but this time not in its relationship with the earth but as a member of the whole cosmic order. And just as the pupil had discovered the secret of the flowers, he now discovered the secret of the metals. The first secret he learnt was the flowers' secret and the second one was the secret of the metals.

This secret or mystery of the metals, which was given expression in the male statue of the Eleusinian Mysteries by means of the great planisphere that I described to you yesterday, still formed part of the education given in Aristotle's time, and in this secret of the metals was revealed the secret of the planets. Human feeling and perception were not so coarse as they are today. When the pupil looked at lead, its blue-grey colour did not appear only to his physical eye but also had a particular effect on his inner eye. In a certain respect this blue-grey of the fresh lead extinguished all the other colours, and the pupil felt as if he were going out to meet this blue-grey metallic nature, as if he were moving with it. He came into a state of consciousness in which he had an experience of something entirely different from the present. He came completely into a mood of soul when—because the present was blotted out by the blue-grey—it was as though the whole past of the earth rose up before him, and the nature of Saturn stood revealed!

In the case of gold, people point to external analogies to account for the fact that the ancients saw in gold a representative of the sun. They were by no means merely toying with an external analogy when they regarded the sun as of great value in the heavens and gold as of great value on earth. Really nothing is too stupid for modern humanity to ascribe to the ancients! In reality, when they looked at gold with its brilliant yellow colour—a colour which is, so to say, self-contained—and see how plain and unpretentious and at the same time how proud it is in its outward appearance, they felt in very truth an immediate connection to their own blood circulation. With regard to the very *quality* of gold, a person had the feeling that he himself was within it; he *felt* his way into it. And through this perception he was able to grasp the nature of the sun and of everything appertaining to it. For he felt how the quality of gold is allied to a quality of the sun which works in human blood.

And so, taking the metals one by one, the pupil of the ancient Mysteries came to a perception of the whole planetary system. And as he learnt to apply his thinking to these things—and we must not imagine this to be as abstract as today's thinking—he came to think of the metals in the following way:

> I ponder on the metals.
> They reveal to me their kinship with the planets.
> Captives on earth are they,
> For they are born of air.

It is a fact that the metals we find in the earth today came out of the cosmos in the form of *air*, and only during the Moon existence did they gradually become fluid. They came first in the form of air, when the earth was in its Old Sun condition; they acquired fluid form during the Moon existence, and it is during Earth existence that they have been taken captive in a set and rigid form. That was the second mystery that was disclosed to the pupil.

The third mystery had to be approached by the pupil learning to observe the differences existing between the peoples and the nations spread out over the earth. If one were to go to the continent of Africa with its characteristic climate, one would find that the people are quite different even in the colour of their skin from the people of Hellas. Or if one were to travel to Asia one would find that the people are different again. The Greeks had a fine feeling for these external differences in human beings.

One of the most interesting writings of Aristotle that has come down to posterity is his book on *Physiognomy*, by which not merely the physiognomy of the face is meant, but a study of the physiognomy of the whole human being was undertaken with the view to becoming familiar in this way with the real nature of the human being. He points out, for example, that a person's hair is curly or smooth according to the climate he lives in, and that it is not only the colour of skin which varies with the climate of the land where he is born but the whole way a human being expresses himself is different.

Just as the pupil learnt from the flowers to see a reflection of the moon mystery and from the metals to see a reflection of the planets, he now learnt from this third teaching the actual mystery of human beings on earth. In the natural science of those times people made tremendous progress in the study of the variety of human characteristics on earth, and they went a long way towards obtaining an answer to the question: what is the archetypal human form at the root of the divine plan and purpose?

And through a living study of human physiognomy over the earth there arose in the inner being of the pupil the secret of the zodiac. For in conjunction with the planetary system and the moon it is the zodiac which influences the earthly elements; it sends the winds in one direction at one season of the year and another direction at another season—now wafting warm air over a particular region, now sweeping it with storms of cold rain. All these conditions affect the human being and enter deeply into his life. And the natural scientists of those times looked for the origins of these natural conditions in the influences that stream down upon the earth from the zodiac, modified by the planets, sun and moon.

Students of natural history in those times were especially interested when they saw someone with black, curly hair, a ruddy complexion, a nose of such and such a shape, and so on, and they said: 'This human being refers me to the sign of Leo—Leo raying out his forces either weakened or strengthened by the planets according to their position. He is a person who, in accordance with his karma, has such and such qualities in his liver. If, for instance, he has a quality in his liver which brings a trace of melancholy into his life of soul, then it is due to the fact that at a certain point of time Venus stood in a particular relation to Jupiter and gave a special character to Leo's rays. I can see cosmic influences in the particular nature of the temperament in connection with the liver. I can extend this to all the qualities of the different peoples on earth. In what human beings experience in connection with the atmosphere of their environment I can see the secret of the zodiac.'

And when the pupil had been led thus far, enlightenment again came from his heart, and he clothed it somewhat in the following words:

> I experience the mysteries of the zodiac
>   in the variety of human beings;
> I behold within me the kinship of this human variety
>   with the fixed stars.
> In their variety human beings live
>   as captives on earth,
> For they are born of warmth.

Born, that is, out of warmth ether—from warmth ether under

the influence of the zodiac. In his physiognomy the human being felt himself to be born out of warmth, and although he had undergone change during the Moon epoch and again during the Earth epoch, what he had attained in the Ancient Saturn epoch was his true and original disposition. Just as he perceived the metallity of the earth to be born of the sun, of the air, and flower nature, plant nature, to be born of the moon, of the water; so did he perceive himself as a human being to be born of warmth.

He had been prepared for all this by the feelings and perceptions stimulated in him when experiencing the nature of the warm and gaseous and the cold and watery.

At the time of Aristotle people learnt from observing human nature that a human being has an effect on the warm and gaseous element in a certain combination with the cold and watery element. By studying a person's physiognomy they were able to answer the question: how much does this person give you of the warm and gaseous element, how much does he take from you of the cold and watery element? The development they had undergone in their souls enabled them to look at the human being accordingly, and gradually they learnt to look at the whole of nature in this way. This prepared the way for the old, really genuine alchemy, which afterwards spread across Africa and Spain and certain parts of Central Europe. This was the way of perceiving everything in nature, everything in the world, every flower, animal, every cloud and rolling mist, sand and stones, sea and river, wood and meadow, according to the impression it gave of being warm and gaseous or cold and damp.

And so people came to acquire in regard to nature a fine faculty of perception for four qualities. When they perceived the warm and gaseous they developed a perception for warmth, but at the same time, in perceiving the air, they felt what warmth was for the gaseous element. And in the cold they developed a perception for what is damp and what is dry. They acquired a fine sensitivity for these differentiations, and this sensitivity helped them to enter with their whole being into everything the world offered.

Having adopted this standpoint it was natural that Aristotle's pupil, Alexander the Great, regarded the whole region in which they both lived from this point of view. And being thoroughly equipped with this sensitivity Alexander perceived all the Greek characteristics, in so far as they manifested in Macedonia, according to the qualities of damp and gaseous, and this determined and constituted the mood of his soul at a particular time in his life. And what, from out of the special kind of initiation he received from Aristotle, he perceived to be the fundamental character of his immediate world he regarded as being only half of what there is. 'This can only be half the world,' he told himself. You see, in those times knowledge of natural things was really brought home to people so that they really *experienced* them. And such experience could lead to learning the following:

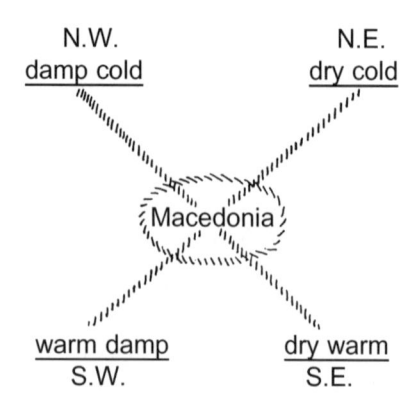

```
       N.W.                  N.E.
     damp cold             dry cold
            ＼              ／
             ＼            ／
              Macedonia
             ／            ＼
            ／              ＼
     warm damp             dry warm
       S.W.                  S.E.
```

Here you have a wind blowing from the north-west (if Macedonia is in the centre), and here a south-westerly wind direction, here again a north-easterly wind and, lastly, here a south-easterly.

Now Aristotle's pupil, Alexander, had learnt from his own experience to feel in what came from the climatic influences and the winds of the north-west the element of moist cold, and in what came from the south-west the element of moist warm. This was a perception of only half the world. In the instruction he was given this perception was completed for him, and he himself was able to feel that what he was taught belonged to what he already knew through his own experience. He learnt that the winds blowing from the north-east brought the element of dry cold, and the winds from the south-east the element of dry warm. So now he had acquired from the four wind directions the perception of dry cold, dry warm, warm moist and cold moist. Being a true man of his time he had the desire to reconcile these opposites. Namely, there in Macedonia one's experience was limited to the cold and moist and the warm and moist; these must be united with the cold and dry and the fiery and dry, with what blows from the north of Asia and what blows from the south of Asia and comes across Asia.

Here you have the source of the irresistible urge that lived in Alexander to go on his Asiatic campaigns. And from this example you may see how different the conditions were then than in more recent times. Think of the education a prince receives today! Imagine a prince who is taught while on the march with his troops. Try to make a clear picture of what kind of relationship exists between the instruction in physics given to a prince by some tutor and what that prince then experiences in the campaign! What is done on war campaigns is not the kind of thing that normally slips out of a retort! Such an example shows particularly well how very far removed, nowadays, the knowledge thought fit to teach a young person and to form his inner being is from what he is in outer life. This was an era in which, from out of a knowledge of these things, they aimed for complete unity between what gives a person inner form and stature and what brings about the way a person relates to the world in his deeds and actions. In those times history began in the classroom. But we must not forget that the classroom in those days was a place that had an affinity to the Mysteries, and the Mysteries meant the world, and the world was seen to be the result of the forces that were in the Mysteries.

It was this which prompted the impulse to take across into Asia the natural sciences of those times. In a considerably filtered down condition they then went across Spain and through Europe. This can still be traced in the way Paracelsus expressed himself, also Jakob Boehme and Gichtl, and the various other people who later had connections with such minds as Basil Valentine. But for the time being knowledge in the form of abstract thought and mere logic was meant to be victorious, and the other part of Aristotle's teachings had to wait.

Now the time has come, however, when these other things have waited long enough and they must be rediscovered as the sum of the natural sciences. Alexander had, fundamentally speaking, to *bury* these secrets of nature in Asia for the time being, for only their corpses were brought across to Europe. It is not our task to galvanize these corpses but to rediscover the original living truth. And we shall only really find the necessary enthusiasm for such a task when we can develop a warm feeling for what existed at that turning-point of time, when we can perceive and appreciate the real purpose of Alexander's campaigns. For only to outward appearance were they campaigns of conquest; in reality their object was to find the other side of the compass, to unravel the mystery of the other half of the world. They were also most certainly a search for a personal experience. A certain discomfort and lack of satisfaction was felt in the milieu restricted to cold and moist and warm and moist, and the feeling of the other half of the compass was needed to create wholeness.

The immense historical significance of this event in the evolution of the whole of the western world will be a theme of the lectures that are to be held in the near future at the Delegates' Meeting on the subject of the occult foundations of the historical life of humanity on earth.

LECTURE 12

The Mysteries of the Samothracian Kabeiroi

During the past weeks I have been lecturing on many forms of the Mysteries. We have been trying to gain insights more especially into those Mysteries which, in a certain sense, were the last of the great Mysteries connecting the inner life of the human being directly with nature, with the spirit of nature existence. These were the Mysteries of Hibernia. And we have seen how, through insight into human nature itself, through insight of an altogether intimate, spiritual kind, individual and personal, the Greek Mysteries penetrated into the inner nature of the human being. One may indeed say: just as in outer nature various regions of the earth bear various kinds of vegetation, so in the course of human evolution there is evidence of the most manifold influences working from the spiritual worlds onto human beings in the different regions of the earth.

If we were now to proceed eastward—as we shall be doing in the course of the next few days in our study of historical connections—we should find there many other forms of the Mysteries. Today, however, since our visitors are not all here yet, I shall not start on something new but add to what we have already been considering.

Looking back on the evolution of humanity, a threefold development appears quite clearly to the Imaginative consciousness. I say 'clearly to the Imaginative consciousness', for if we were to extend further and further into the past the epochs of which I am about to speak we should of course arrive at a greater number than three; and it would be similar if we were to penetrate further and further into the future. Today, however, we will take for our study those middle stages of the evolution of humanity which do not appear only to inspiration but quite clearly already on the imaginative level. We will consider them today from a particular standpoint.

As late as the Egyptian epoch humanity was still at the stage when, for the European-African peoples as well as for the Asian peoples, there was for human consciousness no such thing as what we call matter. There was not even any external coarse substance of any kind as far as human consciousness was concerned, much less those abstractions which we now call carbon, hydrogen, sulphur, and so on. There were none of these things; everything in outer nature was seen directly as the embodiment of divine-spiritual beings manifesting throughout the whole of nature. If nowadays we go into the hills and pick up a stone, we look upon it as a substance like any other. Nothing at all comes into our awareness such as came into the awareness of the ancient Egyptian or ancient oriental.

If nowadays we observe a human being and touch one of his fingers we do not consider this human finger to be an object just like any other. We regard it as belonging to the human organism as a whole. If we were to look, for example, at the last joint of the index finger, we could not do otherwise than to speak of it as a part of the whole organism. That is how it was for the consciousness of the ancient Egyptians and the ancient orientals. If they came upon a stone and picked it up, it was not for them merely a stone as it would be for us today; they did not think of it as ordinary earthly substance at all; it was a part of the divine body which the earth appeared to them to be. People of those olden times regarded the outer surface of the earth just as we in our consciousness regard the human skin. If we meet a person today and become aware that he or she reminds us of someone else we already know but who is not present, and if it afterwards transpires that the person we have met is the brother or sister of the other person, then it immediately comes to our mind that the two of them are of the same flesh and blood; they have certain physical connections with one another. When the ancient Greek or ancient oriental raised his eyes to Mars, Jupiter and Saturn and then looked down to the earth, he saw the earth as the divine body of the earth god, but at the same time as the sister or brother of the planets—in short, he saw a family likeness to the planets revolving around the earth, to Jupiter, Mars and Saturn.

Thus in their perception of the cosmos as a whole and in their perception of the earth as part of the cosmos, these ancient peoples were definitely aware of a soul-spiritual element. You must picture to yourselves what an utterly different experience this was from the way modern human beings experience perception. It meant a very great deal to look on the earth as the body of the Divinity and to see the earth as a member of the great family of the planets of the universe! The people of olden times thought of the whole cosmos as being indwelt by gods. For them not only the whole earth was indwelt by gods but the gods dwelt in each and every one of the great planetary bodies and each and every planetary being. In stone and tree, in river and rock, in cloud and lightning some spiritual being was revealed. This consciousness was there in wide circles of people on the earth, and this consciousness was intensified in the many forms of the Mysteries to be found here and there on earth.

Moving forward to the world of Greece right up to the time when the outer, political greatness of Greece sank into a kind of chaos and the power of Macedonia arose, we find a new current flowing into human knowledge. It is what we came to know last time as Aristotelianism, as that which Alexander the

Great, from a spiritual aspect, chose to be the mission of his people. When we look at the culmination of the greatness of Greece on the one hand and to the fall of Greece and the rise of Macedonia on the other, we are faced, first of all, with what external history tells us, which is in reality a mere legend. But we can also see something else. In the subconsciousness of the deeper thinkers of that time we perceive an impulse which came from those Mysteries to which Aristotle—despite the fact that he never spoke of them outwardly—was very close. They were those Mysteries which, in the deepest sense, awakened to full life in their hearers the consciousness that the whole world was a theogony, a divine process of being, and that we see the world in an altogether illusory way if we believe anything else has being in the world other than gods. It is the gods who manifest in the beings and entities of the world. It is the gods who have experiences in the world, it is gods who perform deeds. And what we see as clouds, what we hear as thunder, what we behold as lightning, what we see on earth as rivers and mountains, what we perceive on earth as the realms of the minerals, all these are revelations, expressions of the progressive development of the destinies of the gods hidden behind them. And what appears outwardly as cloud, lightning, thunder, tree and forest, river and mountain is nothing else but a revelation from out of the omnipresent existence of gods—just as the human skin reveals the inner soul nature of the human being. And if there are gods everywhere then, as the pupils of the Mysteries were taught in northern Greece, human beings must differentiate between the lesser gods who are in single nature beings and nature processes, and the greater gods who manifest as beings of the Sun, Mars and Mercury, and a fourth category who cannot be made externally visible in an image or a form. Those were the 'Great Gods', the great planetary gods, who were presented to

200 MYSTERY KNOWLEDGE AND MYSTERY CENTRES

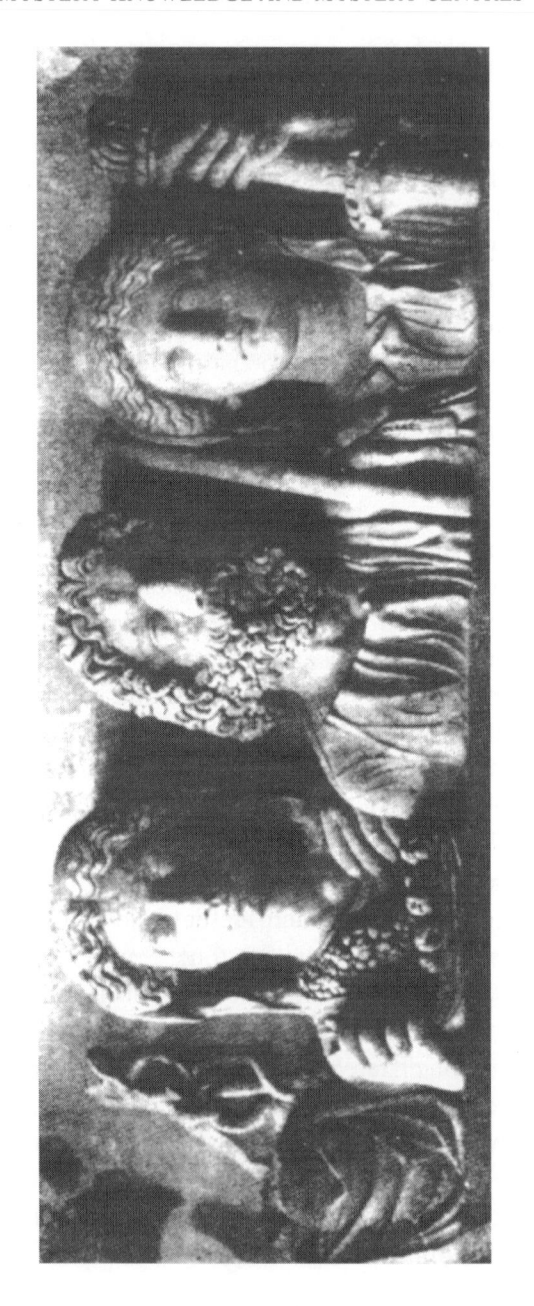

The Great Gods, from the ruins of their temple at the Mystery-site on Samothrace: on the far left the caduceus is all that remains of Kadmilos (Mercury) with, next, Axiokersa (Persephone), Axiokersos (Zeus/Dis) and (far right) Axieros (Demeter).

humanity in such a way that their gaze was led out into the cosmic expanse to see with their own eyes, to see too with their whole heart, what lives in the Sun, Mars and Mercury—yes, and what lives not only out there in one little circle in cosmic space but everywhere in cosmic space, and which above all is connected with humanity.[1]

And then, after what I may call a majestic impulse had been awakened in the pupil of the Mysteries of northern Greece in that his gaze was directed out to the planetary spheres, this insight was deepened within him to such an extent that his eye was so to speak taken hold of by his heart, so that he might see with his soul. Then the pupil understood why three symbolically formed vessels had been placed on the altar before him.

Here in Dornach we once introduced a replica of these vessels in a eurythmic performance of *Faust*. They were presented there exactly as they appeared in the Samothracian Mysteries of northern Greece. The important fact, however, was that in their whole symbolic form these vessels were associated with an act of consecration, an act of sacrifice. A kind of incense was put into them and lighted, and as the smoke rose up three words (of which we shall speak tomorrow) were uttered with mantric power into this smoke by the father who was celebrating, and there appeared the forms of the three Kabeiroi. It happened in the following way. The human breath, as it was exhaled, took shape through the mantric word that was spoken, and communicated its form to the ascending, evaporating substance that had been incorporated in the symbolic jars. When the pupil learnt in this way to read in the stream of his own breath, to read what the stream of his breath wrote in the smoke, he learnt at the same time to read what the mysterious planets said to him from the wide expanses of the cosmos. For now he knew: the form that the first Kabeiros assumed through the power of the mantric word was the form Mercury had in reality; the form shown by the second Kabeiros was the real form of Mars; and the form shown by the third Kabeiros was that of Apollo, the sun.

When we look at those fashionplate figures—if you will forgive such plain speaking—such as we see only too often in galleries of later Greek sculpture, and which are so greatly admired only because people have no idea where they have come from, when we direct our gaze to those figures of an Apollo, a Mars and a Mercury, we must look at them the way Goethe looked at them during his visit to Italy. For then we may acquire some idea of what Greek art really was in the productions that are now lost—lost and destroyed along with so much else in the first centuries of the Christian era in the frightful devastation which befell those times. If we look penetratingly at those late Greek sculptures, held on the one hand to be so great, and rightly so, because they point to something, but on the other hand wrongly so, because they are mere imitative reproductions—if we look through them back to their origins, then we see that in earlier Greek times images of what manifested in the sacrificial rites came into being in the very way I have described, in fact in a much more majestic and magnificent a manner than later on in the Kabeiric Mysteries of Samothrace. We look back to those times when the mantric word was uttered into the sacrificial smoke, and the *real* figure of Apollo, Mars and Mercury appeared.

Those were the times when a human being did not say in the abstract: 'In the beginning was the Word, and the Word was with God, and the Word was a God.' In those times a human being could say something quite different. He could say: 'In me the outgoing breath takes shape, and in shaping itself in an ordered way it manifests as an image of cosmic creating; for it creates for me, out of the sacrificial smoke, forms that are living lines of writing telling me what the planetary worlds want to say to me.'

When the pupil of the Kabeiric Mysteries at Samothrace approached the portals of the places of initiation, then, through the instruction he had received, the feeling came to him: 'Now I am entering the place which holds for me the magic rituals of the celebrating Father' (for the initiate who celebrated these Mysteries was called 'Father'). What did the magic power of the celebrating father reveal to the pupil? Through what was laid within the human being by the gods, through the power of speech, the priestly magician and sage wrote into the sacrificial smoke the writing that expressed the secrets of the universe.

Thus it was that the pupil, as he approached the portal, said in his heart: 'I am entering the place within whose shelter dwells a powerful spirit, within whose shelter dwell the greater gods who unveil on earth the secrets of the universe through sacrificial rites enacted by human beings.'

There a language was being spoken and the kind of writing written which appealed not only to the understanding but to the whole human being. In the Samothracian Mysteries something was still there of a knowledge which by today has of course quite died out. A modern human being is perfectly capable of saying truthfully what a quartz crystal feels like to the touch, or, if you like, a piece of iron or antimony; a person of today can very well say what it feels like to touch hair, the human skin, or animal fur, silk or velvet. In the Samothracian Mysteries something was still present that enabled a human being to say truly what gods feel like. For the sense of feeling, the sense of touch, was still able to do what it could do in ancient times, namely, feel the spiritual element, touch the gods. The wonderful thing is this, and we must certainly go back to more ancient times if we want virtually to speak of human beings being able to say truly: 'I know with my fingertips what the gods feel like to the touch.' In the Samothacian Mysteries, however, there was another way of touching the gods. It was as follows.

When the priest-magician spoke the words into the sacrificial smoke, when he intoned the words on the exhaled breath, then in the outgoing breath he felt as a human being otherwise feels when he stretches out his hand to touch something. And just as one knows that one touches differently with the fingertips in passing them over different substances—in feeling velvet, silk, cat's fur or the human skin—the Samothracian priest-magician perceived his outgoing breath as an expression of something coming from himself. He felt it as an organ of touch reaching out towards the smoke. He felt the smoke, and in the smoke he felt the great gods, the Kabeiroi, coming towards him. He felt the way the smoke took on form, and how these forms approached the exhaled breath, so that the exhaled breath felt: 'Here is something spherical, there is an angularity, there again something is catching hold of me.' The whole divine figure of the Kabeiros was touched and felt by the breath clothed in the form of the word. In the words issuing from his heart the Samothracian sage 'touched' the Kabeiroi, that is, the Greater Gods, descending to him in the sacrificial smoke. It was a living interchange between the logos in the human being and the Logos out in cosmic spaces.

As the initiating father led the pupil to the sacrificial altar and taught him step by step how a human being can sense with speech, and as the pupil progressed more and more and achieved for himself this 'sensing with speech', he eventually reached the stage of inner experience in which he now had a clear awareness of the composition of the form of Mercury or Hermes, of Apollo, or of Ares or Mars. It was as though his whole consciousness were raised out of his body, as if that which the pupil previously knew as the content of his head were up above his head, as if his heart were located in a new place and had thrust its way up out of his chest into his head. Thus in the person who had really gone out beyond himself there arose a knowledge that inwardly formed itself into the words: 'Thus do the Kabeiroi, the Greater Gods, will thee!' From that time onward the pupil knew that Mercury lived in his limbs, the sun in his heart, Mars in his speech.

So you see that in ancient times the pupils were by no means presented only with natural processes and beings in the outer world. What was presented to them was neither one-sidedly naturalistic nor one-sidedly moral, but they were given something in which morality and nature flowed into one. This was the chief secret of the Samothracian world, that an awareness was brought to the pupil: nature is spirit, spirit is nature.

It is in those times, which had their last echo in the Samothracian cult of the Kabeiroi, that the insight originated which brings earthly substances into connection with the heavens. In olden times, when one saw the red-brown mineral with the coppery sheen that we call copper, one could not simply say, as we do today: 'That is copper, that is a constituent of the earth.' They could not think of it like that. For the ancients it was not a constituent of the earth but the deed of Venus manifesting itself as copper. The earth had only suffered rocks and stones to appear, such as sandstone or chalk, in order to be able to take into her lap what the heavens had planted in the earth. Just as we would not venture today to say of a seed which we have planted in the earth, 'This seed has grown out of the earth,' just as little would one have been able to say in those times if, beneath the surface of the earth one had copper ore, 'Copper ore is a constituent of the earth.' One had to say: 'The earth with its sandstone or any other stone is the ground within which the metals have been planted by the planets. The metal is a seed planted in the earth by a planet.' Everything on earth was seen to be sent into the earth by the heavens. Today, when you learn about the earth and its substances, you will see in any mineralogical or geological textbook that only the earth is described. It would never have been done in this way in the science of the ancients. In those times, when a human being let his gaze wander over the earth and saw the substances there, he had to look up to heaven, for there he beheld the essence and reality of the substance. Copper, tin and lead only appear to lie in the earth. They are really the seeds planted during the Old Sun epoch and Moon epoch by the heavens into the earth.

This was still the way the Kabeiroi taught in the Samothracian Mysteries. And this it was, ultimately, that worked upon Aristotle and Alexander—if only as an atmosphere or mood of knowledge. And then a beginning was made for something quite different.

Humanity did not, with regard to their insight, come right down at once onto the earth, but went through an intermediary stage in ancient times. Even in the echoes of those ancient times, namely, the Samothracian Mysteries, when it was a matter of describing metals or any other earthly substances, such as sulphur or phosphorus, they actually described the heavens, just as one describes a plant when one wants to know the nature of a seed. If you have a grain of seed in front of you, you cannot recognize the kind of seed it is if you do not know the plant. What would you make of a grain of seed which looks like *this*, if you did not know what the aniseed plant looks like? 'What would you make of the copper which appears in the earth,' the people of old would have asked, 'if you did not know what Venus looks like, in spirit, soul and body, up there in the heavens?'

The knowledge of the heavens gradually turned into a

knowledge of the atmosphere. So that when people looked at an earthly formation they now no longer described the stars and their beings but said: 'There lives in it in the first place what we see in the solid earth, then there also lives in it the quality of fluid which has the tendency to form drops, and there lives in it too something of an aeriform nature which tends to spread out in every direction, and which lives in the human organism in the breath and in speech. And it also has living within it the fiery element which dissolves separate being, so that from the cleft and scattered parts something new may arise. The elements live in every earthly formation.

And just as in earlier ages, in the ancient Mysteries human beings looked on the substance salt (which, although also of cosmic origin had been shaped and moulded into an earthly substance) and regarded it as the ground into which Mother Earth receives the metals; they regarded as mercury everything that came from the cosmos with the destiny of becoming a metal.

It is really so utterly childish to try to give descriptions, as people do nowadays, of what was thought of as mercury in medieval times! Persistently in the background is the idea that by mercury, even in the Middle Ages, something like quicksilver, or some kind of single metal, is meant. This is not the case. Mercury is *every* metal in so far as it is under the influence of the whole cosmos. For what would happen to copper if the periphery of the cosmos alone worked upon it? Copper would be globular like quicksilver. If the cosmos alone affected it, what would lead become? Lead would be globular like quicksilver. What of tin, if it were affected only by the cosmos? Tin would be globular. Every metal, if affected only by the cosmos, would be quicksilver. All metals are mercury in so far as the cosmos acts upon them. But what of mercury, the actual present-day mercury, which still takes on globular form on earth? What is *that*?

I will tell you. The other metals—let us say lead, copper, tin or iron—have progressed beyond the globular form. While the whole earth was still under the influence of the spherical cosmos, all metals were mercurial. They have now progressed beyond the mercurial form and nowadays they crystallize into other forms. Only actual quicksilver, in the present-day sense of the word, has remained at that stage.

What would the ancient alchemists have said of modern quicksilver, and what in fact did the medieval alchemists say of it? They said: 'Copper, tin, iron and lead are the good metals that have progressed with Providence; quicksilver is the Lucifer among the metals, for it has remained at an earlier stage.' This is how it was in earlier times; when they spoke about earthly things in this way they were in fact speaking of the heavenly aspect.

They went on from this to speaking of what exists between the encircling round and the earth, namely, the earth itself, below, then the watery element, the element of air and the element of fire. Thus the ancients saw everything on the earth from the point of view of the heavens, and the people of the Middle Ages, which did not come to an end until the first third of the fourteenth century, saw everything from the point of view of the surrounding atmosphere. Then, in the fourteenth and fifteenth centuries, came the great turning-point. The human being and his outlook fell right down onto the earth. And now, with regard to his consciousness, the elements of water, air and fire were broken down and split up into sulphur, carbon, hydrogen. Human beings saw everything from the earthly point of view.

This was the beginning of the time I mentioned when describing the Hibernian Mysteries—the time when human beings spanned the earth with their knowledge, and the heavens became a matter of mathematics. Human beings calculate the size of the stars, their movements, their distance, and so on. The heavens became an abstraction.

Nor was it only the heavens that became an abstraction. In the living human being his head is a likeness of the heavens, and what human beings can know of the heavens is in their heads. And since the only knowledge human beings have had of the heavens has been by way of mathematics, that is, the element of logic and abstraction, there now lives in their heads this element only: abstract logic, the realm of concepts and ideas. From this time on there was no way in which human beings could include the spiritual element in their concepts and ideas. And when they looked for the spirit, that great struggle began between what a human being could attain by way of the ideas in his head, in his brain, and what the gods wished to reveal to him from the heavens. This struggle was fought out at its fiercest and in its grandest aspects in Rosicrucianism—in the true forms of what are called the Rosicrucian Mysteries in the Middle Ages.[2] There the helplessness of modern humanity was perceived as a preparation for true knowledge. For indeed, in the circles of true Rosicrucian initiation, something very powerful made itself felt. And it was this. The pupil became—not abstractly, but inwardly—illumined to perceive: as a modern human being you can penetrate only to the world of ideas; thereby, however, you lose the living being of this your humanity.

And the pupil felt that what the new age was giving him could not lead him to the essence of his real being. He felt: either you must despair of knowledge or you must go through a kind of mortification of the arrogance of abstraction. The Rosicrucian pupil—the true Rosicrucian pupil—felt as though his master had given him a blow on the back of his neck to indicate to him that the abstractions of the modern brain are not suited to entering the spiritual worlds, and that he must renounce mere abstraction to enter them.

That was indeed a tremendous preparatory moment for what we may call the Rosicrucian initiation.

LECTURE 13

The Transition from the Spirit of the Ancient Mysteries to the Medieval Mysteries

The Mysteries of the various ages, as I said yesterday, were scattered in various forms over many regions of the earth, and every region, according to its population and other conditions, had its special form of the Mysteries. But now there came a time which was of extraordinary significance for the Mysteries. It was the period in the earth's evolution which began some centuries after the foundation of Christianity.

From my book *Christianity as Mystical Fact* you can see that what happened on Golgotha united in a certain sense what had previously been distributed over the various Mysteries throughout the world. The Mystery of Golgotha, however, differed from all the other Mysteries I have been describing in that it was presented so to say on the stage of history before the eyes of the world, while the older Mysteries were enacted in the obscurity of the inner temples, and they sent out their impulses from the dim twilight of these inner temples.

If we look into the oriental Mysteries or into those I described to you as the Mysteries of Ephesus in Asia Minor, or again if we look into the Greek Mysteries, be they the chthonic or the Eleusinian, or those I spoke of yesterday, the Samothracian, or finally, if we look into those Mysteries I characterized as the Hibernian, we see in every instance how the Mystery in question was enacted in the obscurity of the inner temple from where it sent out its impulses into the world.

Whoever understands the Mystery of Golgotha—and merely to know the historical information available is not to understand it—whoever really understands the Mystery of Golgotha understands all the previous Mysteries.

The Mysteries that preceded the Mystery of Golgotha, and culminated in it, all possessed a particular characteristic in respect of the feelings they aroused. In the Mysteries, many tragic things took place. Whoever attained to initiation was obliged to undergo suffering and pain. You know these things. I have described them to you many times. By and large, before the time of the Mystery of Golgotha, if a candidate was to go through initiation and was warned beforehand that he would have to face many tests and trials, to suffer pain and sorrow, he would still have said: 'I will go through all the fire in the world, for it leads to the light, to the spiritual fields of light where I may attain to a vision of what, in a particular era, can be only dimly divined in ordinary human consciousness on earth!' A really great longing—a longing that was simultaneously joyful—took possession of anyone who sought to find his way to the ancient Mysteries. His joy was certainly solemn, and deep and lofty too, yet joy it certainly was.

Then came an intermediary period. In the lectures that are to follow in a few days I shall have to characterize things from the historical point of view. The intermediary period led ultimately to the fourteenth and fifteenth centuries when, as you know, a new epoch of human evolution began. And now we find an altogether different mood in those who were setting out on the search for knowledge of the higher worlds. It is indeed a fact that when, with the help of the Akashic Records, we look back into the ancient Mysteries, we find joyful faces, deeply serious but fundamentally joyful faces. If I were to describe to you a scene which can be read in the Akashic Records, for example a scene in the Samothracian Mysteries, I should have to say that the countenances of those who entered the innermost temple of the Kabeiroi were meaningful and profound, but nevertheless joyful.

But now came the intermediary period, a time when there was not actually a temple yet there was moral cohesion as there had already been in the ancient Mysteries; we come to what is described as the form of Rosicrucianism of the Middle Ages.

If we want to characterize the Rosicrucian Mystery pupil in the way I have just done for the antique Mysteries we shall have to say something very different. The most important of the personalities striving for knowledge in medieval times, and who undertook research into the spiritual world, bore not joyful but very tragic faces. And this is so true that we can say: those who did not have a deeply tragic expression were certainly not sincere in their efforts. There was abundant reason to have a tragic expression on their faces.

Let me now give you a picture of the way in which those who strove for knowledge in this period culminating in the Rosicrucianism of the fourteenth and fifteenth centuries gradually had to relate differently to the secrets of nature and of the spirit than did the pupils of the Mysteries of ancient times.

Yesterday I already drew your attention to the fact that for the people of olden times the phenomena and processes of nature were nothing less than deeds of the gods. They would as little have thought of treating a phenomenon of nature as an isolated phenomenon as we should think of considering a movement of the human eyes as a thing in itself and not as a revelation of the human soul and spirit. Natural phenomena were considered to be expressions of the gods who manifested through them. For the ancients the earth's surface was as truly the skin of the divine Earth Being as our skin is the skin of an ensouled human being. We really have not the least understanding of the mood of soul of the people of antiquity unless we know that they were speaking of the earth as a body of the gods and of the other planets of our planetary system as brothers and sisters of the earth.

But now this direct relation to the things and processes of nature, which saw in the single object or phenomenon the revelation of the divine principle, changed into a totally different one. The divine part of natural phenomena had, so to speak, withdrawn. Supposing it could happen to one of you that people saw you merely as a body—as we do the earth—neutral and soul-less. It would be absolutely horrible!

But this horrible thing has really happened where modern knowledge is concerned. And medieval scholars felt the horror of it, for from the standpoint of modern knowledge it is as though the divine principle had withdrawn from natural phenomena. And whereas in ancient times the objects and processes of nature were relevations of the divine world, now came the intermediary period when the phenomena of nature were only pictures, no longer revelations but only pictures of divine manifestation.

> Ancient times: natural objects and processes
>   revelations of a divine world
> Medieval times: natural objects and processes
>   pictures of a divine world

However, a modern person does not really have any idea in what way natural processes are pictures of a divine world. Let me give you an example that anyone can be familiar with who knows a smattering of chemistry; it will show you what sort of conception of science those people had who at least still had the view that natural objects and processes are pictures of a divine world.

Do a simple experiment which is continually being done by

chemists today. Take a retort and put into it oxalic acid, which you can get from clover, and mix this oxalic acid with an equal part of glycerine. Then you heat the mixture, and carbon dioxide will be given off. When the carbon dioxide has evaporated, what remains behind is formic acid. The oxalic acid is transformed by the loss of carbon dioxide into formic acid. This experiment can easily be done in a laboratory, and you can look at it as a modern chemist does, namely, as a complete and finished process.

Not so a man of the Middle Ages before the thirteenth and fourteenth centuries. He looked at two different things. He said, oxalic acid is found especially in clover but it occurs in a certain quantity in the whole human organism, in particular in the part of the organism comprising the digestive organs—spleen, liver, and so on. In the area of the digestive tract you have to reckon with processes that are under the influence of oxalic acid.

Now it happens to be the case that this oxalic acid, which plays a part in the human abdomen, is acted upon by the human organism itself in a way which is similar to the action of the glycerine in the retort. Here too we have a glycerine action. And note the remarkable result: under the influence of the activity of glycerine the transformed product of oxalic acid, namely, formic acid, passes into the lungs and the breath. And we breathe out carbon dioxide. We send out our breath and with it we send out carbon dioxide. You can imagine instead of the retort the digestive tract, and where the formic acid is collected you can imagine the lungs, and higher up you have carbon dioxide in the air breathed out from the lungs.

A human being, however, is not a retort! The retort just demonstrates in a dead way what takes place in a human being in a living and feeling way. And this is really how it is: if a human being never produced oxalic acid in his digestive tract he would simply not be able to live. That is to say, his etheric body would have no sort of basis in his organism. If a human being did not change oxalic acid into formic acid his astral body would have no basis in his organism. Human beings need oxalic acid for their etheric body and formic acid for their astral body. Or rather, it is not the substances they need but the inner activity going on in the oxalic acid process and the formic acid process. This is of course something which a present-day physiologist has yet to discover; he still speaks of what goes on in the human being as if these were external processes.

This was the first question put by the student of natural science in medieval times as he sat in front of his retort. He asked himself: 'Such is the external process which I observe; now what is the nature of the similar process in the human being?'

The second question was this: 'What is the same process like in the great world of nature outside?' In the case of the example I have chosen the researcher of those days would have said as follows: 'I look out over the earth and see the world of plants. Oxalic acid is present in a marked degree in wood sorrel and in all kinds of clover. But in reality oxalic acid is contained in all vegetation, even if it is sometimes in homoeopathic doses. There is a touch of it in everything. The ants find it even in decaying wood. The swarms of ants, which we human beings often find so troublesome, get hold of the oxalic acid which occurs all over the fields and meadows and is indeed found wherever there is vegetation, and change it into formic acid. We continually breathe in the formic acid out of the air, although in very small doses, and we are indebted to the work of the insects on the plants for changing the oxalic acid into formic acid.

And the medieval student would say to himself: 'This

metamorphosis of oxalic acid into formic acid takes place within us human beings, and in the activity going on in nature this same metamorphosis is present.'

These two aspects presented themselves to the student with every process he carried out in his laboratory. There was, besides, something else most characteristic of the medieval student, something that has today been completely lost. Today we think, why, anyone can do research in a laboratory! It does not matter in the least whether he is a good or bad person. All the formulae are available; you only have to analyse or synthesize. Anyone can do it. However, in the days when nature was approached quite differently, when people saw in nature the working of divine forces both in humanity as well as in the great world of nature, then it was required of them that a human being who did research should at the same time have an inner piety. He must be ready to turn in soul and in spirit to the divine-spiritual principle in the world. And it was a recognized fact that if a person prepared himself for his experiments as though for a sacred rite, if he were inwardly warmed in soul by the pious exercises he went through beforehand, then he would find that the experiments led him on the one hand inwards to an investigation of the human being, and on the other hand outwards to the examination of external nature. Inner purity and goodness were thus regarded as a preparation for research, and they regarded the answers they received to their questions posed by their laboratory experiments as being willingly given by divine spiritual beings.

This gives you a characteristic picture of the transition from the spirit of the ancient Mysteries to Mysteries such as were able to exist in the Middle Ages. A certain amount of the content of the ancient Mysteries still found a place in the medieval Mysteries as a kind of tradition. Nevertheless it was impossible in the Middle Ages to attain to the greatness and sublimity even of the Mysteries that survived comparatively late, such as those of Samothrace or Hibernia.

In a traditional way what is called astrology has of course been preserved right up to our day, and the same applies to alchemy. But nothing is known today of the conditions necessary for real knowledge of astrology or alchemy, in fact these conditions were hardly known any more even in the twelfth and thirteenth centuries.

It is quite impossible to arrive at astrology through thought or empirical research. If you had suggested such a thing to those who were initiated in the ancient Mysteries, they would have replied: 'You can have just as little hope of being successful in discovering astrology through thought and empirical research as you can have of reaching a person's secrets by those means if he does not tell you them.' Suppose there were a secret known to one person and to no one else, and someone were to contend that he was going to find it out by making experiments or by pondering on it. It would of course be absurd. He can learn the secret only by being told it. And the ancients would have found it equally absurd to try to arrive at a knowledge of astrological matters by pondering on them or by doing experiments or observations. For they knew that it is the gods alone, or, as they were called later, the cosmic Intelligences, who knew the secrets of the starry worlds. They knew them, and they alone could tell them to human beings. Therefore human beings have to pursue the path of knowledge that leads them to a good understanding and relationship with the cosmic intelligences.

A true and genuine astrology depends on a person's ability to understand the cosmic Intelligences. And what of true alchemy? That does not come from doing research after the manner of a chemist of today, but upon being able to perceive the nature spirits within the processes of nature and on being able to come to an understanding with them so that they tell you how the processes take place and what really happens. In those ancient times astrology was no spinning of theories or fancies, neither was it mere research through observation; it was a conversation with the cosmic Intelligences. And alchemy, too, was a conversation with nature spirits. This is the first thing you have to know. If you had approached an Egyptian of ancient times or particularly a Chaldean, he would have told you: 'I have my observatory for the purpose of holding conversations with the cosmic Intelligences; I hold conversations with them by means of my instruments, for my spirit is able to speak with the help of my instruments.' And the pious medieval natural scientist who stood in front of his retort, investigating on the one hand the activity inside the human being and on the other hand the activity of nature as a whole, he would have told you: 'I do experiments because through experiments nature spirits speak to me.' The alchemist was the person who conjured up nature spirits. What was regarded later on as alchemy was no more than a decadent product. The whole of ancient astrology owed its origin to converse with the cosmic intelligences. But by the time of the first centuries after the rise of Christianity, ancient astrology, that is to say, converse with cosmic Intelligences, was a thing of the past. The tradition was still there. When the stars stood in opposition or in conjunction, and so on, then calculations were made accordingly. They still had everything which existed in the way of tradition from the times when the astrologer conversed with cosmic Intelligences. By this time, however, that is to say, a few centuries after the founding of Christianity, although astrology was already over alchemy still remained. Converse with the nature spirits was still possible in these later times.

And if we look into a Rosicrucian alchemical laboratory in

the Middle Ages, let us say in the fourteenth or fifteenth century, we find instruments not unlike those of the present day; at any rate one can gain some idea of them from the instruments in use today. But when we look with spiritual vision into those Rosicrucian Mysteries, we find everywhere the earnest and deeply tragic personality of whom Faust is a later and indeed lesser development, particularly Goethe's Faust. For in comparison with the scholar in the Rosicrucian laboratory with his deeply tragic countenance, who can really no longer cope with life—in comparison with him Goethe's Faust is something like a newspaper print of the Apollo of Belvedere as compared with the real Apollo when he appeared at the altar of the Kabeiroi, taking form in the clouds of sacrificial smoke.

It was so indeed. When one looks into these alchemical laboratories of the eighth, ninth, tenth, eleventh, twelfth and thirteenth centuries one is confronted with a very deep tragedy. This tragic mood, which belonged to the most earnest people of the Middle Ages, is not properly recorded in history books, for the writers of those books have not looked into the depths of the human soul.

But the genuine scholars, who made investigations with retorts to learn about the real nature of the human being and the cosmos, were, in the early Middle Ages, none other than glorified Faustian characters. They were all deeply conscious of one thing. They could all say: 'When we experiment nature spirits speak to us, the spirits of the earth, the spirits of the water, the spirits of fire and the spirits of the air. We hear their whispered murmuring, the coming and going of their voices growing into harmonies and melodies and retreating again. Melodies resound when nature processes take place.' These scholars stood over their retorts and, in piety of heart, steeped themselves in the process that was taking place. For example, in this very process of the transformation of oxalic acid into formic acid, when they asked a question the nature spirit gave answer, so they could make use of the nature spirit for what was going on in the human being. First of all the retort began to speak in colour. They perceived the nature spirits of the earth and the nature spirits of the water rising up out of the oxalic acid and asserting themselves, but then the whole apparition changed into the humming sounds of melodies and harmonies growing and retreating back into itself again. Such was their experience of the process that results in formic acid and carbon dioxide.

And if one was able to enter into the life of this transition from colour into sound, then one could also enter with a deep and living knowledge into what the process could tell one about nature as a whole and about the human being. They arrived at the feeling: the things and processes of nature reveal something more, something which is spoken by the gods; for they are pictures of divine being. And one can turn the knowledge to good account for human beings. Throughout these times the knowledge of healing was closely and intimately bound up with a knowledge of their world view in general.

Now let us imagine we had the task of developing therapy based on such perceptions. We have a human being in front of us. The same complex of external symptoms can of course be an expression of a whole variety of illnesses and their causes. However, with a method that arises from this kind of knowledge—I do not say it can be done today as it was done in the Middle Ages for today of course it has to be quite different, but with such a method we would be able to say: if a certain complex of symptoms occurs, then it shows that the human being is unable to transform enough oxalic acid into formic acid. He has become too weak in some way to do it. We should possibly be able to provide a remedy by giving him formic acid in some form, to give him help from outside if he himself cannot produce formic acid.

Now it might happen in the case of two or three people whom you have diagnosed as not being able to produce formic acid that you treat them with formic acid and it works quite satisfactorily. Then you get a person with a similar complaint to whom you give formic acid and it does not help at all. However, directly you give him oxalic acid it helps immediately. Why is this? Because the deficiency of forces is somewhere else, namely, where the oxalic acid ought to be changed into formic acid. In such a case, if we were to think along the lines of a researcher of the Middle Ages, we should say: 'Yes, under certain circumstances the human organism, on being given formic acid, will reply: "I do not want it. I do not ask for it in the lung or anywhere like that, I do not need it brought into the breath and the circulation. I want to be treated in quite a different place, namely, in the region of the oxalic acid, for I myself want to change the oxalic acid into formic acid. I do not want the formic acid. I want to make it myself."'

This is how different the situation can be. Of course a great deal of swindling and stupidity has gone on under the name of alchemy, but for the genuine scholar who was worthy of the name the subject of his research was always the study of healthy human nature in close connection with human nature when in a sick state.

And this led to nothing less than converse with the nature spirits. The medieval scholar definitely sensed: 'I am associating with nature spirits. There was a time when human beings associated with cosmic intelligences. That is barred to me.'

In fact, my dear friends, since the nature spirits, too, have withdrawn from human ken, and the things and processes of nature have become the abstractions they now appear to be to the physicists and chemists of today, the tragic mood which was there in the Middle Ages no longer arises. For it was the nature spirits, who themselves could just reach back that far, who awakened in the medieval scholar the yearning for the cosmic intelligences. These had been accessible to the ancients, but the medieval scholars could no longer find the way to them with the means of knowledge at their disposal. They could only find their way to the nature spirits. The very fact that they did perceive the nature spirits and were able to draw them into the field of knowledge made it so tragic for them that they were not able to approach the cosmic intelligences by whom the nature spirits themselves were inspired. They perceived what the nature spirits knew, but they could not penetrate through them to the cosmic intelligences beyond. That was the mood of the time.

The real cause of this tragedy was that while the medieval alchemists still acquired knowledge from the nature spirits they had lost touch with the knowledge of the cosmic intelligences. And this in turn was also the cause of the fact that they were unable to attain to a complete knowledge of the human being, although they were still able to divine where such knowledge was to be found. And when Faust says:

And here, poor fool, with all my lore,
I stand, no wiser than before.[1]

we may really take the words as reminiscent of the feeling that prevailed in many a laboratory of the Middle Ages. For ultimately it was the nature spirits who gave the laboratory scholars what they knew, but they could not give them real knowledge of the soul.

By today a great deal has been lost, even in the way of tradition, but it must be found again. These medieval scholars had also heard of reincarnation. When they were in their laboratories, however, the nature spirits were in the habit of speaking about all kinds of things relating to substances or giving descriptions of occurrences in the world, but they never spoke at all about repeated earth lives; they took no interest in the subject at all.

So, my dear friends, I have given you some of the thoughts which gave rise to the fundamentally tragic mood of the medieval natural scientist. He is indeed a remarkable figure, this Rosicrucian scientist of the early Middle Ages, standing in his laboratory with his deeply serious and sorrowful face, not sceptical of human understanding but filled with a profound uncertainty of heart, with no weakness of will but with the awareness: 'I have indeed the will! But how am I to guide it so that it may take the path that leads to the cosmic intelligences?'

Innumerable were the questions arising in the heart of the medieval natural scientist! The monologue at the beginning of *Faust*, with all that follows, is no more than a weak reflection of his endless questioning and striving.

Tomorrow we will take a closer look at this earnest scholar with his deeply moving countenance, who is really the ancestor of Goethe's Faust.

LECTURE 14

The Striving Human Soul during the Middle Ages

We will utilize the last of these lectures to bring together what has been said about the various Mysteries belonging to one or another region of the earth in order to show you, at least from one point of view, the form the Mysteries took during the Middle Ages approximately from the tenth to the fifteenth century.

I do not speak of this epoch because it is particularly complete in itself but because it can be used to show the form human striving was taking during that period in the most civilized parts of the world. The spiritual striving of that period is often described as the Mysteries of the Rosicrucians.[1] This description is in a certain sense quite justifiable, but it must not be confused with the charlatan element we often meet with in literature without realizing how much charlatanry there is in the things we read. The name 'Rosicrucian' must direct our attention to that deeply earnest striving for knowledge which existed during those centuries in almost every region of Europe, central, western and southern. We must realize that the figure of Faust as described by Goethe, with all his deep striving of soul, with all his earnest effort, is a later figure, no longer anything like as profound in soul as many a researcher to be found in the medieval laboratories. These were individuals of whom nothing reaches us by way of history, but who nevertheless laboured earnestly between the tenth and fifteenth centuries. I spoke in the last lecture of the predominantly tragic disposition in the most earnest researchers of the time. Their outstanding trait was the feeling that they had to strive for the greatest knowledge that can be creatively active in human beings; and yet they felt not only that they could in a certain sense never reach this highest goal, but that from a certain point of view it was even a dubious matter whether they ought to strive towards it.

I have said that we do not find among these scientists in their alchemical laboratories a theoretical, trivial knowledge, but a knowledge that had to do with the whole human being, with the innermost feelings and deepest longings of the heart; it was indeed a knowledge of the mind and heart.

What was its origin? You will readily understand it if I try to give you a picture of this tragic scepticism of medieval research. Let me first direct your attention once again to the *form* taken by human cognition in very ancient times.

The most ancient form of human knowledge, intimately bound up as it was with the life of the human being, was not of the kind that would have led people to look up to the planets and perceive the mathematical sublimity, the mathematical movements which people calculate and let their imaginations loose on nowadays. At that time each planet, as well as everything else spread out over the expanses of the heavens, was a living being, and not only living but an ensouled being, a spiritual being. Human beings spoke constantly of the families of the planets, of the families of the heavenly bodies, for they knew that just as a blood relationship exists among the members of a human family there also exists an inner relationship between the members of a planetary system. There was a parallel in their knowledge between what is to be found on the human level and what is revealed out there in the cosmos.

Let us take one region of the earth as an example, and show from that the kind of knowledge human beings came to acquire in the most ancient of the Mysteries when they looked up to the sun. There were Mystery sanctuaries of the kind which were arranged with a specially prepared skylight, so that at certain times of the day they could look at the sun with its light diminished. You must realize that the most important chamber in many an ancient Sun Mystery centre was one with a skylight in the roof, the window of which was filled with some kind of material—not glass of our modern kind but a material through which the orb of the sun was seen as in dim twilight. The pupil was then made ready to observe the solar orb in the right inner mood of soul. He had to make his feeling mind so receptive and perceptive that when, by way of the eye, he opened his soul to the sun with its dimmed-down light it made a strong and lasting impression upon him.

Of course many people look at the sun nowadays through smoked glass, but their perceptive faculty has not been tuned to take the impression into their souls so powerfully that it remains with them as a very special impression. The impression of the dimmed orb of the sun received by the pupils of these Mysteries after they had undergone exercises for a long time was a quite specific one. And anyone who, as Mystery pupil, was able to have this impression, could truly never forget it. It also increased his understanding for certain things. Then, after the pupil had been prepared by the majestic impression made upon him by the sun, he was led to experience the special quality of the substance gold; and through this sun preparation the pupil actually came to a deep understanding of the quality of gold.

If you look into these things it is painful to realize how trivial are the descriptions given in modern history books of why one or another ancient philosopher allocated gold to the sun or gave the same symbol to gold as to the sun. People no longer have any idea that what was known about this in olden times proceeded in reality from long exercise and preparation. A pupil who looked with his whole soul into the dimmed light of the sun was being prepared to understand the gold of the earth. And in what way did he understand it? His attention now awoke to the fact that gold is not receptive to that element which is normally the breath of life for organisms, and to which most other metals are thoroughly receptive, namely, oxygen. Oxygen does not affect or alter gold. This non-receptivity, this obstinacy of gold with regard to the element through which human beings receive life, made a deep impression on the pupil of the ancient Mysteries. He realized that gold cannot approach life directly. Now neither can the sun approach life directly, and the pupil learnt that it is well that neither gold nor the sun can directly approach life. For he was gradually led to realize that because gold has no relationship with oxygen, the breath of life, when it is introduced in a certain dosage into the human organism it has a quite definite effect. It has no relation to the etheric body, no relation to the astral body directly, but it has a direct relation to the quality of thinking.

Just take a look at how far thinking is removed from life, especially in our modern age! A person can sit like a log of wood and think abstractly with great vigour. But, on the other hand, through merely thinking he cannot bring about any change in his organism; human thought has become more and more powerless. However, this thinking is set in motion by the ego organization, and gold introduced in the right dosage into the human organism can bring back power to thought. It restores to the life of thought the power to work down into the astral body and even into the etheric body; thus gold enlivens the human being by way of his thinking.

One of the secrets of these ancient Mysteries was the secret of gold in connection with the sun. The relationship between the substance gold and the cosmic working of the sun made a particular impression on the pupils of these ancient Mysteries.

In a similar way the pupil was led to experience the working of the polar opposite of gold. Gold is an impulse for the quickening of human thinking, so that human thought can work down as far as the etheric body. And what would be the polar opposite to this?

The members of the human organism are ego organization, astral body, etheric body and physical body, and we can say that by means of gold the ego organization becomes capable of working down into the etheric body. The etheric body can then work on the physical body, but gold brings it about that one can actually hold the thoughts in all their power as far as in the etheric body.

What is the polar opposite of this? It is an activity that manifests itself when something attracts the breath of life—oxygen—to itself either in a human being or in nature. And just as gold is unyielding where oxygen is concerned and repels it, and therefore has no direct influence on the etheric or the astral body but only on the thought world of the ego organization, *carbon* has a direct affinity to the oxygen in the human being. As you know, we breathe out carbon dioxide. We make it by combining carbon with oxygen. And the plants require carbon dioxide in order to live. Carbon has the exact opposite properties to gold.

Now carbon played a great part in the oldest Mysteries. In one direction they spoke of gold as a particularly important substance in the study of the human being, and in the other direction they spoke of carbon. In these most ancient of Mysteries they called carbon the 'philosophers' stone'. Gold and the philosophers' stone were very important things in those ancient times—gold and the philosophers' stone. Carbon was the philosophers' stone.

Carbon appears on earth in a variety of forms. Diamond is carbon, a very hard carbon. Graphite is carbon. Coal is carbon. Anthracite is carbon. Carbon appears in the most diverse forms. However, by means of the methods that were customary in the ancient Mysteries, human beings came to understand that there exist still other forms of carbon besides those we find here on earth. And in this connection the pupil in the Mysteries had to undergo another preparation. For besides the sun preparation, which I have already told you about, there was also the moon preparation.

Added to the ancient sanctuaries of the Sun Mysteries we find a kind of observatory in which a human being could open his soul and his physical vision to the forms of the moon. Whereas in the sun training the pupil had to behold the sun at certain times of day in a diminished light, now for weeks at a time he had to expose his eyes to the different forms that the orb of the moon assumes by night. Gazing thus with his whole soul the pupil received a definite inner impression which gave him fresh knowledge. Just as the human being by exposing his soul to the sun became capable of understanding it, similarly, by exposing himself to the phases of the moon the human being became capable of understanding the moon. He learnt what metamorphoses the substance of carbon can undergo. On the earth carbon is coal or graphite, diamond or anthracite, but on the moon this substance is silver. And that was the secret of the ancient Mysteries: carbon is silver on the moon. Carbon is the philosophers' stone, and on the moon it is silver.

The knowledge that was impressed so profoundly on the pupil in the ancient Mysteries was this: any substance whatsoever is only what it seems *in this one place, at this one time*. It was sheer ignorance not to know that carbon is coal, diamond or anthracite only on the earth, and that what exists on the earth as diamond or graphite is, on the moon, silver. If we could at this moment despatch a piece of ordinary black coal to the moon, it would be silver there.[2] A vision of this radical metamorphosis was what the pupil attained in those ancient times. It is the foundation not of that fraudulent alchemy of which one hears today but of true alchemy. This ancient alchemy cannot be acquired by any such abstract means of acquiring knowledge as we have today. Nowadays we observe things or we think about them. Alchemy could not be attained in that way at all. Nowadays a scientist directs his telescope to a certain star, determines parallel axes and the like and does calculation after calculation; or if he wants to discover what a particular substance is he applies the spectroscope, and so on. But everything that can be discovered in this way is infinitely abstract compared with what could once be learnt from the stars! And this ancient wisdom, this true astrology, could only be learnt, as I said yesterday, by establishing a living exchange with the intelligences of the cosmos. When a human being was able to hold converse in his soul, in his spirit, with the intelligences of the cosmos, that itself was attainment of knowledge. What aurum signifies for the human organism is connected with the secret of the sun; and through exposing his soul to the being of the sun a human being entered into a relation with the intelligences of the sun. It was these beings who could tell him of the properties of aurum. In like manner a human being entered into a relation with the intelligences of the moon.

Indeed, human beings came to learn of these intelligences of the moon as those beings who were themselves once in olden times the great teachers of earth humanity when the primeval wisdom was taught on earth. They were the same beings who today send their forces and impulses down from the moon. They withdrew from the moon at a certain time in evolution, and there in the moon they founded a colony after the moon had separated from the earth.

Thus those intelligences who once lived on the earth and are today the moon intelligences have to do with this secret, the carbon-silver secret. Such was the character of knowledge in ancient times.

Let me quote another example. Just as the pupil could receive impressions from the sun and moon, so by means of a further preparation of soul still he could also receive impressions from the other planets; and one of the secrets thus obtained was the one relating to Venus. Venus is studied today through a telescope and is regarded as being like any other star or planet. Just as the human body is studied by investigating, say, a section of the liver and then a section of the brain, actually only investigating their cell structure as though they were not two radically different substances, in the very same way a student will direct his telescope to Mercury, Venus and Mars and so on, believing all of them to be composed of substances of a like nature. In ancient times they knew that if human beings were studying the moon or the sun, they could attain their aims by means of what was directly related to the physical earth: the elements of earth, water, air and fire. If they extended their observation in a spiritual way to the moon, they came to the ether. If, however, they extended their observation to Venus they came to a spiritual world, a purely astral world. What we see physically as Venus is only the external emblem of something which lives and has its being in the astral element, the astral light. Where Venus is concerned physical light is something entirely different from physical sunlight. Physical sunlight still has a relationship with what can live on earth as earth-produced light, whereas Venus light—and it is childish to think of it simply as reflected sunlight—shines forth from the spiritual world. If the pupil exposed his soul to this light, he came to know which intelligences were connected with Venus.

These are intelligences who live in continual opposition to the intelligences of the sun; and a great role was played in the ancient Mysteries by this opposition between the intelligences of Venus and the intelligences of the sun. People spoke with a certain justification of a continual battle between them. There were starting-points for such conflicts when the Venus intelligences began attacking the sun intelligences. There were times of intensified conflicts, there were culminations, catastrophes and crises. And in what lay between an attack and a catastrophe or crisis you had, as it were, a section of that great battle of opposition which is taking place in the spiritual world, and appears in an external form only in the astrological and astronomical relationships between Venus and the sun. It took place in successive phases. And no one can understand what lives on earth in the inner impulses of history if he does not know of this conflict between Venus and the sun. For all that takes place here on earth in the way of conflict, and everything else that happens in the evolution of civilization, is an earthly image of this conflict between Venus and the sun.

Such knowledge existed in the ancient Mysteries because there was a relation between the human beings on the earth and the intelligences of the cosmos. Then came the epoch of which I have spoken, the epoch from the tenth to the fifteenth centuries AD. The medieval investigators in their alchemical laboratories were, in the process of human evolution, no longer able to reach up to the cosmic intelligences, though they could still reach the nature spirits. They made numerous experiments—of which I gave you an instance in the last lecture, when I spoke of the tranformation of oxalic acid into formic acid—numerous experiments of the kind which were to reveal to them the presence and activity of the gods in the processes and things of nature, but they could do so only when they had prepared themselves fittingly through that spirit of piety of which I told you for converse with the nature spirits. Now let us look more closely at the actual situation of such an investigator.

He stood in his laboratory and he could say to himself: 'I bring substances, retorts and heating ovens into my laboratory and I do various experiments. I ask nature certain questions by means of my experiments, and when I do this the nature spirits enter my laboratory with their revelations. I can perceive them.' For this continued right up to the fifteenth century that nature spirits approached a Rosicrucian investigator who was properly prepared. However, he still knew theoretically that in ancient times investigators had not been able merely to reach the nature spirits but could come in touch with the higher cosmic Intelligences who spoke to them of the secret of gold connected with the sun, the secret of silver and of carbon connected with the moon, and of the historically important secret of Venus, and so on. It is true that they had records preserved by way of tradition telling them how there had once been this knowledge, but the records were not especially important to them. If one has once been touched by the spirit then historical documents are not so terribly important as they are for our modern materialistic age. It is really astounding to see how infinitely important it is to many people when some discovery is made such as the recent case of the skeleton of a dinosaur being found in the Gobi desert. Of course it is an important find, but such discoveries are never anything but separate broken fragments, whereas in a spiritual way we can really enter into the secrets of the cosmos. Historical documents were certainly not likely to impress those medieval investigators. It was in another

The laboratory as Rosicrucian temple: from Heinrich Khunrath, Amphitheatrum Sapientiae Eternae (1609).

way that the medieval alchemists acquired knowledge of how human beings had once been able to attain this cosmic knowledge, but that one could now reach only the nature spirits behind the elements of air, fire and water. It was like this: in moments when certain observations of nature were being made or certain experiments being performed, and the investigators approached the sphere of the nature spirits, some of these spirits told them that there had once been human beings who had a connection with the cosmic intelligences. That was the pain which gnawed at the hearts of these medieval investigators, that the nature spirits spoke of a former age when human beings had had a connection with the intelligences of the cosmos. And the investigators had to say: 'These nature spirits can still tell us of a past age which has vanished into the unfathomable depths of human knowledge and human existence.' Thus this ability of the medieval alchemist to reach the nature spirits was really a fraught one. On the one side he approached the spirits of nature, the spirits of air and of water—he approached gnomes, sylphs and undines in their living reality. On the other side there were some among these beings who told him of things that overwhelmed him with despair, telling him how humanity had once been in connection not only with the nature spirits but also with the intelligences of the cosmos, with whom the nature spirits are still connected to this day but whom human beings could no longer reach. That was the feeling of the medieval alchemists, and it often came to expression in a far more sublime, a far more grandiose and tragic manner than we find in Goethe's *Faust* (beautiful and powerful though this is!).

The utterance that Faust addresses to the moon, to the shining silver moonlight in which he longs to bathe,[3] would have been made with much greater depth by the scientists between the tenth and fifteenth centuries when the nature spirits told them about the secret of carbon and silver, a silver which is also closely and intimately connected with the human being. For what was it that these people of olden times experienced alongside those communications? They experienced not only that aurum is connected with the sun but how aurum works in a human being, how argentum (silver) and carbon work in a human being, and similarly how other metals related to the other planets work in a human being. In olden times people experienced these things in the circulation of the blood in their body. They experienced them in a conscious way. They felt the blood streaming and pulsing through their head and at the same time they felt it as a picture of the whole earth, this streaming of their blood through the head. And that sphere where the head is not enclosed by bone, where it opens downwards towards the heart and the chest, they felt to be an image of what rises up from the earth into the atmosphere. Thus in what a human being learnt from the cosmos he recognized the metamorphoses that went on in his own organism; he could follow the planet in its passage through all his organs. We find here a confirmation of the penetrating words of Mephistopheles where he says: 'Blood is a very special fluid.'[4] For in its metamorphosis our blood reflects those wonderful metamorphoses from carbon to silver. All this also lives in human blood.

Thus did the medieval scientist regard the loss of knowledge of the cosmic intelligences as a loss of his own humanity. And it is in reality but a faint reflection of this experience that we find in Faust when he opens the Book of the Macrocosm and endeavours to rise to the cosmic Intelligences, then shuts the book again because he is unable to do so, and contents himself with the spirit of the earth. We have here only a faint echo of the dreadfully tragic mood we find in these medieval scientists—

whose names have not even come down to us—when, on entering the sphere of the nature spirits through their alchemical investigations, they heard from them how human beings had once had a connection with the cosmic intelligences.

Now all this is deeply linked with what had to develop in ancient Greece when it became necessary for the Mysteries of Samothrace, the Mysteries of the Kabeiroi, to be reduced to the philosophy of Aristotle, which then played such an important role in the Middle Ages. All the time, below the surface of what we know as Aristotelianism, there continued to work powerfully, although tragically, right on into the fifteenth century, what I have been able to sketch for you in this fragment of those times. Indeed, it was the case that behind the Macedonian epoch there were Mysteries that reach as far as Greece (there will be more about this in the coming historical lectures), Mysteries that saw deeply into the secrets of the cosmic substances and their connection with the cosmic intelligences, Mysteries that for the first time began to descend from the cosmic Intelligences to the nature spirits. It was as though they were deliberately prevented from seeing as far as the cosmic intelligences and had their attention directed instead to the nature spirits. This was the crisis that came about at the time of Aristotle and Alexander. In all that happened at that time we can still see that the abstractions of Aristotle are rooted in the old Mysteries. Anyone who knows about the carbon-silver secret and then reads the observations of Aristotle that have come down to posterity—his most important ones have not survived—reads what is written there relating to the secret of the moon, will understand at once the connection with those olden times.

More light will be shed on these very things in the lectures I intend to give on the historical development of humanity from the standpoint of anthroposophy.[3]

APPENDIX 1

Original German texts of Verses

Lecture 3

Winter Wille
O Welten-Bilder
Ihr schwebet heran
Aus Raumesweiten
Ihr strebet nach mir,
Ihr dringet ein
In meines Hauptes
Denkende Kräfte.

Sommer Wille
Ihr meines Hauptes
Bildende Seelenkräfte,
Ihr erfüllet mein Eigensein,
Ihr dringet aus meinem Wesen,
In die Weltenweiten,
Und einigt mich selbst
Mit Weltenschaffensmächten.

Lecture 6

Schaue den Logos
Im sengenden Feuer;
Finde die Lösung
In Dianens Haus.

Lecture 7

Ich bin das Bild der Welt,
Sieh, wie das Sein mir fehlt.
Ich lebe in deiner Erkenntnis,
Ich werde in dir nun Bekenntnis.

Ich bin das Bild der Welt,
Sieh, wie Wahrheit mir fehlt.
Willst du mit mir zu leben wagen,
So werd' ich dir zum Behagen.

Ich bin die Erkenntnis.
Aber was ich bin ist kein Sein.
Ich bin die Phantasie,
Aber was ich bin hat keine Wahrheit.

(First Priest:)
Nimm das Wort und die Kraft dieses Wesens
In dein Herz auf.

(Second Priest:)
Und von ihm empfange,
Was die beiden Gestalten geben wollten:
WISSENSCHAFT und KUNST.

Lecture 8

In den Weiten sollst du lernen.
Wie im Blau der Ätherfernen
Erst das Weltensein entschwindet
Und in dir sich wiederfindet.

In den Tiefen sollst du lösen
Aus dem heiss-erfiebernden Bösen,
Wie die Wahrheit sich entzündet
Und durch dich im Sein sich ergründet.

Lerne geistig Wintersein schauen
Und dir wird der Anblick des Vorirdischen.

Lerne geistig Sommersein träumen
Und dir wird das Erleben des Nachirdischen.

Lecture 11

1. *Pflanzengeheimnis* (secret of the plants)
Ich schaue in die Blumen;

Ihre Verwandschaft mit dem Mondensein offenbaren sie;
Sie sind erdbezwungene nun, denn sie sind Wassergeborene.

2. *Metallgeheimnis* (secret of the metals)
Ich denke über die Metalle;
Ihre Verwandschaft mit den Planeten offenbaren sie;
Sie sind erdbezwungen, denn sie sind Luftgeborene.

3. *Menschengeheimnis* (secret of human beings)
Ich erlebe die Geheimnisse des Tierkreises in der Mannigfaltigkeit der Menschen;
Die Verwandschaft dieser Mannigfaltigkeit der Menschen mit den Fixsternen steht vor meiner Seele;
Denn die Menschen leben mit dieser Mannigfaltigkeit erdbezwungen; sie sind Wärmegeborene.

APPENDIX 2

The Mystery of Transformation in Ovid's Metamorphoses

In Lecture 4 of this book, Rudolf Steiner refers to the survival of the ancient Mystery feeling for the transformation processes in man and nature, which he finds reflected in the long and fascinating masterpiece of the Roman poet Ovid, *Metamorphoses*.

Though one of the most influential literary works in the Western canon, Ovid's linked recital of mythical tales, each concerned with the transformation of one thing into another, also has a certain baffling quality that has led many to seek deeper meanings than meet the eye. The poet was himself keenly aware of the instability of life—and indeed suffered the fate of exile and disgrace, banished to the margins of the Roman world where he ended his career by writing miserable verse-letters home and a poem on the fishes of the Black Sea. But his great work, the *Metamorphoses*, seems to suggest that by grasping constant change we can reach to enduring patterns of things, and that (as his later imitator Spenser expressed it) man likewise may be mortal and perishing:

> Yet is eterne in mutabilitie,
> And by succession made perpetuall,
> Transformed oft, and chaunged diverslie...

Thus Ovid's poem, beginning with the transformation of chaos into ordered creation, somewhat paradoxically grounds upon this idea of change his permanent claim to immortality in its last lines. In Book XV, Pythagoras is represented teaching his philosophy of change, and there is little doubt that his message is also Ovid's own. This part was translated into verse that matches the original in self-conscious brilliance by John Dryden for his *Fables Ancient and Modern* of 1700. Pythagoras is speaking:

Now since the God inspires me to proceed,
Be that, whate'er inspiring Pow'r, obey'd.
For I will sing of mighty Mysteries,
Of Truths conceal'd before, from human Eyes,
Dark Oracles unveil, and open all the Skies.
Pleas'd as I am to walk along the Sphere
Of shining Stars, and travel with the Year,
To leave the heavy Earth, and scale the height
Of *Atlas*, who supports the heav'nly weight;
To look from upper Light, and thence survey
Mistaken Mortals wandring from the way,
And wanting Wisdom, fearful for the state
Of future Things, and trembling at their Fate!

   Those I would teach; and by right Reason bring
To think of Death, as but an idle Thing.
Why thus affrighted at an empty Name,
A dream of Darkness, and fictitious Flame?
Vain Themes of Wit, which but in Poems pass,
And Fables of a World, that never was!
What feels the Body when the Soul expires,
By time corrupted, or consum'd by Fires?
Nor dies the Spirit, but new Life repeats
In other Forms, and only changes Seats.

   Ev'n I, who these mysterious Truths declare,
Was once *Euphorbus* in the *Trojan* War;
My Name and Lineage I remember well,
And how in Fight by *Sparta*'s King I fell.
In *Argive Juno*'s Fane I late beheld
My Buckler hung on high, and own'd my former Shield.

   Then, Death, so call'd, is but old Matter dress'd
In some new Figure, and a vary'd Vest:
Thus all Things are but alter'd, nothing dies;
And here and there th' unbodied Spirit flies,
By Time, or Force, or Sickness dispossest,
And lodges, where it lights, in Man or Beast;

Or hunts without, till ready Limbs it find,
And actuates those according to their kind;
From Tenement to Tenement is toss'd;
The Soul is still the same, the Figure only lost:
And, as the soften'd Wax new Seals receives,
This Face assumes, and that Impression leaves:
Now call'd by one, now by another Name;
The form is only chang'd, the Wax is still the same:
So Death, so call'd, can but the Form deface,
Th' immortal Soul flies out in empty space;
To seek her Fortune in some other Place.

   Then let not Piety be put to flight,
To please the taste of Glutton-Appetite;
But suffer inmate Souls secure to dwell,
Lest from their Seats your Parents you expel;
With rabid Hunger feed upon your kind,
Or from a Beast dislodge a Brother's Mind.

   And since, Like *Tiphys* parting from the Shore,
In ample Seas I sail, and Depths untry'd before,
This let me further add, that Nature knows
No steadfast Station, but, or Ebbs, or Flows:
Ever in motion; she destroys her old,
And casts new Figures in another Mold.
Ev'n Times are in perpetual Flux; and run
Like Rivers from their Fountain rowling on;
For Time no more than Streams, is at a stay:
The flying Hour is ever on her way;
And as the Fountain still supplies her store,
The Wave behind impels the Wave before;
Thus in successive Course the Minutes run,
And urge their predecessor Minutes on,
Still moving, every new: For former Things
Are set aside, like abdicated Kings:
And every moment alters what is done,
And innovates some Act till then unknown.

Darkness we see emerges into Light,
And shining Suns descend to Sable Night;
Ev'n Heav'n it self receives another die,
When weari'd Animals in Slumbers lie,
Of Midnight Ease: Another when the gray
Of Morn preludes the Splendor of the Day.
The disk of *Phoebus* when he climbs on high,
Appears at first but as a bloodshot Eye;
And when his Chariot downward drives to Bed,
His Ball is with the same Suffusion red;
But mounted high in his Meridian Race
All bright he shines, and with a better Face:
For there, pure Particles of *Aether* flow,
Far from th' Infection of the World below.

Now equal Light th' unequal Moon adorns,
Or in her wexing or her waning Horns.
For ev'ry Day she wanes, her Face is less,
But fath'ring into Globe, she fattens at increase.

Perceiv'st thou not the process of the Year,
How the four Seasons in four Forms appear,
Resembling human Life in ev'ry Shape they wear?
Spring first, like Infancy, shoots out her Head,
With milky Juice requiring to be fed:
Helpless, tho' fresh, and wanting to be led.
The green Stem grows in Stature and in Size,
But only feeds with hope the Farmer's Eyes;
Then laughs the childish Year with Flourets crown'd,
And lavishing perfumes the Fields around,
But no substantial Nourishment receives,
Infirm the Stalks, unsolid are the Leaves.

Proceeding onward whence the Year began
The Summer grows adult, and ripens into Man.
This Season, as in Men, is most repeat,
With kindly Moisture, and prolifick Heat.
Autumn succeeds, a sober tepid Age,

Not froze with Fear, nor boiling into Rage;
More than mature, and tending to decay,
When our brown Locks repine to mix with odious Grey.

   Last Winter creeps along with tardy pace,
Sour is his Front, an furrow'd is his Face;
His Scalp if not dishonour'd quite of Hair,
The ragged Fleece is thin, and thin is worse than bare.

   Ev'n our own Bodies daily change receive,
Some part of what was theirs before, they leave;
Nor are to Day what Yesterday they were;
Nor the whole same to Morrow will appear.

   Time was, when we were sow'd, and just began
From some few fruitful Drops, the promise of Man;
Then Nature's Hand (fermented as it was)
Moulded to Shape the soft, coagulated Mass;
And when the little Man was fully form'd,
The breathless Embryo with a Spirit warm'd;
But when the Mothers Throws begin to come,
The Creature, pent within the narrow Room,
Breaks his blind Prison, pushing to repair
His stiffled Breath, and draw the living Air;
Cast on the Margin of the World he lies,
A helpless, Babe, but by Instinct he cries.
He next essays to walk, but downward press'd
On four Feet imitates his Brother Beast:
By slow degrees he gathers from the Ground
His Legs, and to the rowling Chair is bound;
Then walks alone; a Horseman now become
He rides a Stick, and travels round the Room:
In time he vaunts among his youthful Peers,
Strong-bon'd, and strung with Nerves, in pride of Years,
He runs with Mettle his first merry Stage,
Maintains the next abated of his Rage,
But manages his Strength, and spares his Age.
Heavy the third, and stiff, he sinks apace,

And tho' 'tis down-hill all, but creeps along the Race.
Now sapless on the verge of Death he stands,
Contemplating his former Feet, and Hands;
And *Milo*-like, his slacken'd Sinews sees,
And wither'd Arms, once fit to cope with Hercules,
Unable now to shake, much less to tear the Trees.

   So *Helen* wept when her too faithful Glass
Reflected to her Eyes the ruins of her Face:
Wondring what Charms her Ravishers cou'd spy,
To force her twice, or ev'n but once enjoy!

   Thy Teeth, devouring Time, thin, envious Age,
On Things below still exercise your Rage:
With venom'd Grinders you corrupt your Meat,
And then at lingring Meals, the Morsels eat.

   Nor those, which Elements we call, abide,
For to this Figure, nor to that are ty'd:
For this eternal World is said of Old
But four prolifick Principles to hold,
Four different Bodies; two to Heaven ascend,
And other two down to the Center tend:
Fire first with Wings expanded mounts on high,
Pure, void of weight, and dwells in upper Sky;
Then Air, because unclogg'd in empty space
Flies after Fire, and claims the second Place:
But weighty Water as her Nature guides,
Lies on the lap of Earth; and Mother Earth subsides.

   All Things are mix'd of these, which all contain,
And into these are all resolv'd again:
Earth rarifies to Dew; expanded more,
The subtil Dew in Air begins to soar;
Spreads as she flies, and weary of her Name
Extenuates still, and changes into Flame;
Thus having by degrees Perfection won,
Restless they soon untwist the Web they spun,

and Fire begins to lose her radiant Hue,
Mix'd with gross Air, and Air descends to Dew:
And Dew condensing, does her Form forego,
And sinks, a heavy lump of Earth below.

   Thus are their Figures never at a stand,
But chang'd by Nature's innovating Hand;
All Things are alter'd, nothing is destroy'd,
The shifted Scene, for some new Show employ'd.
Then to be born, is to begin to be
Some other Thing we were not formerly:
And what we call to Die, is not t' appear,
Or be the Thing that formerly we were.
Those very Elements which we partake,
Alive, when Dead some other Bodies make:
Translated grow, have Sense, or can Discourse,
But Death on deathless Substance has no force.

   That Forms are chang'd I grant; that nothing can
Continue in the Figure it began:
The Golden Age, to Silver was debas'd:
To Copper that; our Mettal came at last.

   The Face of Places, and their Forms decay;
And that is solid Earth, that once was Sea:
Seas in their turn retreating from the Shore,
Make solid Land, what Ocean was before;
And far from Strands are Shells of Fishes found,
And rusty Anchors fix'd on Mountain-Ground:
And what were Fields before, now wash'd and worn
By falling Floods from high, to Valley's turn,
And crumbling still descend to level Lands;
And Lakes, and trembling Bogs are barren Sands:
And the parch'd Desart floats in Streams unknown;
Wondring to drink of Waters not her own.

Notes

Notes to Introduction

1 The lectures and discussions referred to have now been made available in full in English: Rudolf Steiner, *The Christmas Conference for the Foundation of the General Anthroposophical Society 1923–1924*, with an Introduction by Virginia Sease (New York 1990). They include not only the discussion on the statutes of the new Society but a series of detailed approaches to the central 'Foundation Stone Meditation' and an important lecture on the Mystery-background to the burning of the First Goetheanum in relation to the temple of Artemis in ancient Ephesus.
2 Otherwise such 'Victory' figures would appear only on temples commemorating divinely aided victories. The *Nike* now in the Louvre, originating from the Mystery-complex of the Great Gods at Samothrace, is not the one from the acroterion of the Temple but from a related monument on the site. One might speculate about the link between these figures and the 'seraphic' figure in Steiner's statue *The Representative of Man between Lucifer and Ahriman*. Described as the 'Spirit of Humour', it likewise suggests transcendence and victory that does not cancel out the suffering and effort in the main figures.
3 Steiner, *The Christmas Conference*, pp. 68ff. He places the idea of threefoldness expressed there among 'the most important findings of recent years' in the unfolding of anthroposophy. He had expounded it originally in 1917; the passage is to be found in Steiner, *The Case for Anthroposophy*, ed. Owen Barfield (London 1970), pp. 69ff. Although his later thought must not be reduced to a mechanical application of this principle, it led him to formulate a view of the threefold relationship of human beings to society as a living dimension of the different aspects of their being. Everyone is related to others in all three ways, but the principle underlying each sphere of relationships is different. Firstly, everyone exists as an individual, in freedom and inde-

pendence (this is not just a fact but already socially significant); likewise in a relationship of brotherly or sisterly collaboration and exchange, where individuals must find ways of working together, changing themselves to achieve shared goals; and in a network of common responsibilities which all equally must share, and in relationship to which all are to be treated equally. None of these relationships is merely external; each has its spirituality, and whereas much of Steiner's discussion focuses on ways in which they could have been realized through social reconstruction after the War, some of the broader implications are explored for instance in his wide-ranging cultural comparison and analysis, *The Tension between East and West* (London 1963). In fact, we can see that each sphere had its representative spiritual forms in previous cultures—though the several spheres were often very unequally developed in comparison with the situation (despite its confusions) that prevails in advanced societies today.

4 The sphere of work/transformation/exchange (including economics) is highly developed today, but attempts to subject it to laws often lead away from the human experience of work. The spirituality belonging to this sphere has in particular failed to keep pace. Instead of a static 'belief' in the spirit, Steiner stressed 'that as human evolution in different regions takes on different forms in successive periods, so it is with everything that we call the nature of the Mysteries ... For reasons that we can easily recognize, the principle of initiation must also change in successive epochs of humanity': *Mysteries of the East and Christianity* (London 1972), p. 9. Elsewhere he emphasized that in spiritual teaching 'one must create a link with something which already exists in contemporary civilization': *The Anthroposophic Movement* (Bristol 1993), p. 31—in contrast to the view taken by some other spiritual movements. The intensification of individual consciousness, together with the increased scale of modern life and its pressures, has often left people without those very resources of creative change associated with the Mysteries and their secret wisdom in the past. Renewal of the Mysteries needed an understanding of the spiritual values in all three spheres. For an account of Rudolf Steiner's path towards this task, see S.

Prokofieff, *Rudolf Steiner and the Founding of the New Mysteries* (London and New York 1986).
5 Steiner, *Occult Science* (London 1969), pp. 194ff. For the continuation of one central strand, connected with 'Know thyself' as the focal statement 'regarded in antiquity as an oracle of Apollo', into modern thought, see Steiner, *Eleven European Mystics* (New York 1971), pp. 103ff. He treats the 'mystics' not as alien to their world but as intermediaries between the oracular statement and the individual consciousness of our own time, pioneers of modern individuality and knowledge. For some information on the Greek situation, c.f. H.W. Parke, *The Greek Oracles* (London 1967); for crucial influence on Socrates, p. 112.
6 Steiner, *Christianity as Mystical Fact* (New York 1997), p. 3. For the Mysteries' connection with scepticism, not a negative but a spiritually questioning attitude, pp. 16ff. For a collection of Steiner's ideas on the subject generally, see Welburn (ed.), *The Mysteries. Rudolf Steiner's Writings on Spiritual Initiation* (Edinburgh 1997); and further material in Steiner, *Wonders of the World* (London 1963); and *The Easter Festival in Relation to the Mysteries* (London 1968). A useful aid to study is M. Meyer, *The Ancient Mysteries. A Source-book* (New York 1987). Anthroposophical perspectives on the Mysteries and spiritual life in B.C.J. Lievegood, *Mystery Streams in Europe and the New Mysteries* (New York 1982).
7 Below, p. 175.
8 *Christianity as Mystical Fact*, p. 100. For more on this 'World Pentecost' as the foundation for anthroposophy, cf. Prokofieff, *Rudolf Steiner and the Founding of the New Mysteries*, pp. 271ff. Steiner's Christology does not deny the perspective of humanity's historical 'going astray' and need for grace as traditionally understood, but complements and balances it with the restored perspective of the Mysteries and their view of man's striving. Acceptance of the working of the 'Christ-impulse' in humanity universally is not in contradistinction to the new Mysteries but their presupposition. Cf. Steiner, *The Christ-Impulse and the Evolution of Ego-Consciousness* (New York 1976).
9 *Christianity as Mystical Fact*, loc. cit.

10 Thus Steiner gives to the idea of the Church, the universal community, its full scope which has usually been compromised by the institutional needs of the particular churches which have claimed the title. See in particular Steiner, *Love and its Meaning in the World* (London 1960). Wherever the ideal of global community arises, the Christ-impulse is at work—and in comparison with this openness to recognize Christ in others any exclusivism condemns itself. In 1918 Steiner spoke already of the need to fashion the new Mystery, centred on a new form of the Isis-Sophia figure, but its aim is not to bring us to Christ: 'We have not lost Osiris-Christ—we have lost that being equivalent for us to Isis... With the power which we do not understand, but which is nevertheless in us, with the power of Christ the new Osiris we must set out on our quest...' He calls upon us to create a new myth that will express the truth of our time, when Mystery-wisdom has faded into the abstractions that we project upon the cosmos, the luciferic empty abstractions which are inwardly empty. The true Mystery-wisdom of modern times would not bring us to Christ but it adds a light of consciousness to the power working within us, to the 'Christ who remains hidden for us in darkness if we do not illuminate Him with divine Wisdom': *Ancient Myths and the New Isis-Mystery* (New York 1994), p. 173. Thus the vehicle of the new Mystery, the Anthroposophical Society, is wholly different from a Church—whose role is precisely to bring us to Christ and incorporate us in his community.

11 The way to heal the rift might once more be approached via the threefold model of spirituality. It is essential to Steiner's idea that the three spheres are not separate societies but integral aspects of society. Everyone belongs to all three, though he or she may now be most strongly active in one or another, or an institution may be centred in one while including the others in lesser degree. Thus a Church as a human reality cannot actually exist in the form of pure communality. It needs to work for specific people, and requires moments of conscious reminding of the realities which gave it birth, i.e. enactments derived from the Mysteries. Priesthood was thus reintroduced into Christianity, for instance, and Steiner points out that the ordination of priests 'was an attempt by the Church to establish a kind of continuation of the

ancient principle of initiation': *Building Stones for an Understanding of the Mystery of Golgotha* (London 1972), p. 171. But it has to remain a reminder within the Church/universality sphere (cf. Luke 22:19) and not turn back into an old temple cult. Here we see the danger of the Church's forgetting that originally the initiates did properly enter the temple sphere in the Mysteries. For the Church, suppressing that knowledge, ascribes to itself what is really an echo or reminiscence of the Mystery-experience and may, for example, withold the sacraments from the laity in some part. The way for spiritual life to develop freely is for each of the spheres to acknowledge the others, and the need for each to be echoed also within the others since human beings belong to all three. The Anthroposophical Society will likewise acknowledge the attempts of the Church-sphere to build upon the universality of the working of the Christ-impulse, and even its own dependence upon a certain echo of the 'congregational' experience as a secondary element in itself—just as it also has a place for enquiring individuals. While it was still based on the anthroposophical movement (see p. 26 below), it was still an undifferentiated mixture of principles belonging to the different spheres: it gave Steiner an individual platform for his teaching, it brought people together to hear and adopt spiritual values, and performed many other functions in a rather *ad hoc* way. By bringing the anthroposophical movement fully into the Society and making it a Mystery, he was not going back to the old esoteric form but integrating the Mystery fully with the other spheres of contemporary life. He showed the way to do this in principle—though in practice much remains to be done.

12 A valuable sketch introducing many of these aspects is R. Lissau, *Rudolf Steiner: life, work, inner path and social initiatives* (Stroud 1987).

13 Steiner, *The Easter Festival in Relation to the Mysteries*, p. 34. Cf. the important statement of Cicero concerning the Mysteries that 'just as they are called initiations, so in actual fact we have learned from them the fundamental initiatives of life'. The play on words is typical of the hinting, ambiguous way the ancients used in alluding to the importance of the secret rites: Cicero, *de legibus*, II, 14, 36.

14 Manfred Schmidt-Brabant rightly answered in the negative the question 'Was Rudolf Steiner a Freemason?': see his article in *Die Drei* (1988), 4. Steiner did acquire a Masonic charter from Theodor Reuss, but the activities developed in his esoteric school at the same period are not Freemasonry, as can be seen from *Zur Geschichte und aus den Inhalten der ersten Abteilung der esoterischen Schule*, vol. I (Dornach 1984) and vol. II (Dornach 1987). For the significance of Rosicrucianism in giving initiation a form related to modern knowledge, see *Esoteric Christianity and the Mission of Christian Rosenkreutz* (London 1984).

15 Rudolf Steiner, *The Mission of the Archangel Michael* (New York 1961).

16 Our own cultural epoch, says Steiner, cannot look to a past model as could those up to the fourth post-Atlantean age (Graeco-Roman civilization). Our age 'must look to the future rather than the past. It must look towards the future, when all the gods must arise again. This reunion with the gods was prepared in the time of the bursting-in of the Christ-force, which worked so powerfully that it could again endow man with a godly consciousness ... Only if man looks forward will life again become spiritual. In the fifth post-Atlantean period, consciousness must become apocalyptic': *Egyptian Myths and Mysteries* (New York 1971), p. 25.

17 *True and False Paths in Spiritual Investigation* (London 1969).

18 *Man as Symphony of the Creative Word* (London 1970).

19 *The Four Seasons and the Archangels* (London 1968).

20 *Ancient Myths and the New Isis-Mystery*, pp. 170ff.

Notes to Lecture 1

1 On the relationship of these lectures to the Christmas Conference, see the Introduction. For the published records of the Conference, see the work referred to there (note 1).

2 These articles are published in English as: Rudolf Steiner, *On the Life of the Soul* (New York 1985).

3 Steiner, *The Philosophy of Freedom* (London 1970): see Chapter 3, 'Thinking in the Service of Knowledge'.

4 For these paintings and their relationship to the overall conception of the building, see Hilde Raske, *The Language of Colour in the First Goetheanum* (Dornach n.d.), which includes many colour reproductions.

Notes to Lecture 2

1 Rudolf Steiner had recently spoken about this event. See his lectures *The Evolution of Consciousness* (London 1966), pp. 148ff: 'Once, in a long-past period of human evolution, divine-spiritual beings dwelt on earth together with men. They did not always make their presence known ... but they did reveal themselves if a person was led to them in the right way through the servants of the Mystery-temples. This happened only in the Mysteries, and through the Mysteries these beings became companions of earthly men. Since then they have withdrawn from the earth to the moon, where they now dwell as in a cosmic citadel...'
2 Steiner, *Cosmology, Religion and Philosophy*, London 1930.
3 Steiner, *How to Know Higher Worlds* (New York 1994): this book has previously been published under other titles, *The Way of Initiation*, *Knowledge of Higher Worlds*, etc.
4 Steiner quotes the first lines respectively of Homer's *Iliad*, Homer's *Odyssey* and of the modern epic by 'the German Milton', F.G. Klopstock, *The Messiah* (*Der Messias*, 1773).

Notes to Lecture 3

1 See Goethe's poem 'Ins Innere der Natur' which Steiner paraphrases here. Albrecht von Haller is best remembered for his distinction between the 'irritable' and 'sensible' responses of the human nervous system in his treatise of 1752.
2 On the transformation of these forces (with some educational implications) see further Steiner, *The Study of Man* (London 1966), pp. 149ff.
3 For a far-reaching description of the Hierarchies in relation to the cosmos and to our inner life, see Steiner's lectures *The Spiritual Hierarchies and their Reflection in the Physical World* (New York 1970). In Goethe's *Faust*, when Faust opens the Book of the

Macrocosm he sees a vision of the Hierarchies transforming earthly substance, handing it up the ladder of being in 'golden vessels' (Part I, line 450).
4. See Steiner's Mystery-play *The Soul's Awakening*, Scene 3.
5. The Akashic Record is the living experience of the past accessible to an initiate: 'Whatever a person has done and accomplished is recorded in that imperishable book of history.' For further remarks and warnings about the confusing nature of the Akasha images, see Steiner, *At the Gates of Spiritual Science* (London 1970), pp. 23–24.

Notes to Lecture 4

1. See further Steiner, *True and False Paths in Spiritual Investigation* (London 1969), Lectures 3 to 5.
2. See Steiner, *Occult Science—An Outline* (London 1969), pp. 102ff.
3. The *Metamorphoses* is the chief work of the Roman poet Ovid (Publius Ovidius Naso); it has been many times translated into English, e.g. the recent version by Melville (Oxford 1986). See further the Appendix below, for a passage giving the underlying philosophy of the poem.

Notes to Lecture 5

1. See further Steiner, *Cosmic Memory: Atlantis and Lemuria* (New York 1971), pp. 71ff: *Occult Science*, pp. 173ff.
2. *Occult Science*, pp. 115ff.

Notes to Lecture 6

1. The temple itself (or Artemision) stood outside the ancient city of Ephesus, but in a wider sense the whole city was sacred to the goddess, who could be regarded conversely as a personification of the divine power present in the place (Dio Chrysostom, *Orations*, 31, 87). The cult was ancient, antedating the arrival of the Greeks, who in accordance with their practice of 'syncretism' (see Introduction) identified its virgin goddess with their Artemis. However, Near Eastern, especially Iranian influences, remained strong, as

can be seen from the presence of the Persian priestly dynasty, the Megabyzoi. Diodorus of Sicily refers to Mysteries celebrated in honour of the Persian Artemis (V, 77, 7–8), i.e. the great goddess Anahit, and the cult of Ephesian Artemis (which has virtually no connections to the native religion of the Greeks) evidently continues their traditions in a special local form. As such, the Ephesian Artemis was worshipped in other places, and her Mysteries were also performed, e.g. at Cremna in Pisidia (see R. Strelan, *Paul, Artemis and the Jews in Ephesus* (Berlin and New York 1996), pp. 47, 67 and 79–80). But Ephesus was her sacred city and the place where she dwelt above all.

Contrary to assumptions sometimes made about her, the Ephesian Artemis was not a fertility goddess. The multiple 'breasts' shown on her images from at least the fourth century BC have been variously interpreted (e.g. as testicles, alluding to her castrated priests!) but are most plausibly understood as ova around the goddess as queen bee (a recurring symbol of her). She is a perpetual virgin, and was specially worshipped by girls before marriage; married women were forbidden upon pain of death from entering her sanctuary. Men were admitted if pure, and could hold the office of priesthood although women clearly dominated the cult, which in mythology is connected with the Amazons, or virginal warrior women. Though there are exceedingly few references in ancient literature to her Mysteries, it appears that these were celebrated annually, with the initiation of girls and boys at puberty into her cult with dancing and the recital of the sacred myths. 'The myths of the ceremonies were "secret", that is, they belonged to the tribe and were taught only by the initiated to the uninitiated on their initiation ... These myths were chanted or sung and danced in the ceremony, and their performance was believed to re-present the powers of creation and of transition, as boys became men, girls became women' (Strelan, op. cit. p. 54). The goddess herself was thus present in her sacred Logos/recital, and those who took part in it were said to be 'in Artemis' (so Philostratus, *Epistles*, 65): a remarkable parallel to the Mystery language used in the Gospel of John (being 'in God', 'in the Father', etc.), again pointing to links between John and these Mysteries which Rudolf Steiner indicates.

Since the myths were secret, we know nothing of their content and symbolism. However, subsequent legend holds that the philosopher Heraclitus deposited his book *On Nature* in the temple of Artemis. In reality it is highly unlikely that Heraclitus' doctrine was presented in book form at all, so that the legend seems rather to be expressing symbolically a perception of the inner link between his teachings and those of the Mysteries. Heraclitus' ideas about the transmutations of fire are particularly close to Steiner's descriptions of the Mystery-teaching in this lecture. For Heraclitus and the Mysteries see further Steiner's comments in *Christianity as Mystical Fact* (New York 1997), pp. 22ff.

Notes to Lecture 7

1 See Steiner's Mystery-play *The Portal of Initiation*, Scene 7. Hibernia is the Roman name for ancient Ireland, which was already inhabited by Celtic peoples with a distinctive culture. However, since that culture was an oral one, literary evidence about their beliefs and initiation practices can be drawn only from the Roman writers who described them (often uncomprehendingly) or from the writing down of native traditions at a much later date (often distorted by Christian polemic). Caesar's remarks about the Druids (in *Gallic War*, VI, 13–19) probably apply to Ireland as well as to the situation in the rest of Britain and Gaul (France). Indeed, he claims that the institution of Druids originated in Britain (13). 'Druid' probably means 'knowledge of the oak', and the sacredness of the oak is one of the many features that link the ancient Celts with their common Indo-European religious brethren. Caesar describes also 'seers' (Latin *vates*) and 'bards' as sacred officials alongside the Druids.

The 20 years or more needed for the training of a bard (possibly comprised within the training of a Druid) was evidently divided into several stages of initiation (see Steiner's reference to what may be called, as in other Mystery-complexes such as Eleusis, the higher or Great Mysteries). But the congregating of large numbers of young men mentioned by Caesar suggests that the higher callings developed on the basis of communal initiations, through which the youths were made into full members of society, with the appropriate knowledge taught by the Druids. The latter were thus vehicles for the flowing out of the sacred into every aspect of society, and excommunication from their rites was the ultimate sanction of the community. The initiation of leaders and kings would naturally have formed part of the complex of social and religious rites. But in the nature of things we have very little evidence apart from the spiritual-scientific researches such as those in these lectures as to what was recited or enacted in the rites. '[The Druids] do not think it proper to commit this teaching to writing and ... they do not want their teaching spread abroad' (Caesar, op. cit. 14). A rare exception pointed out by John Sharkey is the account of a royal initiation in pagan Ulster by the medieval writer Gerald of Wales, in his *Description of Ireland*. Though shocked in tone it may be accurate in detail about the procedures involved. 'The whole people of the country being gathered in one place, a white mare is led into the midst of them, and he who is to be inaugurated, not as a prince [in my opinion] but as a brute, not as a king but as an outlaw, comes before the people on all fours, confessing himself a beast ... The mare being immediately killed and cut into pieces and boiled, a bath is prepared for him from the broth. Sitting in this he eats of the flesh which is brought to him, the people standing around and partaking of it also. He is then required to drink of the broth in which he bathes, not drinking it in any vessel nor even in his hand but lapping it with his mouth. These unrighteous rites duly accomplished, his royal authority and dominion are ratified' (cited in Sharkey, *Celtic Mysteries*, London 1975, p. 13). The elaborate assimilation to the sacrifice, the human-animal symbolism and the communion are typical of Mystery-rites and, more specifically, Sharkey recognizes in it the very ancient Indo-European 'horse-sacrifice', already characterized in almost identical terms in the *Verdas*, the *aśvamedha*. In it the horse represented the primordial power of creation to be reactualized in the king, renewing society and indeed the cosmic order. Mircea Eliade notes also that the Vedic accounts 'emphasize the relations between the horse and the primordial waters. Now in India the waters represent the cosmogonic element *par excellence*. But this complex rite also constitutes a "mystery" of the esoteric type. "Indeed, the *aśvamedha* is all, and he who, being

a Brahmin, knows nothing of the *aśvamedha*, knows nothing at all, he is not a Brahmin ..." Śatapatha Brahmana, 13.4.2.17.' (Eliade, *History of Religious Ideas*, Vol. I, London 1979, pp. 218–9.) In fact, the Indo-European system of sacrifices possess in general the pattern of an initiation, and he who performs them is 'reborn'. If Sharkey is right, the Irish Celts were still in medieval times heirs to these extremely archaic Mysteries of esoteric renewal.
2 Caesar (*Gallic War*, VI, 16) mentions in connection with supposed human sacrifices offered by the Druids that 'some of them use huge images of the gods, and fill their limbs which are woven from wicker, with living people', whom he claims are then consumed by fire. Caesar is naturally keen to present the Druids as barbarians, justifying his violent suppression of them in the war. But Mysteries were often misunderstood as human sacrifice, since in them people were said to die prior to rebirth on a higher plane. Evidence for actual human sacrifice among the Celts is actually very thin. More likely these figures (note the plural) are a reminiscence of events in the Mysteries like those Steiner describes.
3 On the nature of this experience, see further Steiner, *Occult Science* (London 1969), pp. 281ff.

Notes to Lecture 8

1 Steiner distinguishes now between our normal ability to have mental images, which are echoes of outer perception or subjective 'fantasy', and spiritual Imagination: a perception of the realities of the spiritual world through images and pictures. It leads on to still higher faculties of spiritual perception which he distinguishes by the technical terms Inspiration and Intuition. See again *Occult Science* (London 1969), pp. 260ff.

Notes to Lecture 9

1 See Steiner, *Occult Science* (London 1969), pp. 137ff.
2 Op. cit. pp. 115ff.
3 Caesar (*Gallic War*, VI, 14) says of the Druids: 'The principal doctrine they attempt to impart is that souls do not die but after

death cross from one person to another ... Besides this, they debate many subjects and teach them to their young men—for example, the stars and their movements, the size of the universe and the earth, the nature of things, and the strength and power of the immortal gods.'

4 This fundamental text of Rosicrucianism is available in translation in P.M. Allen (ed.), *A Christian Rosencreutz Anthology* (New York 1968). See, in addition to the lectures below, Steiner's lectures *Esoteric Christianity and the Mission of Christian Rosenkreutz* (London 1984).

Notes to Lecture 10

1 The latter cults were distinguished by the term *chthonic*, meaning that they were related to the forces in the inner depths of the earth (*chthon*). They were distinguished in many ways from the cults of the sky-gods, e.g. in the specification of animals that were to be sacrificed, etc. At Eleusis, the centre of the most famous Mysteries in the ancient world, each candidate for initiation had to sacrifice a pig, the *chthonic* animal *par excellence*. For Steiner's comments on the Eleusinian Mysteries, with their relationship to modern discoveries, see Welburn (ed.), *The Mysteries. Rudolf Steiner's Writings on Spiritual Initiation* (Edinburgh 1997), pp. 39ff.

2 We now know that the Eleusinian, Orphic and other Mysteries in Greece interacted in complex ways. Although it cannot directly be related to Eleusis, the symbolism of the Orphic relief from Modena (reproduced in Welburn [ed], *The Mysteries* as cited in note 1 above, Frontispiece) evokes many of the elements of this teaching.

3 Compare the ritual formula from the Eleusinia, preserved by Hippolytus, *Refutation of Heresies*, V, 7, 34, as: 'Rain (down)! Conceive!' M. Meyer, *The Ancient Mysteries* (New York 1987), p. 19 interprets this 'as a command to the sky to emit rain and the earth to conceive'. But what the earth-goddess Persephone conceives is not just natural growth, but a divine child.

4 The divine child-god Iacchos (identified with Dionysus) was mentioned constantly in the hymns and processions which preceded the holy events of the Mysteries, but he remains extremely

obscure. Statues of the kind described by Steiner are virtually unknown, but a few have been discovered—for instance, in connection with Persephone's important cult-centre at Selinus in Sicily. (It was from Sicily, it may be recalled, that the goddess was carried away into the underworld.) She is there shown nurturing a mysterious boy-child—a 'Greek Madonna'. as Zuntz remarks: see his *Persephone* (Oxford 1971), p. 151.

5 Greek *telos*.

6 In Antiquity, Aristotle was known and famous only for his 'Platonic' writings—which were, however, lost and only his logical and analytical works remained to be rediscovered.

Notes to Lecture 11

1 See Steiner, *The Riddles of Philosophy* (New York 1973), pp. 39ff.
2 See further Steiner, *True and False Paths in Spiritual Investigation* (London 1969), Lectures 3 to 5.

Notes to Lecture 12

1 In the Mystery-complex on Samothrace, excavated by archaeologists in the 1950s, there is evidence that the three figures were represented in the so-called Hall of the Lords. The central figure was Mercury-Hermes, called in the pre-Greek language of the cult Kadmilos; the others were shown as youths with erect phalli, with arms uplifted in an ancient gesture of epiphany. A similar picture is implied by Hippolytus, *Refutation of Heresies*, V, 8, 9 who interprets them as aspects of Archetypal Man. Strictly speaking it is the two accompanying youths who are Kabeiroi (a term widely used, however, for divine beings of non-Olympian type, e.g. at Thebes in mainland Greece); in the old language they may have been known as Dardanos and Aetion, whose names survive as those of the mythical founders of the Samothracian cult. They were intimately associated in the Mysteries with a Mother goddess, called Axieros in the old language and mystically present in the rocky landscape of the island. 'A curious feature of the cult of the Mother of the Rocks here is that she manifested her power, which was immanent in stones, in loadstones of magnetic iron of which

rings were fashioned, seemingly in the Sanctuary. Worn by the worshippers, they tied them to the Great Goddess' (K. Lehmann, *Samothrace*, New York 1966, p. 22). In addition to the Mother and the Kabeiroi, also important in the Mysteries were the heaven-and-underworld god, identified by the Greeks both with their Zeus and Dis, king of heaven and king of the dead, and his spouse. In the local language these were Axiokersos and Axiokersa. The group were properly worshipped under their title of the Great Gods.

Later the names and stories about the Great Gods were mixed with Greek features; the Kabeiroi, for instance, were identified with the Dioskouroi, Castor and Pollux. But in the Mysteries that were celebrated on Samothrace archaic wisdom and practices continued, and the Mysteries acquired a fame and veneration second only to Eleusis in the ancient world. The process certainly included the revelation of a sacred story, and the explanation of the sacred symbols. 'In Samothrace, Herodotus tells us, the *mystes* learned to understand the deeper significance of the ithyphallic images of Hermes-Kadmilos and, centuries later, a man of the intellectual level of Varro claims that certain symbols shown in the Samothracian Mysteries symbolized Heaven and Earth' (Lehmann, op. cit. pp. 28–29). A higher degree of initiation like that at Eleusis is also attested for Samothrace, and it appears that the condition of self-knowledge and the ritual confession of guilt gave the Greater Mysteries in particular an elevated moral character. The term for the higher Mystery-experience, *epopteia*, implies that it was a vision or revelation—but although some of the sacrificial procedure of the rites can be reconstructed, including a sort of baptism, very little can be recovered of the inner sequence except what we may glean from Rudolf Steiner's account here.

2 See Steiner, *Rosicrucianism and Modern Initiation* (London 1982).

Notes to Lecture 13

1 Goethe, *Faust*, Part I, lines 358–59.

Notes to Lecture 14

1 See Introduction, pp. 17ff.

2 Readers may find this sentence a stumbling block in an age of space exploration, when carbon-containing spacecraft (and astronauts) have landed on the moon with impunity. But Dr Steiner's phrase needs to be understood in the context of what precedes and follows it.

For the true alchemists the metals were not merely substances but embodied cosmic *activities* come to rest on earth. Silver is thus an embodiment of the moon's activity on earth, tin an embodiment of Jupiter, and so on. In this context carbon may be understood as the metal of the earth, embodying in substance the essential activity or character of the planet on which we live. For the Mystery experiences Dr Steiner is here describing, carbon—the characteristic metal of the earth—becomes metamorphosed into silver on the moon, into iron on Mars, and so on.

Just as the planets are ruled by the sun, so the metals are ruled by gold. From this point of view each planet reveals *one aspect* of the sun's nature and activity in the cosmos. Similarly, each planetary metal embodies one aspect of 'gold'. Carbon, the philosophers' stone, must thus contain within its darkness a hidden presence of the sun. The human spirit, clothed with the help of carbon in a physical body, can strive to awaken to its own sunlike nature, and find strength to transform the grave of physical existence (lead) into a spiritual one (gold). It is within this context of true alchemical experience that Rudolf Steiner's remarks about carbon and silver need to be understood.

3 See Steiner, *World History and the Mysteries in the Light of Anthroposophy* (London 1997).

Publisher's Note Regarding Rudolf Steiner's Lectures

The lectures contained in this volume have been translated from the German which is based on stenographic and other recorded texts that were in most cases never seen or revised by the lecturer. Hence, due to human errors in hearing and transcription, they may contain mistakes and faulty passages. Every effort has been made to ensure that this is not the case. Some of the lectures were given to audiences more familiar with anthroposophy; these are the so-called 'private' or 'members' lectures. Other lectures, like the written works, were intended for the general public. The differences between these, as Rudolf Steiner indicates in his *Autobiography*, is twofold. On the one hand, the members' lectures take for granted a background in and commitment to anthroposophy; in the public lectures this was not the case. At the same time, the members' lectures address the concerns and dilemmas of the members, while the public work speaks directly out of Steiner's own understanding of universal needs. Nevertheless, as Rudolf Steiner stresses: 'Nothing was ever said that was not solely the result of my direct experience of the growing content of anthroposophy. There was never any question of concessions to the prejudices and preferences of the members. Whoever reads these privately printed lectures can take them to represent anthroposophy in the fullest sense. Thus it was possible without hesitation—when the complaints in this direction became too persistent—to depart from the custom of circulating this material "for members only". But it must be borne in mind that faulty passages do occur in these reports not revised by myself.' Earlier in the same chapter, he states: 'Had I been able to correct them [the private lectures] the restriction [for members only] would have been unnecessary from the beginning.'